P9-DGN-361

Publication Manual

of the American Psychological Association

Third Edition

American Psychological Association
Washington, DC

Printed in the United States of America.

Thirteenth Printing January 1993

Copies may be ordered from:
Order Department
American Psychological Association
P.O. Box 2710
Hyattsville, MD 20784

Library of Congress Cataloging in Publication Data
Main entry under title:

Publication manual of the American Psychological Association

    Rev. ed. of: Publication manual. 2nd ed. 1974.
    Bibliography: p. 181
    Includes index.
. 1. Communication in psychology.   2. Psychology—Authorship.
I. American Psychological Association.   II. Publication manual.   [DNLM:
1. Writing. WZ 345 A518p]
BF76.7.P83 1983   808'.02   83-2521
ISBN 0-912704-57-8

Design by Elizabeth Elliott, Concepts Unlimited, Washington, DC
Composition by York Custom Graphics, York, Pennsylvania
Printing by Lancaster Press, Inc., Lancaster, Pennsylvania
Keystroking and coding by Marian Wood

Table of Contents

Manuscript Checklist	**Inside Front Cover**
Note to Students	**Inside Back Cover**
Foreword	**9**
Introduction	**11**
Organization of the Third Edition	11
Specific Style Changes in the Third Edition	12
How to Use the Manual	14

1   Content and Organization of a Manuscript

Quality of Content	**19**
1.01 Designing and Reporting Research	19
1.02 Evaluating Content	19
Characteristics of Authorship and Articles	**20**
1.03 Authorship	20
1.04 Types of Articles	21
1.05 Length, Headings, and Tone	22
Parts of a Manuscript	**22**
1.06 Title Page	22
1.07 Abstract	23
1.08 Introduction	24
1.09 Method	25
1.10 Results	27
1.11 Discussion	27
1.12 Multiple Experiments	28
1.13 References	28
1.14 Appendix	28
Quality of Presentation	**29**

2   Expression of Ideas

Writing Style	**32**
2.01 Orderly Presentation of Ideas	32
2.02 Smoothness of Expression	32
2.03 Economy of Expression	33
2.04 Precision and Clarity in Word Choice	34
2.05 Strategies to Improve Writing Style	35
Grammar	**36**
2.06 Verbs	36
2.07 Agreement of Subject and Verb	37
2.08 Pronouns	38
2.09 Misplaced and Dangling Modifiers	39
2.10 Relative Pronouns and Subordinate Conjunctions	40
2.11 Parallel Construction	41
Consideration of the Reader	**43**
2.12 Guidelines for Nonsexist Language in APA Journals	43
2.13 Avoiding Ethnic Bias	44

continued

3   APA Editorial Style

Punctuation	**52**
3.01 Period	52
3.02 Comma	52
3.03 Semicolon	52
3.04 Colon	53
3.05 Dash	53
3.06 Quotation Marks	53
3.07 Parentheses	54
3.08 Brackets	55

Spelling	**55**
3.09 Preferred Spelling	55
3.10 Hyphenation	55

Capitalization	**57**
3.11 Words Beginning a Sentence	57
3.12 Major Words in Titles and Headings	58
3.13 Proper Nouns and Trade Names	59
3.14 Nouns Followed by Numerals or Letters	60
3.15 Titles of Tests	60
3.16 Names of Conditions or Groups in an Experiment	60
3.17 Names of Factors, Variables, and Effects	60

Italics	**61**
3.18 Underlining Words	61

Abbreviations	**63**
3.19 Use of Abbreviations	63
3.20 Explanation of Abbreviations	63
3.21 Abbreviations Accepted as Words	64
3.22 Abbreviations Used Often in APA Journals	64
3.23 Latin Abbreviations	64
3.24 Abbreviations of Units of Measurement and Statistics	64
3.25 Use of Periods With Abbreviations	65
3.26 Plurals of Abbreviations	65
3.27 Abbreviations Beginning a Sentence	65

Headings and Series	**65**
3.28 Organizing a Manuscript With Headings	65
3.29 Levels of Headings	66
3.30 Selecting the Levels of Headings	66
3.31 Seriation	67

Quotations	**68**
3.32 Quotation of Sources	68
3.33 Accuracy	69
3.34 Double or Single Quotation Marks	70
3.35 Changes From the Source Requiring No Explanation	70
3.36 Changes From the Source Requiring Explanation	70
3.37 Citation of Sources	70
3.38 Permission to Quote	71

Numbers	**71**
3.39 Numbers Expressed in Figures	71
3.40 Numbers Expressed in Words	73
3.41 Combining Figures and Words to Express Numbers	74
3.42 Ordinal Numbers	74
3.43 Decimal Fractions	74
3.44 Arabic or Roman Numerals	74
3.45 Commas in Numbers	74
3.46 Plurals of Numbers	75

Metrication	**75**
3.47 Policy on Metrication	75
3.48 Style for Metric Units	75
3.49 Metric Tables	76

Statistical and Mathematical Copy	**80**
3.50 Selecting the Method of Analysis and Retaining Data	80
3.51 Selecting Effective Presentation	80
3.52 References for Statistics	80
3.53 Formulas	80
3.54 Statistics in Text	80
3.55 Statistical Symbols	81
3.56 Spacing, Alignment, and Punctuation	82
3.57 Equations in Text	82
3.58 Displayed Equations	83

Tables	**83**
3.59 Tabular Versus Textual Presentation	83
3.60 Relation of Tables and Text	84
3.61 Relation Between Tables	86
3.62 Table Numbers	86
3.63 Table Titles	86
3.64 Headings	87
3.65 Body of a Table	90
3.66 Notes to a Table	91
3.67 Ruling of Tables	93
3.68 Size of Tables	93
3.69 Tables From Another Source	93
3.70 Table Checklist	94

Figures	**94**
3.71 Deciding to Use Figures	94
3.72 Standards for Figures	95
3.73 Types of Figures	95
3.74 Line Art Versus Halftone	98
3.75 Size and Proportion	98
3.76 Mechanical Preparation of Figures	100
3.77 Drawing Graphs	102
3.78 Using Photographs	102
3.79 Identifying and Citing Figures	103
3.80 Figure Captions and Legends	103
3.81 Submitting Figures	104
3.82 Figure Checklist	105

Footnotes and Notes	**105**
3.83 Footnotes in Text	105
3.84 Notes to Tables	106
3.85 Author Identification Notes	106

continued

Reference Citations in Text **107**
3.86 One Work by a Single Author — 107
3.87 One Work by Two or More Authors — 107
3.88 Corporate Authors — 108
3.89 Works With No Author or With an Anonymous Author — 109
3.90 Authors With the Same Surname — 109
3.91 Two or More Works Within the Same Parentheses — 109
3.92 Specific Parts of a Source — 110
3.93 Personal Communications — 110
3.94 References to Legal Materials — 110
3.95 References in Parenthetical Material — 111

Reference List **111**
3.96 Agreement of Text and Reference List — 111
3.97 Construction of an Accurate and Complete Reference List — 111
3.98 APA Style — 112
3.99 References to Legal Materials — 113
3.100 Order of References in the Reference List — 115
3.101 Application of APA Reference Style — 116

4 Typing Instructions and Sample Paper

Author's Responsibilities **136**
Typist's Responsibilities **136**
General Instructions **136**
4.01 Paper — 136
4.02 Type Element — 136
4.03 Double-Spacing — 137
4.04 Margins — 137
4.05 Order of the Manuscript Pages — 137
4.06 Page Numbers and Short Titles — 138
4.07 Corrections — 138
4.08 Paragraphs and Indentation — 138
4.09 Uppercase and Lowercase Letters — 139
4.10 Headings — 139
4.11 Spacing and Punctuation — 140
4.12 Seriation — 140
4.13 Quotations — 141
4.14 Statistical and Mathematical Copy — 141

Instructions for Typing the Parts of a Manuscript **143**
4.15 Title Page — 143
4.16 Abstract — 144
4.17 Text — 144
4.18 References — 145
4.19 Appendixes — 145
4.20 Footnotes and Notes — 145
4.21 Tables and Table Titles, Notes, and Rules — 146
4.22 Figures and Figure Captions — 146

Sample Paper and Outlines **147**

5 Submitting the Manuscript and Proofreading

Submitting the Manuscript **158**
5.01 Number of Copies — 158
5.02 Cover Letter — 158

5.03 *Contents of Package*		158
5.04 *Editor Acknowledgment of Manuscript Submission*		159
5.05 *Interim Correspondence*		159
5.06 *Copyright Transfer*		159
5.07 *Future Correspondence*		159

Reviewing the Copy-Edited Manuscript — **159**

Proofreading — **161**
5.08 *Reading Proofs*		161
5.09 *Author's Alterations*		161
5.10 *Returning Proofs and Manuscript*		163
5.11 *Reprints*		163

After the Article Is Published — **163**
5.12 *Retaining Raw Data*		163
5.13 *Correction Notices*		163

6 Journal Program of the American Psychological Association

Policies Governing the Journals — **166**
6.01 *Selection of Editors*		166
6.02 *Page Allocations*		166
6.03 *Publication Lag*		167
6.04 *Primary Publication*		167
6.05 *Author's Copyright on an Unpublished Manuscript*		168
6.06 *Copyright and Permission to Reproduce APA Material*		169
6.07 *Other Copyrighted Material*		169

Editorial Management of Manuscripts — **169**
6.08 *Editorial Responsibilities*		169
6.09 *Date of Receipt of Manuscripts*		170
6.10 *Order of Publication of Articles*		170
6.11 *Procedures in Editorial Review*		170
6.12 *Blind Review*		172
6.13 *Evaluation of Manuscripts*		172

The APA Journals — **173**
6.14 *Policy Statements on Journal Coverage*		173

Journal-Related Periodicals — **178**

7 Bibliography
7.01 *History of the Publication Manual*		181
7.02 *References Cited in This Edition*		181
7.03 *Suggested Reading*		183

Appendix: Material Other Than Journal Articles

Theses, Dissertations, and Student Papers — **189**
A.01 *Final Manuscript*		189
A.02 *Content Requirements*		190
A.03 *Typing Requirements*		191

Material for Oral Presentation — **192**

continued

Material Published in Abbreviated Form   **193**
A.04 *Psychological Documents*   193
A.05 *Brief Reports*   193
A.06 *NAPS*   194

Index   **195**

List of Tables

1. Guidelines for Nonsexist Language in APA Journals   45
2. Guide to Hyphenating Psychological Terms   56
3. Prefixes Not Requiring Hyphens   58
4. Prefixed Words Requiring Hyphens   59
5. Use of Italics   61
6. International System (SI) Base and Supplementary Units 76
7. International System (SI) Prefixes   77
8. International System (SI) Derived Units With
   Special Names   77
9. Other International System (SI) Derived Units   78
10. Examples of Conversions to International System
    (SI) Equivalents   79
11. Mean Numbers of Words Reported as a Function of
    Interstimulus Interval [sample table]   84
12. Mean Attribution Scores for Experiment 1 [sample table] 85
13. Recognition Memory for Words and Nonwords as a
    Function of Age and Viewing Condition [sample table]   85
14. Intercorrelations Between Subscales for Students
    and Older Adults [sample table]   85
15. Mean Numbers of Correct Responses by Children
    With and Without Pretraining [sample table]   89
16. Abbreviations for States and Territories   113
17. Elements and Examples of References in APA Style   118

List of Figures

1. Sample Line Graph   96
2. Sample Bar Graph   96
3. Sample Scatter Graph   97
4. Sample Drawing   99
5. Sample Photograph   99
6. Effects of Reducing Letters and Symbols
   Frequently Used in Figures   101
7. Sample One-Experiment Paper   148
8. Outline of the Text of a Sample Two-Experiment Paper   155
9. Outline of the Text of a Sample Review Paper   156
10. Proofreader's Marks   160
11. Marking Proofs   162
12. The APA Publication Process   171

Foreword

In 1928 editors and business managers of anthropological and psychological journals met to discuss the form of journal manuscripts and to write instructions for their preparation. The report of this meeting of the Committee on Form of Manuscript, which was chaired by Madison Bentley and sponsored by the National Research Council, was the forerunner of this book. The report was published as a seven-page article in the February 1929 issue of the *Psychological Bulletin*, a journal of the American Psychological Association (APA). The group agreed that it would not dictate to authors; instead, it recommended "a standard of procedure, to which exceptions would doubtless be necessary, but to which reference might be made in cases of doubt" ("Instructions," 1929, p. 57; see section 7.02 for references cited in the *Manual*).

That first effort was succeeded in 1944 by a 32-page guide authorized by the APA's Board of Editors. This guide, which appeared in the *Psychological Bulletin* as an article by John Anderson and Willard Valentine, stated that one of its aims was to encourage young members of the profession who might be writing for the first time.

In 1952 the APA Board of Editors (now called the Council of Editors) expanded the 1944 article into a 60-page supplement to the *Bulletin*. Laurance Shaffer coordinated the task of revision. This revision, which was the first to carry the title *Publication Manual*, marked the beginning of a recognized APA journal style. Two revisions followed as separate publications: One, in 1957, was done by the Council of Editors, coordinated first by C. M. Louttit and then by Laurance Shaffer. The other, in 1967, was coordinated by Estelle Mallinoff in the APA Publications Office, under the direction of Helen Orr.

In 1974 APA published the second edition of the *Manual* under the authorization of its Publications and Communications Board. The second edition was prepared by a task force, consisting of APA members Charles Cofer, Robert Daniel, Frances Dunham, Walter Heimer, and William Mikulas, and by Susan Bunker, a member of APA's journal staff, working under the direction of Anita DeVivo, Executive Editor of the Publications Division of APA. Arthur W. Melton served as special advisor. Subsequent modifications of the *Manual* were published in two change sheets, one issued in 1975 and one in 1977.

The second edition gained wide acceptance. The style set forth in the second edition was adopted in whole or in part by more than 200 non-APA journals. In addition, many graduate and undergraduate departments of psychology adopted the requirements in the 1974 edition for the preparation of dissertations, theses, and student papers.

In response to users' suggestions for improvements to the *Manual*, the Publications and Communications Board authorized a revision of the second edition. In preparation for this third edition, a questionnaire was distributed in 1979 to authors whose articles were in press in APA journals, to chairs of graduate departments of psychology (who were asked to distribute copies to faculty and graduate students), to editors of non-APA journals using the second edition, to editors of APA journals, to APA production editors, and to other individuals whose comments had been helpful in the development of the second edition. The questionnaire asked which sections of the second edition were most confusing and which were most useful, what specific improvements could be made, and what additional information on manuscript preparation would be helpful. The respondents' answers and comments helped to guide the preparation of the third edition.

Every edition of the *Manual* has been intended to aid authors in the preparation of manuscripts. The 1929 guide could gently advise authors on style because there were then only about 200 authors who published in the 4 existing APA journals. Today, the editors of APA's 18 journals consider close to 6,500 manuscript submissions a year (of which approximately 1,400 reach print). Without APA style conventions, the time and effort required to review and edit manuscripts would prohibit timely and cost-effective publication and would make clear communication harder to achieve.

This third edition of the *Manual* continues to reflect the maturing of the language of psychology and incorporates current national and international standards of scientific communication. The *Manual* presents explicit style requirements but acknowledges that alternatives are sometimes necessary; authors should balance the rules of the *Manual* with good judgment. Because the written language of psychology changes more slowly than psychology itself, the *Manual* does not offer solutions for all stylistic problems. In that sense, it is a transitional document: Its style requirements are based on the existing scientific literature rather than imposed on the literature.

Preparation of this edition was initiated in 1978 by Anita DeVivo. Subsequently, Ann Mahoney, Managing Editor of the Publications Division, and Leslie Cameron, Coordinator of the *Publication Manual* revision, assumed the direction of the project. Charles Cofer, Robert Daniel, Frances Dunham, and Walter Heimer, members of the task force that served for the second edition, continued to serve for the third edition. Members of the APA Central Office staff and many other volunteers, especially Bruce R. Dunn, David T. Goldman, Robert B. McCall, Nancy Perrigo, and Elyce Zenoff, contributed their time, energy, and knowledge to the preparation of the third edition.

As the principal advisory body, the APA Council of Editors reviewed the changes of policy appearing in the third edition. At its meeting in June 1982, the Publications and Communications Board enthusiastically endorsed the third edition as a means of improving the quality of the communication of psychology.

Earl A. Alluisi
Chair, Publications and Communications Board
September 1982

Introduction

Rules for the preparation of manuscripts should contribute to clear communication. Take, for example, the rule that some editors consider the most important: Double-space everything. A double-spaced manuscript allows each person in the publication process to function comfortably and efficiently: Authors and editors have space for handwritten notes; typists and printers can easily read all marks. Such mechanical rules, and most style rules, are usually the result of a confluence of established authorities and common usage. These rules introduce the uniformity necessary to convert manuscripts written in many styles to printed pages edited in one consistent style. They spare readers from a distracting variety of forms throughout a work and permit readers to give full attention to content.

The rules provided in the *Publication Manual* are drawn from an extensive body of psychological literature, from editors and authors experienced in psychological writing, and from recognized authorities on publication practices. Writers who conscientiously use the *Manual* will express their ideas in a form and a style both accepted by and familiar to a broad, established readership in psychology.

Early editions of the *Manual* were intended exclusively for APA authors. Recognizing a need for commonly accepted guidelines in psychology as a whole, the Association published the 1974 second edition for a much wider audience. The widespread adoption of the second edition by publishers of non-APA journals and by members of graduate and undergraduate departments of psychology indicates that the second edition has met this important need.

The third edition aims to be an even more useful guide for authors, editors, students, typists, and publishers. It amplifies and refines some parts of the second edition, reorganizes other parts, and presents new material. Instructions about style and policy that were confusing have been clarified. A more thorough index and more examples have been added to help the user more easily find and apply style and policy rules. The following paragraphs give a brief description of each chapter and indicate more specifically the changes and additions in this new edition.

Organization of the Third Edition

Chapter 1, Content and Organization of a Manuscript, describes review and theoretical articles as well as empirical studies. As in the second edition, authorship is specifically defined. In order to provide specific guidelines on determining authorship, in this edition Principle 7f (Professional Relations) of the "Ethical Principles of Psychologists" (APA, 1981) is reprinted. Also, instructions on the preparation of abstracts are developed more extensively. Part of the second edition's chapter 1 material on quality of content is now part of the discussion on review procedures and the editorial process in chapter 6.

Chapter 2, Expression of Ideas, emphasizes the importance of organizing one's thinking and writing and of making every word contribute to clear and concise communication. New aids for the writer include a section on common grammatical errors, the "Guidelines for Nonsexist Language in APA Journals" (formerly Change Sheet 2 to the second edition), and suggestions for avoiding ethnic bias in language.

Chapter 3, APA Editorial Style, describes many of the mechanical aspects of editorial style as it is applied in APA journals, including punctuation, spelling, capitalization, italics, abbreviations, quotations, mathematical copy, headings, illustrations, footnotes, and references. All sections have been clarified and expanded. The section on references has been substantially revised: Reference notes are now incorporated into the reference list, and the year of publication cited in the reference list now appears immediately after the author's name, a style that conforms to a uniform system of citation that many publishers in the social, physical, and biological sciences recognize. The *Manual* now provides more kinds of reference examples, including legal references, and all examples of references are incorporated into the section on references. This chapter is intended not to determine all points of style but rather to resolve the questions that occur most frequently in manuscripts written for psychological journals. It defines the forms that over the years have been accepted in APA journals and that now are described as APA style.

Chapter 4, Typing Instructions and Sample Paper, provides instructions to typists on preparing the final manuscript. In addition to a complete one-experiment sample paper, it now includes outlines for a two-experiment paper and a theoretical or review paper. The sample paper and outlines illustrate the format and application of APA style.

Chapter 5, Submitting the Manuscript and Proofreading, provides instructions to authors on procedures for submitting the manuscript and for handling the manuscripts and proofs of articles accepted for publication.

Chapter 6, Journal Program of the American Psychological Association, discusses the general policies that govern all APA journals and describes the management of manuscripts by APA journal editors and by APA's journal office. In addition, it describes the Association's journals and related publications and their fields of coverage.

Chapter 7, the Bibliography, lists works on the history of the *Manual*, references cited in the *Manual*, and annotated, selected references for further reading on subjects discussed in the *Manual*.

The **appendix** describes material other than journal articles: theses, dissertations, student papers, material for oral presentation, and brief reports.

The **index** has been expanded, and topics are now indexed by page number rather than by section number.

Specific Style Changes in the Third Edition

Readers who are familiar with the second edition of the *Manual* will find, besides the revisions and additions outlined above, the following specific changes in style requirements introduced with the third edition.

Typing the Manuscript
- Type every page of a manuscript with a $1\frac{1}{2}$-in. (4-cm) margin on all sides. (p. 137)
- Do not break words at the end of a typed line. (p. 137)

Writing Style
- Avoid language that can be construed as sexist. (pp. 43–44)

Parts of a Manuscript
- Use 100 to 150 words for the abstract of a report of an empirical study; use 75 to 100 words for the abstract of a review or theoretical paper. (pp. 23–24)

APA Editorial Style
Abbreviations
- Use the International System of Units abbreviation for *second* (s rather than sec) when the unit is accompanied by a numeric value. (p. 76, Table 6)
- Omit periods in abbreviations for nonmetric measurements (ft, lb), except in the abbreviation for inch (in.). (p. 65)
- Never abbreviate the following units of time: day, week, month, and year. (p. 64)
- In reference lists, use the official two-letter U.S. Postal Service abbreviations for the names of states. (pp. 112–113, Table 16)

Statistical and Mathematical Copy
- Report sample size with chi-square analyses. (p. 81)
- Report descriptive statistics when reporting inferential statistics. (pp. 80–81)
- Use a zero before the decimal point in numbers that are less than one unless the decimal fraction cannot be greater than one (e.g., levels of statistical significance). (p. 74)
- Use figures to express sample or population size even when the number is less than 10. (p. 72)

References
- In reference lists, place the year of publication in parentheses immediately after the author's name. (pp. 119–120, Table 17)
- Reference notes have been eliminated; therefore, include all references except personal communications in the reference list. Mention personal communications only in the text. (p. 110)
- Prepare legal references according to the new guidelines described in the *Manual*'s section on references. (pp. 110–111, 113–115)
- In references to articles or chapters in books, add the inclusive page numbers of the articles or chapters. (p. 126, Table 17)

Changes in requirements for manuscript preparation may initially be inconvenient and annoying to persons submitting papers. Such changes are often unavoidable, however, because of changes in APA policy, in printing technology, in the economy, or in the state of science. Should future changes in requirements occur before the preparation of another edition of the *Manual*, they will be published in the *American Psychologist* and keyed to this edition. The announcements of changes will be listed in the table of contents of the *American Psychologist* and in its annual index.

Although the *Manual* does provide some specific rules of usage and grammar, it does not address general problems of writing and language, which are adequately dealt with elsewhere. Nor does it deal with exceptional writing situations in psychology in which style precedents may need to be set. When one is without a rule or a reference and the answer to a question can be narrowed to several reasonable and equally defensible choices, the *Manual* suggests that simplicity, plain language, and direct statements will always suffice.

How to Use the *Manual*

The *Publication Manual* describes requirements for the preparation and submission of manuscripts for publication. Chapters in the *Manual* provide substantively different kinds of information and are arranged in the sequence in which one considers the elements of manuscript preparation, from initial concept through publication. Although each chapter is autonomous, each chapter also develops from the preceding chapter. For example, chapter 1 explains how to organize the parts of a manuscript, and chapter 2 describes how to express specific ideas within the manuscript. Chapter 4, which concerns typing a manuscript, provides information you will use only after you have reviewed the first three chapters—that is, you will not type your manuscript until you have organized and written it. To use the *Manual* most effectively, you should be familiar with the contents of all the chapters before you begin writing. If you are already familiar with the second edition of the *Manual,* see the list on page 13 of specific style changes introduced with the third edition.

The design of the third edition of the *Manual* provides specific aids that allow you to locate information quickly. Format aids, such as changes in typeface and horizontal rules, will help you easily locate and identify the answers to questions on style and format. Organizational aids, such as checklists and cross-references to other sections, will help you organize and write the manuscript and check major points of style and format when you have finished. Do not use these aids independently of the explanatory text; they highlight important information, but they do not include everything you need for preparing your manuscript. Some of these format and organizational aids are listed below.

Format aids:
- The examples of points of style or format that appear in chapters 3 and 4 are in a typeface that looks like that produced on a typewriter. This typeface not only helps you locate the examples quickly but shows how material appears when typed:

    ```
    This is an example of the typewriter typeface.
    ```

- A detailed table of contents, which lists the sections for each chapter, helps you locate categories of information quickly.
- A list of tables and a list of figures, which appear in the table of contents, help you locate specific tables and figures.
- Each page of the table of reference examples carries a tab so that you can immediately open the *Manual* to the reference examples without first going to the table of contents or the index.

- The comprehensive index helps you locate page numbers for specific topics quickly.

Organizational aids:
- A section on evaluating content (section 1.02) lists questions you can use—before you begin writing—to decide whether the research is likely to merit publication.
- A section at the end of chapter 1 on the quality of presentation lists questions you can use to evaluate the organization and presentation of information in the manuscript.
- Sample Tables 11–15 show how tables should be prepared. A table checklist (section 3.70) provides a final review of major points of table style and format.
- Sample Figures 1–5 show how figures should be prepared. A figure checklist (section 3.82) provides a final review of major points of figure style and format.
- Sample papers and outlines (Figures 7–9) are provided: The sample one-experiment paper shows how a typical manuscript looks as prepared on a typewriter. The outlines for a sample two-experiment and a sample review paper show the typical organization of these kinds of papers.
- The manuscript checklist on the inside front and back covers provides a final review of major points of style and format and directs you to the text section that describes in detail each element of the checklist.
- Section 7.03 of the Bibliography lists publications that provide more information on topics discussed in the *Manual*.

1 Content and Organization of a Manuscript

Research is complete only when the results are shared with the scientific community. Although such sharing is accomplished in a variety of formal and informal ways, the traditional medium for communicating research results is the scientific journal.

The scientific journal is the repository of the accumulated knowledge of a field. In the literature are distilled the successes and failures, the information, and the perspectives contributed by many investigators over many years. Familiarity with the literature allows an individual investigator to avoid needlessly repeating work that has been done before, to build on existing work, and in turn to contribute something new. A literature built of meticulously prepared, carefully reviewed contributions thus fosters the growth of a field.

Although writing for publication is sometimes tedious, the rewards of publication are many for the writer, the reader, and the science. The writing process initially requires a thorough review and evaluation of previous work in the literature, which helps acquaint one with the field as a whole and establishes whether one's idea is truly new and significant. Authors beginning the writing process will find there is no better way to clarify and organize their ideas than by trying to explain them to someone else. In fact, scientists "will get to really know a field only if [they] become sufficiently involved to contribute to it" (Orne, 1981, p. 4; see section 7.02 for references cited in the Manual). Thus the content and the organization of a scientific manuscript reflect the logical thinking in scientific investigation, and the preparation of a manuscript for journal publication is an integral part of the individual research effort.

Just as each investigator benefits from the publication process, so the body of scientific literature depends for its vitality on the active participation of individual investigators. And individual scientific articles contribute most to the literature when they communicate material clearly and concisely.

This chapter discusses several considerations authors

should weigh before writing for publication—considerations both about their own research and about the scientific publishing tradition in which they are to take part. First, the answers to questions about the quality of the research will determine whether the study is worth writing or is publishable. Second, consideration of authorship and types of articles will suggest who gets credit, how that credit is given, and what basic organization of the article would be most effective. Consistency of presentation and format within and across journal articles is an aspect of the scientific publishing tradition that enables authors to present material systematically and enables readers to locate material easily. Finally, consideration of the traditional structure of the manuscript allows writers to judge the thoroughness, originality, and clarity of their work and to communicate more easily with other individuals within the same tradition.

Quality of Content

No amount of skill in writing can disguise research that is poorly designed or managed. Indeed, such defects are a major cause for the rejection of manuscripts. Before committing a report to manuscript form, you as a would-be author should critically review the quality of research and ask if the research is sufficiently important and free from flaws to justify publication. If the report came from another researcher, would you read it? Would it influence your work? Most researchers have in a back drawer one or more studies that failed to meet this test. No matter how well written, a paper that reflects poor methods is unacceptable.

1.01 Designing and Reporting Research

You, as an author, should familiarize yourself with the criteria and standards that editors and reviewers use to evaluate manuscripts. (See chapter 6 for a discussion of the review process.) Editors find in submitted papers the following kinds of defects in the design and reporting of research:

- piecemeal publication, that is, the separation of a single substantial report into a series of overlapping papers;
- the reporting of only a single correlation—even a significant correlation between two variables rarely has any interpretable value;
- the reporting of negative results, unless repeated studies contradict a strong theoretical or empirical base for or against a relationship;
- failure to build in needed controls, often for a subtle but important aspect of the study;
- exhaustion of a problem—there is a difference between ongoing research that explores the limits of the generality of a research finding and the endless production of papers that report trivial changes in previous research.

1.02 Evaluating Content

Before preparing a manuscript, you should evaluate the research and judge that it is an important contribution to the field. An editorial by Brendan A. Maher (1974) will be found helpful in making that judgment, and a humorous account by Robert R. Holt (1959, "Researchmanship or How to Write a Dissertation in Clinical Psychology Without Really Trying") makes some sharp but pertinent points about research design. The following checklist (based on Bartol, 1981) may also help in assessing the quality of content and in deciding whether the research is likely to merit publication.

- Is the research question significant, and is the work original and important?
- Have the instruments been demonstrated to have satisfactory reliability and validity?
- Are the outcome measures clearly related to the variables with which the investigation is concerned?
- Does the research design fully and unambiguously test the hypothesis?

- Are the subjects representative of the population to which generalizations are made?
- Did the researcher observe ethical standards in the treatment of subjects—for example, if deception was used for human subjects?
- Is the research at an advanced enough stage to make the publication of results meaningful?

Characteristics of Authorship and Articles

1.03 Authorship

Authorship is reserved for persons who receive primary credit and hold primary responsibility for a published work. Authorship encompasses, therefore, not only those who do the actual writing but also those who have made substantial scientific contributions to a study. This concept of authorship is discussed in Principle 7f of the "Ethical Principles of Psychologists" (APA, 1981). Principle 7f is reprinted here:

Principle 7f. Publication credit is assigned to those who have contributed to a publication in proportion to their professional contributions. Major contributions of a professional character made by several persons to a common project are recognized by joint authorship, with the individual who made the principal contribution listed first. Minor contributions of a professional character and extensive clerical or similar nonprofessional assistance may be acknowledged in footnotes. . . . Acknowledgment through specific citations is made for unpublished as well as published material that has directly influenced the research or writing. Psychologists who compile and edit material of others for publication publish the material in the name of the originating group, if appropriate, with their own name appearing as chairperson or editor. All contributors are to be acknowledged and named. (p. 637)

Substantial professional contributions may include formulating the problem or hypothesis, structuring the experimental design, organizing and conducting the statistical analysis, interpreting the results, or writing a major portion of the paper. Those who so contribute are listed in the by-line. Lesser contributions, which do not constitute authorship, may be acknowledged in a note (see section 3.85 for suggested note forms). These contributions may include such supportive functions as designing or building the apparatus, suggesting or advising about the statistical analysis, collecting the data, modifying or structuring a computer program, and arranging for research subjects. Combinations of these (and other) tasks, however, may justify authorship. In any case, the writer should always obtain a person's consent before including that person's name in a by-line or in a note.

Authors are responsible for determining authorship and for specifying the order in which two or more authors' names appear in the by-line. The general rule is that the name of the principal contributor should appear first, with subsequent names in order of decreasing contribution.

Authors are also responsible for the factual accuracy of their contributions. The Association and the editors of its journals assume no responsibility for the statements and opinions advanced by contributors to APA journals.

1.04 Types of Articles

Journal articles are usually reports of empirical studies, review articles, or theoretical articles.

Reports of empirical studies are reports of original research. They typically consist of distinct sections that reflect the stages in the research process and that appear in the sequence of these stages:
- **introduction:** development of the problem under investigation and statement of the purpose of the investigation;
- **method:** description of the method used to conduct the investigation;
- **results:** report of the results that were found; and
- **discussion:** interpretation and discussion of the implications of the results.

(See Figure 7 for a sample one-experiment paper and Figure 8 for an outline of a sample two-experiment paper.)

Review articles are critical evaluations of material that has already been published. By organizing, integrating, and evaluating previously published material, the author of a review article considers the progress of current research toward clarifying a problem. In a sense, a review article is tutorial in that the author
- defines and clarifies the problem;
- summarizes previous investigations in order to inform the reader of the state of current research;
- identifies relations, contradictions, gaps, and inconsistencies in the literature; and
- suggests the next step or steps in solving the problem.

The components of review articles, unlike the sections of reports of empirical studies, are arranged by relationship rather than by chronology. (See Figure 9 for an outline of a sample review paper.)

Theoretical articles are papers in which the author draws upon existing research literature to advance theory in any area of psychology. Review and theoretical articles are often similar in structure, but theoretical articles present empirical information only when it affects theoretical issues. The author traces the development of theory in order to expand and refine theoretical constructs. Ordinarily, the author presents a new theory. Alternatively, the author may analyze existing theory, pointing up flaws or demonstrating the superiority of one theory over another. In this type of theoretical analysis, the author customarily examines a theory's internal and external consistency, that is, whether a theory is self-contradictory and whether the theory and empirical observation contradict each other. The sections of a theoretical article, like those of a review article, are usually ordered by relationship rather than by chronology.

Other, less frequently published types of articles in APA journals include brief reports, comments and replies, discussions of quantitative methods, case histories, and monographs. Although the contents of these articles are dissimilar, the manuscripts should still be logically and coherently organized, according to the guidelines described in the previous paragraphs. Authors should refer to the journal to which they are submitting the manuscript for specific information regarding these kinds of articles.

Most journal articles published in psychology are reports of empirical studies, and therefore the next section of this chapter emphasizes their preparation.

1.05 Length, Headings, and Tone

Before beginning to write, you should consider the following three major characteristics of a journal article: length, headings, and tone.

Length. Determine the typical length of an article in the journal for which you are writing and do not exceed that length unless you are writing a monograph or some other exceptional material. To estimate how long the manuscript might run in printed pages, count *every* manuscript page (including the title and abstract pages, tables, and figures) and divide the number of manuscript pages by 3 (i.e., 1 printed page = 3 manuscript pages).

Discursive writing often obscures an author's main points, and long manuscripts are frequently improved by condensation. If a paper is too long, shorten it by stating points clearly and directly, confining the discussion to the specific problem under investigation, deleting or combining tabular material, eliminating repetition, and writing in the active voice.

Headings. Carefully consider your material and the sequence and levels of importance of the ideas you wish to present. Headings help a reader grasp the paper's outline and the relative importance of the parts of the paper (see section 3.28).

Tone. Although scientific writing differs in form from literary writing, it need not and should not lack style or be dull. In describing your research, present the ideas and findings directly but aim for an interesting and compelling manner that reflects your involvement with the problem (see chapter 2 on writing style).

Parts of a Manuscript

1.06 Title Page

Title. A title should summarize the main idea of the paper simply and, if possible, with style. It should be a concise statement of the main topic and should identify the actual variables or theoretical issues under investigation and the relation between them. An example of a good title is "Effect of Transformed Letters on Reading Speed."

A title should be fully explanatory when standing alone. Although its principal function is to inform readers about the study, a title is also used as a statement of article content for abstracting and information services, such as APA's *Psychological Abstracts* and PsycINFO Database. A good title easily compresses to the short title used for editorial purposes and to the running head used with the published article (see page 23 and section 4.15).

Titles are commonly indexed and compiled in numerous reference works. Therefore, avoid words that serve no useful purpose; they increase length and can mislead indexers. For example, the words *method* and *results* do not normally appear in a title, nor should such redundancies as "A Study of" or "An Experimental Investigation of" begin a title. Do not use abbreviations in a title: Spelling out all terms will help ensure accurate, complete indexing of the article. The recommended length for a title is 12 to 15 words.

Author's name and affiliation. Every manuscript has a by-line consisting of two parts: the name of the author and the institution where the investigation was conducted (without the words *by* or *from the*).

Author's name. The preferred form of an author's name is first name, middle initial, and last name. This designation reduces the likelihood of mistaken identity. Use the same by-line designation on all manuscripts; that is, do not use initials on one manuscript and the full name on a later one. Omit all titles (e.g., Dr., Professor) and degrees (e.g., PhD, MD).

Affiliation. The affiliation identifies where the author or authors conducted the investigation and is usually an institution. Include a dual affiliation only if two institutions contributed substantial financial support to the study. Add the author's department in the by-line only if it is other than a department of psychology. When an author has no institutional affiliation, list the city and state of residence below the author's name. If the institutional affiliation has changed since the work was completed, give the current affiliation in the author identification notes. (See section 1.03 for a discussion about what constitutes authorship.)

Running head. The running head is an abbreviated title that is printed at the top of the pages of a published article to identify the article for readers. The head should be a maximum of 50 characters, counting letters, punctuation, and spaces between words.

1.07 Abstract

An abstract is a brief, comprehensive summary of the contents of the article; it allows readers to survey the contents of an article quickly and, like a title, is used by abstracting and information services to index and retrieve articles. All APA journals except *Contemporary Psychology* require an abstract.

A well-prepared abstract can be the single most important paragraph in the article. An abstract (a) is read first, (b) may be the only part of an article that is actually read (readers frequently decide, on the basis of the abstract, whether to read the entire article), and (c) is an important means of access in locating and retrieving the article. A good abstract is
- **accurate:** Ensure that an abstract correctly reflects the purpose and content of the manuscript. Do not include in an abstract information that does not appear in the body of the paper. Comparing an abstract with an outline of the paper's headings is a useful way to verify the accuracy of an abstract.
- **self-contained:** Define all abbreviations and acronyms. Spell out names of tests and drugs (use generic names for drugs). Define unique terms. Paraphrase rather than quote. Include names of

authors and dates of publication in citations of other publications (and give a full bibliographic citation in the article's reference list). Include key words for indexing purposes.

- **concise and specific:** Make each sentence maximally informative, especially the lead sentence. Be as brief as possible. Only abstracts of the longest and most complex papers require as many as 150 words.
- **nonevaluative:** Report rather than evaluate; do not add to or comment on what is in the body of the manuscript.
- **coherent and readable:** Write in clear and vigorous prose. Use verbs rather than the noun equivalents and the active rather than the passive voice. Use the present tense to describe results with continuing applicability or conclusions drawn; use the past tense to describe specific variables manipulated or tests applied.

An abstract of a *report of an empirical study* should describe in 100 to 150 words

- the problem under investigation, in one sentence if possible;
- the subjects, specifying pertinent characteristics, such as number, type, age, sex, and species;
- the experimental method, including the apparatus, data-gathering procedures, and complete test names or generic names and the dosage of any drugs, particularly if the drugs are novel or important to the study;
- the findings, including statistical significance levels; and
- the conclusions and the implications or applications.

An abstract for a *review or theoretical article* should describe in 75 to 100 words

- the topic, in one sentence if possible;
- the purpose, thesis, or organizing construct and the scope (comprehensive or selective) of the article;
- the sources used (e.g., personal observation, published literature); and
- the conclusions and the implications or applications.

An abstract that is accurate, succinct, quickly comprehensible, and informative will increase the audience and the future retrievability of your article. For information on how abstracts are used to retrieve articles, consult the *PsycINFO Psychological Abstracts Information Services Users Reference Manual* (1981).

1.08 Introduction

Introduce the problem. The body of a paper opens with an introduction that presents the specific problem under study and describes the research strategy. Because the introduction is clearly identified by its position in the article, it is not labeled. Before writing the introduction, consider

- What is the point of the study?
- How do the hypothesis and the experimental design relate to the problem?
- What are the theoretical implications of the study, and how does the study relate to previous work in the area? What are the theoretical propositions tested, and how were they derived?

A good introduction answers these questions in a paragraph or two and, by summarizing the relevant arguments and the data, gives the reader a firm sense of what was done and why.

Develop the background. Discuss the literature but do not include an exhaustive historical review. Assume that the reader has knowledge in the field for which you are writing and does not require a complete digest. Although you should acknowledge the contributions of others to the study of the problem, cite only that research pertinent to the specific issue and avoid references with only tangential or general significance. If you summarize earlier works, avoid nonessential details; instead, emphasize pertinent findings, relevant methodological issues, and major conclusions. Refer the reader to general surveys or reviews of the topic if they are available.

Demonstrate the logical continuity between previous and present work. Develop the problem with enough breadth and clarity to make it generally understood by as wide a professional audience as possible. Do not let the goal of brevity mislead you into writing a statement intelligible only to the specialist.

Controversial issues, when relevant, should be treated fairly. A simple statement that certain studies support one conclusion and others support another conclusion is better than an extensive and inconclusive discussion. Whatever your personal opinion, avoid animosity and *ad hominem* arguments in presenting the controversy. Do not support your position or justify your research by citing established authorities out of context.

State the purpose and rationale. After you have introduced the problem and developed the background material, you are in a position to tell what you did. Make this statement in the closing paragraphs of the introduction. At this point, a definition of the variables and a formal statement of your hypotheses give clarity to the paper. Questions to bear in mind in closing the introduction are, What variables did I plan to manipulate? What results did I expect and why did I expect them? The logic behind "Why did I expect them?" should be made explicit. Clearly develop the rationale for each hypothesis.

1.09 Method

The Method section describes in detail how the study was conducted. Such a description enables the reader to evaluate the appropriateness of your methods and the reliability and the validity of your results. It also permits experienced investigators to replicate the study if they so desire.

If you refer the reader to another source for details of the method, give a brief synopsis of the method in this section. (See section 1.12 for treatment of multiple experiments.)

Identify subsections. It is both conventional and expedient to divide the Method section into labeled subsections. These usually include descriptions of the *subjects*, the *apparatus* (or *materials*), and the *procedure*. If the design of the experiment is complex or the stimuli require detailed description, additional subsections or subheadings to divide the subsections may be warranted to help readers find specific information. Your own judgment is the best guide on what number and type of subheadings to use (see section 3.30 for guidelines).

Include in these subsections only the information essential to comprehend and replicate the study. Given insufficient detail, the reader is left with questions; given too much detail, the reader is burdened with irrelevant information.

Subjects. The subsection on subjects answers three questions: Who participated in the study? How many participants were there? How were they selected? Give the total number of participants and the number assigned to each experimental condition. If any participants did not complete the experiment, give the number of participants and the reasons they did not continue.

When humans are the participants, report the procedures for selecting and assigning subjects and the agreements and payments made. Give major demographic characteristics such as general geographic location, type of institutional affiliation, sex, and age. When a demographic characteristic is an experimental variable, describe the group specifically: for example, "The second group comprised 40 men between the ages of 20 and 30 years, all of whom had emigrated from Scandinavia, were permanent residents of the United States for at least 15 years, and lived in a major city in Minnesota."

When animals are the participants, report the genus, species, and strain number or other specific identification, such as the name of the supplier. Give the number of animals and the animals' sex, age, weight, and physiological condition. In addition, specify all essential details of their treatment and handling so that the investigation can be successfully replicated.

When you submit your manuscript, indicate to the journal editor that the treatment of participants (human or animal) was in accordance with the ethical standards of the APA (see Principle 9, Research With Human Participants, and Principle 10, Care and Use of Animals, in the "Ethical Principles of Psychologists," APA, 1981).

Apparatus. The subsection on apparatus briefly describes the apparatus or materials used and their function in the experiment. Standard laboratory equipment, such as furniture, stopwatches, or screens, can usually be mentioned without detail. Identify specialized equipment obtained from a commercial establishment by the firm's name and the model number of the equipment. Complex or custom-made equipment may be illustrated by a drawing or photograph, although such figures do add to manuscript preparation and printing costs. A detailed description of complex equipment may be included in an appendix.

Procedure. The subsection on procedure summarizes each step in the execution of the research. Include the instructions to the participants, the formation of the groups, and the specific experimental manipulations. Describe randomization, counterbalancing, and other control features in the design. Summarize or paraphrase instructions, unless they are unusual or compose an experimental manipulation, in which cases they may be presented verbatim. Most readers are familiar with standard testing procedures; unless new or unique procedures are used, do not describe them in detail.

Remember that the Method section should tell the reader *what* you did and *how* you did it.

1.10 Results

The Results section summarizes the data collected and the statistical treatment of them. First, briefly state the main results or findings. Then report the data in sufficient detail to justify the conclusions. Discussing the implications of the results is not appropriate here. Mention all relevant results, including those that run counter to the hypothesis. Do not include individual scores or raw data, with the exception, for example, of single-subject designs or illustrative samples.

Tables and figures. To report the data, choose the medium that presents them clearly and economically. Tables provide exact values and can efficiently illustrate main effects; they are less expensive than figures to reproduce. Figures of professional quality attract the reader's eye and best illustrate interactions and general comparisons, but they are imprecise and are expensive to reproduce.

Although summarizing the results and the analysis in tables or figures may be helpful, avoid repeating the same data in several places and using tables for data that can be easily presented in a few sentences in the text. If you do use tables or figures, use as few as possible and be certain to mention all of them in text. Refer to all tables as *tables* and to all graphs, pictures, or drawings as *figures*. Tables and figures supplement the text; they cannot do the entire job of communication. Always tell the reader what to look for in tables and figures and provide sufficient explanation to make them readily intelligible (see sections 3.59 to 3.82 for detailed information on tables and figures).

Statistical presentation. When reporting inferential statistics (e.g., *t* tests, *F* tests, chi-square), include information about the obtained magnitude or value of the test, the degrees of freedom, the probability level, and the direction of the effect. Be sure to include descriptive statistics (e.g., means or standard deviations). (See section 3.54 on statistical presentation.) Assume that your reader has professional knowledge of statistics. Basic assumptions, such as rejecting the null hypothesis, should not be reviewed. If there is a question about the appropriateness of a particular test, however, be sure to justify the use of that test.

1.11 Discussion

After presenting the results, you are in a position to evaluate and interpret their implications, especially with respect to your original hypothesis. In the Discussion section, you are free to examine, interpret, and qualify the results, as well as to draw inferences from them. Emphasize any theoretical consequences of the results and the validity of your conclusions. (When the discussion is relatively brief and straightforward, some authors prefer to combine it with the previous Results section, yielding *Results and Conclusions* or *Results and Discussion*.)

Open the discussion with a clear statement of the support or nonsupport for your original hypothesis. Similarities and differences between your results and the work of others should clarify and confirm your conclusions. Do not, however, simply reformulate and repeat points already made; each new statement should contribute to your position and to the readers' understanding of the problem. You may remark on certain shortcomings of the study, but do not dwell compulsively on every flaw. Negative results should be accepted as such without an undue attempt to explain them away.

Avoid polemics, triviality, and weak theoretical comparisons in your discussion. Speculation is in order only if it is (a) identified as such, (b) related closely and logically to empirical data or theory, and (c) expressed concisely. Identifying the practical and theoretical implications of your study, suggesting improvements on your research, or proposing new research may be appropriate, but keep these comments brief. In general, be guided by these questions:
- What have I contributed here?
- How has my study helped to resolve the original problem?
- What conclusions and theoretical implications can I draw from my study?

The responses to these questions are the core of your contribution, and readers have a right to clear, unambiguous, and direct answers.

1.12 Multiple Experiments

If you are integrating several experiments in one paper, describe the method and results of each experiment separately. If appropriate, include for each experiment a short discussion of the results or combine the discussion with the description of results (e.g., *Results and Discussion*). Always make the logic and rationale of each new experiment clear to the reader. Always include a comprehensive general discussion of all the work after the last experiment.

The arrangement of sections reflects the structure described above. Label the experiments Experiment 1, Experiment 2, and so forth. These labels are centered main headings (see section 3.29 on levels of headings). They organize the subsections and make referring to a specific experiment convenient for the reader. The Method and Results sections (and the Discussion section, if a short discussion accompanies each experiment) appear under each experimental heading. (Refer to Figure 8 for the form of a multiple-experiment paper.)

1.13 References

Just as data in the paper support interpretations and conclusions, so reference citations document statements made about the literature. All citations in the manuscript must appear in the reference list, and all references must be cited in text. Choose references judiciously and cite them accurately. The standard procedures for citation ensure that references are accurate, complete, and useful to investigators and readers (see sections 3.86 to 3.101 on citations and references).

1.14 Appendix

An appendix, although seldom used, is helpful if the detailed description of certain material is distracting in, or inappropriate to, the body of the paper. Some examples of material suitable for an appendix are (a) a new computer program specifically designed for your research and unavailable elsewhere, (b) an unpublished test and its validation, (c) a complicated mathematical proof, (d) a list of stimulus materials (e.g., those used in psycholinguistic research), or (e) a detailed description of a complex piece of equipment. Include an appendix only if it helps readers to understand, evaluate, or replicate the study.

Quality of Presentation

A manuscript that is important enough to write deserves thoughtful preparation. You should evaluate the content and organization of the manuscript just as you evaluated the investigation itself. The following questions (based on Bartol, 1981) may help you assess the quality of your presentation.

- Is the topic appropriate for the journal to which the manuscript is submitted?
- Is the introduction clear and complete?
- Does the statement of purpose adequately and logically orient the reader?
- Is the literature adequately reviewed?
- Are the citations appropriate and complete?
- Is the research question clearly identified, and is the hypothesis explicit?
- Are the conceptualization and rationale perfectly clear?
- Is the method clearly and adequately described? That is, can the study be replicated from the description provided in the paper?
- If observers were used to assess variables, is the interobserver reliability reported?
- Are the techniques of data analysis appropriate, and is the analysis clear? Are the assumptions underlying the statistical procedures clearly met by the data to which they are applied?
- Are the results and conclusions unambiguous, valid, and meaningful?
- Is the discussion thorough? Does it stick to the point and confine itself to what can be concluded from the significant findings of the study?
- Is the paper concise?
- Is the manuscript prepared according to APA style? (Use the checklist on the inside front and back covers of the *Manual* as a guide.)

2 Expression of Ideas

Good writing is an art and a craft, and instructing in its mastery is beyond the scope of the Publication Manual. *Instead, this chapter provides some general principles of expository writing, demonstrates how correct grammar can facilitate clear communication, and suggests ways to assess and improve writing style. Just as a disciplined scientific investigation contributes to the growth and development of a field, so does carefully crafted writing contribute to the value of scientific literature. Thoughtful concern for the language can yield clear and orderly writing that sharpens and strengthens your personal style and allows for individuality of expression and purpose.*

Clear communication, which is the prime objective of scientific reporting, may be achieved by presenting ideas in an orderly manner and by expressing oneself smoothly and precisely. By developing ideas clearly and logically, you invite readers to read, encourage them to continue, and make their task agreeable by leading them smoothly from thought to thought. Some guides listed in section 7.03 elaborate on these objectives.

Writing Style

The style requirements in the *Publication Manual* are intended to facilitate clear communication. The requirements are explicit, but alternatives to prescribed forms are permissible if they ensure clearer communication. In all cases, the use of rules should be balanced with good judgment.

2.01 Orderly Presentation of Ideas

Thought units—whether single words, a sentence or paragraph, or longer sequences—must be orderly. So that readers will understand what you are presenting, you must aim for continuity in words, concepts, and thematic development from the opening statement to the conclusion. Readers will be confused if you misplace words or phrases in sentences, abandon familiar syntax, shift the criterion for items in a series, or clutter the sequence of ideas with wordiness or irrelevancies.

Continuity can be achieved in several ways. For instance, punctuation marks contribute to continuity by showing relationships between ideas. They cue the reader to the pauses, inflections, subordination, and pacing normally heard in speech. Use the full range of punctuation aids available: Neither overuse nor underuse one type of punctuation, such as commas or dashes. Overuse may annoy the reader; underuse may confuse. Instead, use punctuation to support meaning (see sections 3.01 to 3.08 for details on accepted use of punctuation).

Another way to achieve continuity is through the use of transition words. These words help maintain the flow of thought, especially when the material is complex or abstract. A pronoun that refers to a noun in the preceding sentence not only serves as a transition but also avoids repetition. Be sure the referent is obvious. Other transition devices are time links (*then, next, after, while, since*), cause–effect links (*therefore, consequently, as a result*), addition links (*in addition, moreover, furthermore, similarly*), or contrast links (*however, but, conversely, nevertheless, although, whereas*).

A few transition words (e.g., *while, since*) create confusion because they have been adopted in informal writing style and in conversation for transitions other than time links. For example, *since* is often used when *because* is meant. Scientific writing, however, must be precise; therefore, only the original meaning of these transition words is acceptable (see section 2.10 for rules and examples).

2.02 Smoothness of Expression

Scientific prose serves a different purpose than creative writing does. Devices that are often found in creative writing, for example, setting up ambiguity, inserting the unexpected, omitting the expected, and suddenly shifting the topic, tense, or person, can confuse or disturb readers of scientific prose. Therefore, these devices should be avoided in writing that aims for clear and logical communication.

Because you have spent so much time close to your material and have thus lost some objectivity, you may not immediately see certain problems, especially inferred contradictions. A reading by a col-

league may uncover such problems. You can usually catch omissions, irrelevancies, and abruptness by putting the manuscript aside and rereading it later. If you also read the paper aloud, you have an even better chance of finding problems of abruptness.

If, on later reading, you do find that your writing is abrupt, more transition from one topic to another may be needed. Possibly you have abandoned an argument or theme prematurely; if so, you need to amplify the discussion.

Abruptness is often the result of sudden shifts in verb tense and the capricious use of different tenses within the same paragraph or in adjacent paragraphs. By being consistent in the use of verb tenses, you can help ensure smooth expression. Past tense (e.g., *Smith showed*) or present perfect tense (e.g., *researchers have shown*) is appropriate for the literature review and the description of the procedure if the discussion is of past events. Stay within the chosen tense. Use past tense (e.g., *the subjects performed*) to describe the results. Use the present tense (e.g., *the data indicate*) to discuss the results and to present the conclusions. By reporting conclusions in the present tense, you allow readers to join you in deliberating the matter at hand. (See section 2.06 for details on the use of tense.)

Many writers strive to achieve smooth expression by using synonyms or near synonyms to avoid repeating a term. The intention is commendable, but by using synonyms you may unintentionally suggest a subtle difference. Therefore, choose synonyms with care. The discreet use of pronouns can often relieve the monotonous repetition of a term without introducing ambiguity.

2.03 Economy of Expression

Say only what needs to be said. The author who is frugal with words not only writes a more readable manuscript but also increases the chances that the manuscript will be accepted. Editors work with limited numbers of printed pages and therefore often request authors to shorten submitted papers. You can tighten overly long papers by eliminating redundancy, wordiness, jargon, evasiveness, circumlocution, and clumsiness. Weed out overly detailed descriptions of apparatus, subjects, or procedure; gratuitous embellishments; elaborations of the obvious; and irrelevant observations or asides.

Short words and short sentences are easier to comprehend than long ones. A long technical term, however, may be more precise than several short words, and technical terms are inseparable from scientific reporting. Yet the technical terminology in a paper should be understood by psychologists throughout the discipline. An article that depends upon terminology familiar to only a few specialists does not sufficiently contribute to the literature.

The main causes of uneconomical writing are jargon and wordiness. Jargon is the continuous use of a technical vocabulary even in places where that vocabulary is not relevant. Jargon is also the substitution of a euphemistic phrase for a familiar term (e.g., *monetary felt scarcity* for *poverty*), and, as such, it should be scrupulously avoided. Federal bureaucratic jargon has had the greatest publicity, but scientific jargon also grates on the reader, encumbers the communication of information, and often takes up space unnecessarily.

Wordiness is every bit as irritating and uneconomical as jargon and can impede the ready grasp of ideas. Change *based on the fact that* to *because*, *at the present time* to *now*, and *for the purpose of* to a simple *for* or *to*. Change *there were several students who completed* to *several students completed*. *Reason* and *because* often appear in the same sentence; however, they have the same meaning, and therefore they should not be used together. Unconstrained wordiness lapses into embellishment and literary elegance, which are clearly inappropriate in scientific style. Mullins (1977) comprehensively discusses examples of wordiness found in the social science literature.

Writers often become redundant in a mistaken effort to be emphatic. Use no more words than are necessary to convey the meaning. In the following examples, the italicized words are redundant and should be omitted:

They were *both* alike	*one and* the same
a total of 68 subjects	in *close* proximity
Four *different* groups saw	*completely* unanimous
instructions, which were *exactly* the same as those used	*just* exactly
	very close to significance
	period of time
absolutely essential	summarize *briefly*
has been *previously* found	the reason is *because*
small *in size*	

Although writing only in short, simple sentences produces choppy and boring prose, writing exclusively in long, involved sentences creates difficult, sometimes incomprehensible material. Varied sentence length helps readers maintain interest and comprehension. When involved concepts do require long sentences, the components should march along like people in a parade, not dodge about like broken-field runners. Direct, declarative sentences with simple, common words are usually best.

Similar cautions apply to paragraph length. Single-sentence paragraphs may be abrupt. Paragraphs that are too long, a more typical fault in manuscripts, are likely to lose the reader's attention. New paragraphs provide a pause for the reader—a chance to store one step in the conceptual development before beginning another. If your paragraphs run longer than a page in typescript, you are probably straining the reader's thought span. Look for a logical place to make a break or reorganize the material. Unity, cohesiveness, and continuity should characterize all paragraphs.

2.04 Precision and Clarity in Word Choice

Make certain that every word means exactly what you intend it to mean. Sooner or later most authors discover a discrepancy between their accepted meaning of a term and its dictionary definition. In informal style, for example, *feel* broadly substitutes for *think* or *believe*, but such latitude is not acceptable in scientific style.

Likewise, avoid colloquial expressions (e.g., *write up* for *report*), which diffuse meaning. Approximations of quantity (e.g., *quite a large part*, *practically all*, or *very few*) are interpreted differently by different readers or in different contexts. They weaken statements, especially those describing empirical observations.

Pronouns confuse readers unless the referent for each pronoun is obvious; readers should not have to search previous text to determine the meaning of the term. Simple pronouns are the most troublesome, especially *this*, *that*, *these*, and *those* when they refer to a previous sentence. Eliminate ambiguity by writing, for example, *this test*, *that trial*, *these subjects*, and *those reports*. (See also section 2.08.)

Omission of key verbs is another cause of ambiguity, as in the sentence, "Ten-year-olds were more likely to play with age peers than 8-year-olds." Does this sentence mean that 10-year-olds were more likely than 8-year-olds to play with age peers? Or does it mean that 10-year-olds were more likely to play with age peers and less likely to play with 8-year-olds? Thoughtful attention to good sentence structure and word choice reduces the chance of this kind of ambiguity.

Inappropriately or illogically attributing action in the name of objectivity can be misleading. For example, writing "The experimenter instructed the subjects" when "the experimenter" refers to yourself is at best ambiguous and may even give the impression that you disavow your own study. (For a study of editorial preferences for first- or third-person writing style, see Polyson, Levinson, & Miller, 1982.) In addition, do not attribute human functions to nonhuman sources (e.g., "The community program was persuaded to allow five of the observers to become tutors"). An experiment cannot *attempt to demonstrate*, *control unwanted variables*, or *interpret findings*. Use *I* or *we*, that is, the author or authors, as the subject of these verbs (but never use *we* in the editorial sense).

2.05 Strategies to Improve Writing Style

Authors use a variety of strategies in putting their thoughts on paper, and there is little basis for selecting one over another. Very likely the fit between author and strategy is more important than the particular strategy used. Three approaches to achieving professional and effective communication are (a) writing from an outline; (b) putting aside the first draft, then rereading it after a delay; and (c) asking a colleague to criticize the draft for you.

Writing from an outline helps preserve the logic of the research itself. It identifies main ideas, defines subordinate ideas, disciplines your writing, maintains the continuity and pacing, discourages tangential excursions, and points out omissions.

Rereading your own copy after setting it aside for a few days permits a fresh approach. Reading the paper aloud enables you not only to see faults that "were never there" on the previous reading but to hear them as well. When these problems are corrected, give a polished copy to a colleague—preferably a person who has published but who has not been close to your own work—for a critical review. Even better, get critiques from two colleagues, and you have a trial run of a journal's review process.

These strategies, particularly the latter, may require you to invest more time in a manuscript than you had anticipated. The results of these strategies, however, may be greater accuracy and thorough-ness and clearer communication.

Grammar

Incorrect grammar and careless construction of sentences distract the reader, introduce ambiguity, and generally obstruct communi-cation. For example, the sentence "We scheduled a 10-min break between each test" suggests that each test was interrupted by a break. The sentence should read, "We scheduled 10-min breaks be-tween the tests" or "We scheduled a 10-min break after each test." Correct grammar and thoughtful construction of sentences ease the reader's task and facilitate unambiguous communication.

The examples in the next section of this chapter represent the kinds of problems of grammar and usage that occur frequently in manuscripts submitted to APA journals. These examples of incor-rect and correct usage should help authors steer clear of the most common errors. For discussions of problems not addressed in this section and for more comprehensive discussions of grammar and usage in general, authors should consult appropriate authoritative manuals (see also the sources on writing style in section 7.03 of the Bibliography).

2.06 Verbs

Verbs are vigorous, direct communicators. Use the active rather than the passive voice and select tense or mood carefully.

Use the active voice.

Poor: The experiment was designed by Gould (1970).
Better: Gould (1970) designed the experiment.

Use the past tense to express an action or a condition that occurred at a specific, definite time in the past. (See also section 2.02 on verb tense.)

Incorrect: Ramirez (1980) shows the same results.
Correct: Ramirez (1980) showed the same results.

Use the present perfect tense to express a past action or condition that did not occur at a specific, definite time or an action beginning in the past and continuing to the present.

Incorrect: Since that time investigators from several studies used this method.
Correct: Since that time investigators from several studies have used this method.

Use the subjunctive to describe only conditions that are contrary to fact or improbable; do not use the subjunctive to describe simple conditions or contingencies.

Incorrect: If the experiment was not designed this way, the subjects' performances would suffer.
Correct: If the experiment were not designed this way, the sub-jects' performances would suffer.

Incorrect: If the subject were finished answering the questions, the data are complete.

> *Correct:* If the subject is finished answering the questions, the data are complete.

Use *would* with care. *Would* can correctly be used to mean habitually, as "The child would walk about the classroom," or to express a conditional action, as "We would sign the letter if we could." Do not use *would* to hedge; for example, change *it would appear that* to *it appears that*.

2.07 Agreement of Subject and Verb

A verb must agree in number (i.e., singular or plural) with its subject despite intervening phrases that begin with such words as *together with, including, plus,* and *as well as.*

> *Incorrect:* The percentage of correct responses as well as the speed of the responses increase with practice.
> *Correct:* The percentage of correct responses as well as the speed of the responses increases with practice.

The plural form of some nouns of foreign origin, particularly those that end in the letter *a,* may appear to be singular and can cause authors to select a verb that does not agree in number with the noun:

> *Incorrect:* The data indicates that Terrence was correct.
> *Correct:* The data indicate that Terrence was correct.
> *Incorrect:* The phenomena occurs every 100 years.
> *Correct:* The phenomena occur every 100 years.

Also beware that some nouns of foreign origin that in their singular form end in the letter *a* form the plural by adding an ending other than the letter *s*; for example, the plural form of the word *schema* is *schemata,* not *schemas.* Consult the dictionary when in doubt about the plural form of nouns of foreign origin.

Collective nouns (e.g., *series, set, faculty,* or *pair*) can refer either to several individuals or to a single unit. If the action of the verb is on the group as a whole, treat the noun as a singular noun. If the action of the verb is on members of the group as individuals, treat the noun as a plural noun. The context (i.e., your emphasis) determines whether the action is on the group or on individuals.

> *Singular in context:*
>> The number of people in the state is growing.
>> A pair of animals was in each cage.
>> The couple is surrounded.
>
> *Plural in context:*
>> A number of people are watching.
>> A pair of animals were then yoked.
>> The couple are separated.

The pronoun *none* can also be singular or plural. When the noun that follows it is singular, use a singular verb; when the noun is plural, use a plural verb. If you mean "not one," use *not one* instead of *none* and use a singular verb.

> *Singular in context:*
>> None of the information was correct.

Plural in context:

None of the children were finished in the time allotted.

but

Not one of the children was finished in the time allotted.

When the subject is composed of a singular and a plural noun joined by *or* or *nor*, the verb agrees with the noun that is closer.

Incorrect: Neither the subjects nor the confederate were in the room.

Correct: Neither the subjects nor the confederate was in the room.

or

Neither the confederate nor the subjects were in the room.

If the number of the subject changes, retain the verb in each clause.

Incorrect: The positions in the sequence were changed, and the test rerun.

Correct: The positions in the sequence were changed, and the test was rerun.

2.08 Pronouns

Pronouns replace nouns. Each pronoun should refer clearly to its antecedent and should agree with the antecedent in number and gender.

A pronoun must agree in number (i.e., singular or plural) with the noun it replaces.

Incorrect: The group improved their scores 30%.
Correct: The group improved its scores 30%.

Incorrect: Neither the highest scorer nor the lowest scorer in the group had any doubt about their competence.
Correct: Neither the highest scorer nor the lowest scorer in the group had any doubt about his or her competence.

A pronoun must agree in gender (i.e., masculine, feminine, or neuter) with the noun it replaces. This rule extends to relative pronouns (pronouns that link subordinate clauses to nouns). Use *who* for human beings; use *that* or *which* for nonhuman animals and for things.

Incorrect: The rats who completed the task successfully were rewarded.
Correct: The rats that completed the task successfully were rewarded.

(See section 2.10 for further discussion of the use of relative pronouns.)

Pronouns can be subjects or objects of verbs or prepositions. Use *who* as the subject of a verb and *whom* as the object of a verb or a preposition. You can determine whether a relative pronoun is the subject or object of a verb by turning the subordinate clause around and substituting a personal pronoun. If you can substitute *he* or *she, who* is correct; if you can substitute *him* or *her, whom* is the correct pronoun.

Incorrect: Name the subject whom you found scored above the median. [you found *him* or *her* scored above the median]

Correct: Name the subject who you found scored above the median. [you found *he* or *she* scored above the median]

Incorrect: The subject who I identified as the youngest dropped out. [I identified *he* or *she* as the youngest]

Correct: The subject whom I identified as the youngest dropped out. [I identified *him* or *her* as the youngest]

In a phrase consisting of a pronoun or noun plus a present participle (e.g., *running, flying*) that is used as an object of a preposition, the participle can be either a noun or a modifier of a noun, depending on the intended meaning. When you use a participle as a noun, make the other pronoun or noun possessive.

Incorrect: We had nothing to do with them being the winners.

Correct: We had nothing to do with their being the winners.

Incorrect: The significance is questionable because of one subject performing at incredible speed.

Correct: The significance is questionable because of one subject's performing at incredible speed. [The significance is questionable because of the performance, not because of the subject.]

> **but**

We spoke to the person sitting at the table. [The person, not the sitting, is the object of the preposition.]

2.09 Misplaced and Dangling Modifiers

An adjective or an adverb, whether a single word or a phrase, must clearly refer to the word it modifies.

Misplaced modifiers, because of their placement in a sentence, ambiguously or illogically modify a word. You can eliminate these by placing an adjective or an adverb as close as possible to the word it modifies.

Unclear: The investigator tested the subjects using this procedure. [The sentence is unclear about whether the investigator or the subjects used this procedure.]

Clear: Using this procedure, the investigator tested the subjects.

Clear: The investigator, using this procedure, tested the subjects.

Many writers have particular problems with the word *only*. Place *only* next to the word or phrase it modifies.

Incorrect: These data only provide a partial answer.

Correct: These data provide only a partial answer.

Incorrect: We found a mean of 7.9 errors on the first trial and only a mean of 1.3 errors on the second trial.

Correct: We found a mean of 7.9 errors on the first trial and a mean of only 1.3 errors on the second trial.

Dangling modifiers have no referent in the sentence. Many of these are results of the use of passive voice. By writing in the active voice, you can avoid many dangling modifiers.

Incorrect: After separating the subjects into groups, Group A was tested.

Correct: After separating the subjects into groups, I tested Group A. [I, not Group A, separated the subjects into groups.]

Incorrect: The subjects were tested using this procedure.

Correct: Using this procedure, I tested the subjects. [I, not the subjects, used the procedure.]

Incorrect: To test this hypothesis, the subjects were divided into two groups.

Correct: To test this hypothesis, we divided the subjects into two groups. [We, not the subjects, tested the hypothesis.]

Incorrect: Congruent with other studies, Black and Smith (1981) found that this group performed better.

Correct: Black and Smith (1980) found that this group performed better, results that are congruent with those of other studies. [The results, not Black and Smith, are congruent.]

Adverbs can be used as introductory or transition words. Adverbs modify verbs, adjectives, and other adverbs and express manner or quality. Some adverbs, however, such as *fortunately, similarly, certainly, consequently, conversely,* and *regrettably,* can also be used as introductory or transition words as long as the sense is confined to, for example, "it is fortunate that" or "in a similar manner." Use adverbs judiciously as introductory or transition words. Ask yourself first whether the introduction or transition is needed and second whether the adverb is being used correctly.

The adverb most often misused as an introductory or transition word is *hopefully. Hopefully* means "in a hopeful manner" or "full of hope"; *hopefully* should not be used to mean "I hope" or "it is hoped."

Incorrect: Hopefully, this is not the case.

Correct: I hope this is not the case.

2.10   Relative Pronouns and Subordinate Conjunctions

Relative pronouns (*who, whom, that, which*) and subordinate conjunctions (e.g., *since, while, although*) introduce an element that is subordinate to the main clause of the sentence and reflect the relationship of the subordinate element to the main clause. Therefore, select these pronouns and conjunctions with care; do not interchange them. (See section 2.08 for further discussion of relative pronouns.)

Relative pronouns
That versus *which*
That clauses (called restrictive) are essential to the meaning of the sentence:

The animals that performed well in the first experiment were used in the second experiment.

Which clauses (called nonrestrictive) merely add further information:

> The animals, which performed well in the first experiment, were not proficient in the second experiment.

Subordinate conjunctions
While and *since*

Some style authorities accept the use of *while* and *since* when they do not refer strictly to time; however, words like these, with more than one meaning, can cause confusion. Because precision and clarity are the standards in scientific writing, the *Manual* restricts *while* and *since* to their temporal meanings. (See also section 2.04 on precision and clarity.)

> Bragg (1965) found that subjects performed well while listening to music.
>
> Several versions of the test have been developed since the test was first introduced.

While versus *although*

Use *while* only to link events occurring simultaneously; do not use *while* in place of *although*, *whereas*, *and*, or *but*.

Incorrect: Bragg (1965) found that subjects performed well, while Bohr (1969) found that subjects did poorly.

Correct: Bragg (1965) found that subjects performed well, whereas Bohr (1969) found that subjects did poorly.

Incorrect: While these findings are unusual, they are not unique.

Correct: Although these findings are unusual, they are not unique.

> *or*
>
> These findings are unusual, but they are not unique.

Since versus *because*

Use *since* in reference only to time (to mean "after that"); do not use *since* in place of *because*.

Incorrect: Data for 2 subjects were incomplete since these subjects did not report for follow-up testing.

Correct: Data for 2 subjects were incomplete because these subjects did not report for follow-up testing.

2.11 Parallel Construction

For accuracy, parallel ideas require parallel or coordinate form. Make certain that all elements of the parallelism are present before and after the coordinating conjunction (i.e., *and*, *but*, *or*, *nor*).

Incorrect: The results showed that such changes could be made without affecting error rate and latencies continued to decrease over time.

Correct: The results showed that such changes could be made without affecting error rate and that latencies continued to decrease over time.

With coordinating conjunctions used in pairs (*between . . . and*, *both . . . and*, *neither . . . nor*, *either . . . or*, *not only . . . but also*), place the first conjunction immediately before the first part of the parallelism.

Between and *and*

Incorrect: We recorded the difference between the performance of subjects who completed the first task and the second task.

Correct: We recorded the difference between the performance of subjects who completed the first task and the performance of those who completed the second task. [The difference is between the subjects' performances, not between the performance and the task.]

Both and *and*

Incorrect: The names were both difficult to pronounce and spell.

Correct: The names were difficult both to pronounce and to spell.

Never use *both* with *as well as*: The resulting construction is redundant.

Incorrect: The names were difficult both to pronounce as well as to spell.

Correct: The names were difficult to pronounce as well as to spell.

Neither and *nor* and *either* and *or*

Incorrect: Neither the responses to the auditory stimuli nor to the tactile stimuli were repeated.

Correct: Neither the responses to the auditory stimuli nor the responses to the tactile stimuli were repeated.

Incorrect: The subjects either gave the worst answer or the best answer.

Correct: The subjects either gave the worst answer or gave the best answer.

or

The subjects gave either the worst answer or the best answer.

Not only and *but* (*also*)

Incorrect: It is not only surprising that pencil-and-paper scores predicted this result but that all other predictors did less well.

Correct: It is surprising not only that pencil-and-paper scores predicted this result but (also) that all other predictors did less well.

Elements in a series should also be parallel in form.

Incorrect: The subjects were told to make themselves comfortable, to read the instructions, and that they should ask about anything they did not understand.

Correct: The subjects were told to make themselves comfortable, to read the instructions, and to ask about anything they did not understand.

When you develop a clear writing style and use correct grammar, you show a concern not only for accurately presenting your knowledge and ideas but also for easing the reader's task. Another consideration in writing is that of maintaining the reader's focus of attention. Such a concern demands the thoughtful use of language. The next section discusses the importance of choosing words that are appropriate to your subject and free from bias, another way to achieve disciplined writing and precise, unambiguous communication.

Consideration of the Reader

Help the reader focus on the content of your paper by avoiding language that may cause irritation, flights of thought, or even momentary interruptions. Such sources of distraction include linguistic devices and constructions that might imply sexual, ethnic, or other kinds of bias.

Devices that attract attention to words, sounds, or other embellishments instead of to ideas are inappropriate in scientific writing. Avoid heavy alliteration, accidental rhyming, poetic expressions, and clichés. Use metaphors sparingly; although they can help simplify complicated ideas, metaphors can be distracting. Avoid mixed metaphors (e.g., *a theory representing one branch of a growing body of evidence*) and words with surplus or unintended meaning (e.g., *cop* for *police officer*), which may distract if not actually mislead the reader. Use figurative expressions with restraint and colorful expressions with care; these expressions can sound strained or forced.

APA as a publisher accepts journal authors' word choices unless those choices are inaccurate, unclear, or ungrammatical. Because APA as an organization is committed both to science and to the fair treatment of individuals and groups, however, authors of journal articles are required to avoid writing in a manner that reinforces questionable attitudes and assumptions about people.

2.12 Guidelines for Nonsexist Language in APA Journals

Language that reinforces sexism can spring from subtle errors in research design, inaccurate interpretation, or imprecise word choices. An investigator may unintentionally introduce bias into the research design, for example, by using stimulus materials and measures that suggest to one sex or the other what responses are "appropriate." Or, in interpretation, an investigator may make unwarranted generalizations about both men and women from data about one sex. Imprecise word choices, which occur frequently in journal writing, may be interpreted as biased, discriminatory, or demeaning even if they are not intended to be.

Advice on research design and interpretation is beyond the scope of the APA *Publication Manual*. However, in the spirit of the discussion on writing style in this chapter, the *Manual* does contain guidelines on nonsexist language to help authors recognize and change instances in which word choices may be inaccurate, misleading, or discriminatory (see Table 1).

In 1977 the APA adopted guidelines for nonsexist language, which appeared as Change Sheet 2 for the 1974 edition of the *Manual*. In

1982 the APA Publications and Communications Board adopted a policy that requires authors who are submitting their manuscripts to an APA journal to use nonsexist language, that is, to avoid in their manuscripts language that could be construed as sexist. The guidelines on nonsexist language adopted in 1977 are reproduced in Table 1 with minor editorial improvements and updating (also see the sources on nondiscriminatory language in section 7.03).

Sexism in journal writing may be classified into two categories: problems of designation and problems of evaluation.

Problems of designation. When you refer to a person or persons, choose words that are accurate, clear, and free from bias. Long-established cultural practice can exert a powerful, insidious influence over even the most conscientious author. For example, the use of *man* as a generic noun can be ambiguous and may convey an implicit message that women are of secondary importance. You can choose nouns, pronouns, and adjectives to eliminate, or at least to minimize, the possibility of ambiguity in sex identity or sex role. In the examples in Table 1, problems of designation are divided into two subcategories: *ambiguity of referent*, when it is unclear whether the author means one sex or both sexes, and *stereotyping*, when the writing conveys unsupported or biased connotations about sex roles and identity.

Problems of evaluation. Scientific writing, as an extension of science, should be free of implied or irrelevant evaluation of the sexes. Difficulties may derive from the habitual use of clichés or familiar expressions, such as "man and wife." The use of *man* and *wife* together implies differences in the freedom and activities of each and may inappropriately prompt the reader to evaluate the roles. Thus, *husband* and *wife* are parallel, and *man* and *woman* are parallel, but *man* and *wife* are not. In the examples in Table 1, problems of evaluation, like problems of designation, are divided into *ambiguity of referent* and *stereotyping*.

Avoiding sexist language. The task of changing language may seem awkward at first. Nevertheless, careful attention to meaning and practice in rephrasing will overcome any initial difficulty (cf. Bass, 1979). The result of such effort, and the purpose of the Table 1 guidelines, is accurate, unbiased communication.

2.13 Avoiding Ethnic Bias

Like language that may be interpreted as sexist, language that may be construed as ethnically biased can be classified into problems of designation and problems of evaluation.

Problems of designation. Styles and preferences for nouns referring to ethnic groups change over time. In some cases, even members of a group disagree about the preferred name at a specific time. You should try to ascertain the most acceptable current terms and use them. Consideration for your audience should prevail.

Problems of evaluation. The majority of instances of implied irrelevant evaluation seem to occur when the writer uses one group (usually the writer's *own* group) as the standard against which others are assessed. Unfortunately, the basis for negative comparisons is usually established during the planning of the research, for example, by the choice of empirical measures.

At the writing stage, avoid language that suggests evaluation. An example of implied evaluation is found in the term *culturally deprived* when it is used to describe a single group rather than to compare two or more groups. Using the term to describe one group of subjects—*without the supporting data required in scientific writing*—implies that one culture is a universally accepted standard against which others are judged. As a test of implied evaluation, substitute another group (e.g., your own) for the group being discussed. If you are offended by the revised statement, there is probably bias in the original statement.

TABLE 1

Guidelines for Nonsexist Language in APA Journals

Examples of common usage	Alternatives
Problems of Designation: Ambiguity of Referent	
1. The *client* is usually the best judge of the value of *his* counseling.	The *client* is usually the best judge of the value of counseling. [Comment: *His* deleted]
	The client is usually the best judge of the value of his *or her* counseling. [Comment: *Or her* added (Use sparingly to avoid monotonous repetition.)]
	Clients are usually the best judges of the value of the counseling *they* receive. [Comment: Changed to plural]
	The best judge of the value of counseling is usually *the client.* [Comment: Rephrased]
2. *Man's search* for knowledge has led *him* into ways of learning that bear examination.	*The search* for knowledge has led *us* into ways of learning that bear examination. [Comment: Rephrased in first person]
	People have continually sought knowledge. The search has led *them* into ways of learning that bear examination. [Comment: Changed to plural and rewritten in two sentences]
3. man, mankind	people, humanity, human beings, humankind, human species
man's achievements	human achievements, achievements of the human species
the average man	the average person, people in general
man a project	staff a project, hire personnel, employ staff
man–machine interface	user–system interface, person–system interface, human–machine interface
manpower	work force, personnel, workers, human resources
	[Comment: Various terms substituted for each example]

continued

(Table 1 continued)

4.	The use of experiments in psychology presupposes the mechanistic nature of *man*.	The use of experiments in psychology presupposes the mechanistic nature of the *human being*. [Comment: Noun substituted]
5.	This interference phenomenon, called learned helplessness, has been demonstrated in rats, cats, fish, dogs, monkeys, and *men*.	This interference phenomenon, called learned helplessness, has been demonstrated in rats, cats, fish, dogs, monkeys, and *humans*. [Comment: Noun substituted]
6.	Responsivity in the premature *infant* may be secondary to *his* heightened level of autonomic arousal.	Responsivity in the premature *infant* may be secondary to *the* heightened level of autonomic arousal. [Comment: *His* changed to *the*] Responsivity in premature *infants* may be secondary to *their* heightened levels of autonomic arousal. [Comment: Rewritten in the plural]
7.	First the *individual* becomes aroused by violations of *his* personal space, and then *he* attributes the cause of this arousal to other people in *his* environment.	First *we* become aroused by violations of *our* personal space, and then *we* attribute the cause of this arousal to other people in *the* environment. [Comment: First-person pronouns substituted for the noun and *he* and *his*; *his* changed to *the*] First *one* becomes aroused by violations of personal space, and then *one* attributes the cause of this arousal to other people in *the* environment. [Comment: *One* substituted; *his* omitted or changed to *the*]
8.	Much has been written about the effect that a *child's* position among *his* siblings has on *his* intellectual development.	Much has been written about the relationship between sibling position and intellectual development in *children*. [Comment: Rewritten; plural introduced]
9.	Subjects were 16 girls and 16 boys. Each *child* was to place a car on *his* board so that two cars and boards looked alike.	Each child was to place a car on *his* or *her* board so that two cars and boards looked alike. [Comment: *His* changed to *his or her* or to *her or his* (Use sparingly to avoid monotonous repetition.)]
10.	Each person's alertness was measured by the difference between *his* obtained relaxation score and *his* obtained arousal score.	Each person's alertness was measured by the difference between *the* obtained relaxation and arousal scores. [Comment: *His* changed to *the*; plural introduced]
11.	The client's husband *lets* her teach part-time.	The client's husband "*lets*" her teach part-time. The husband says he "*lets*" the client teach part-time. The client *says her husband* "*lets*" her teach part-time. [Comment: Punctuation added to clarify that the location of the bias is with the husband and wife, not with the author. If necessary, rewrite to clarify as allegation. (See Example 24.)]

Problems of Designation: Stereotyping

12. males, females	men, women, boys, girls, adults, children, adolescents [Comment: Specific nouns reduce possibility of stereotypic bias and often clarify discussion. Use *male* and *female* as adjectives where appropriate and relevant (female experimenter, male subject). Avoid unparallel usage such as 10 *men* and 16 *females*.]
13. Research scientists often neglect their *wives* and *children*.	Research scientists often neglect their *spouses* and *children*. [Comment: Alternative wording acknowledges that women as well as men are research scientists.]
14. When a *test developer* or *test user* fails to satisfy these requirements, *he* should . . .	When *test developers or test users* fail to satisfy these requirements, *they* should . . . [Comment: Same as Example 13]
15. the psychologist . . . *he* the therapist . . . *he* the nurse . . . *she* the teacher . . . *she*	psychologists . . . *they;* the psychologist . . . *she* therapists . . . *they;* the therapist . . . *she or he* nurses . . . *they;* nurse . . . *he* teachers . . . *they;* teacher . . . *he* [Comment: Be specific, change to plural if discussing women as well as men, or use *he or she*. Do not use *s/he*.]
16. woman doctor, lady lawyer, male nurse	doctor, physician, lawyer, nurse [Comment: Specify sex only if it is a variable or if sex designation is necessary to the discussion ("13 female doctors and 22 male doctors"). *Woman* and *lady* are nouns; *female* is the adjective counterpart to *male*.]
17. mothering	parenting, nurturing (or specify exact behavior) [Comment: Noun substituted]
18. chairman (of an academic department)	Use *chairperson* or *chair;* use *chairman* only if it is known that the institution has established that form as an official title. [Comment: *Department head* may be appropriate; however, the term is not synonymous with *chair* and *chairperson* at all institutions.]
chairman (presiding officer of a committee or meeting)	chairperson, chair, moderator, discussion leader [Comment: In parliamentary usage, *chairman* is the official term and should not be changed. Alternatives are acceptable in most writing.]
19. Only *freshmen* were eligible for the project.	No alternative if academic standing is meant
All the students had matriculated for 3 years, but the majority were still *freshmen*.	No alternative if academic standing is meant
	[Comment: *First-year student* is often an acceptable alternative to *freshman,* but in these examples, *freshmen* is used for accuracy.]

continued

(Table 1 continued)

20. foreman, policeman, mailman	supervisor or superintendent, police officer, postal worker or letter carrier [Comment: Noun substituted]

Problems of Evaluation: Ambiguity of Referent

21. The authors acknowledge the assistance of *Mrs. John Smith.*	The authors acknowledge the assistance of *Jane Smith.* [Comment: Use given names.]
22. men and women, sons and daughters, boys and girls, husbands and wives	women and men, daughters and sons, girls and boys, wives and husbands [Comment: Vary the order if content does not require traditional order.]

Problems of Evaluation: Stereotyping

23. men and girls	men and women, women and men, boys and girls [Comment: Use parallel terms. Of course, use *men* and *girls* if that is literally what is meant.]
24. The client's husband lets her teach part-time.	The client teaches part-time. [Comment: The author of this example intended to communicate the working status of the woman but inadvertently revealed a stereotype about husband–wife relationships. (See Example 11.)]
25. ambitious men and aggressive women	ambitious women and men, ambitious people
	aggressive men and women, aggressive people
cautious men and timid women	cautious women and men, cautious people
	timid men and women, timid people
	[Comment: Some adjectives, depending on whether the person described is a man or a woman, connote bias. The examples illustrate some common usages that may not always convey exact meaning, especially when paired, as in column 1.]
26. The boys chose typically male toys. The client's behavior was typically female.	The boys chose (specify). The client's behavior was (specify). [Comment: Being specific reduces possibility of stereotypic bias.]
27. woman driver	driver [Comment: If specifying sex is necessary, avoid biased clichés. Use *female driver,* or write "The driver was a woman."]
28. The *girls* in the office greeted all clients.	receptionists, secretaries, office assistants [Comment: Noun substituted]
29. coed	student [Comment: Noun substituted. If specification of sex is necessary, use *female student.*]

30. women's lib, women's libber	women's movement, feminist, supporter of women's movement [Comment: Noun substituted]
31. Subjects were 16 men and 4 women. *The women were housewives.*	The men were (specify), and the women were (specify). [Comment: Women and men described in parallel terms or description of both omitted. Do not use *housewife* to identify occupation, a term that indicates sex and marital status and excludes men. Use *homemaker*, which includes men.]

3 APA Editorial Style

When editors or printers refer to style, they usually do not mean writing style; they mean editorial style, the rules or guidelines a publisher observes to ensure clear, consistent presentation of the printed word. Editorial style concerns uniform use of punctuation and abbreviations, construction of tables, selection of headings, and citation of references, as well as many other elements that are part of every manuscript.

The author of a book may have considerable freedom in choosing editorial style, but an author writing for a journal must follow the style rules established for that journal to avoid inconsistencies among articles. For example, without rules of style, three different articles might use sub-test, subtest, and Subtest in one issue of a journal. Although the meaning of the word is the same and the choice of one style over the other may seem arbitrary (in this case, subtest is APA style), such variations in style may distract or confuse the reader.

This chapter describes the editorial style for APA journals. It omits general rules explained in widely available style books and examples of usage with little relevance to APA journals. Among the most helpful general guides to editorial style are Words into Type *(Skillin & Gay, 1974) and the* Chicago Manual of Style *(University of Chicago Press, 1982), both used in developing this section. Style manuals agree more often than they disagree; where they disagree, the APA* Manual, *because it considers the special requirements of psychology, takes precedence for the APA journals.*

Punctuation

3.01 Period

Use a period at the end of a complete sentence. For other uses of periods, see the following sections: Abbreviations (section 3.25), Quotations (sections 3.34–3.37), Numbers (section 3.43), and References (Table 17).

3.02 Comma

Use a comma:
- before *and* and *or* in a series of three or more items. (See section 3.31 for use of commas in numbered or lettered series.)

  ```
  the height, width, or depth
  in a study by Thomas, Beck, and Gilbert (1981)
  ```
- to set off a nonessential or nonrestrictive clause, that is, a clause that the sentence can do without.

  ```
  Switch A, which was on a panel, controlled the
  recording device.
  ```
- to separate two independent clauses joined by a conjunction.

  ```
  Cedar shavings covered the floor, and paper was
  available for shredding and nest building.
  ```
- to separate groups of three digits in most numbers of 1,000 or more (see section 3.45).

Do not use a comma:
- before an essential or restrictive clause, that is, a clause that identifies, limits, or defines the word it modifies.

  ```
  The switch that stops the recording device also
  controls the light.
  ```
- between the two parts of a compound predicate.

  ```
  The results contradicted Smith's hypothesis and
  indicated that the effect of intervening problems
  was nonsignificant.
  ```

3.03 Semicolon

Use a semicolon:
- to separate two independent clauses that are not joined by a conjunction.

  ```
  The subjects in the first study were unpaid
  volunteers; those in the second study were paid
  for their participation.
  ```
- to separate elements that already contain commas. (See section 3.31 for the use of semicolons in numbered or lettered series.)

  ```
  The color order was red, white, blue; blue, white,
  red; or white, red, blue.
  ```
  ```
  (Adams & Baker, 1982; Jones, 1980)
  ```

3.04 Colon

Use a colon:
- before a final phrase or clause that illustrates, extends, or amplifies preceding material. If the final clause is a complete sentence, it begins with a capital letter.

      The digits were shown in the following order:
      3, 2, 4, 1.

      They have agreed on the outcome: Informed
      subjects perform better than do uninformed
      subjects.

- in ratios and proportions.

      The proportions (salt:water) were 1:8, 1:4, and
      1:2.

- in references between place of publication and publisher.

      New York: Wiley.

      St. Louis, MO: Mosby.

3.05 Dash

Punctuation within a sentence marks a pause in the thought; different kinds of punctuation indicate different kinds and lengths of pauses. Use the dash to indicate only a sudden interruption in the continuity of a sentence. Overuse weakens the flow of material.

      These two subjects——one from the first group, one
      from the second group——were tested separately.

3.06 Quotation Marks

Observe the following guidelines for uses of double quotation marks other than in material quoted directly from a source. See section 3.34 for a discussion of double and single quotation marks in quoted material.

Use double quotation marks:
- to introduce a word or phrase used as an ironic comment, as slang, or as an invented or coined expression. Use quotation marks the first time the word or phrase is used; thereafter, do not use quotation marks.

      considered "normal" behavior

      the "bad guy" variable . . . the bad guy
      variable [no quotation marks after the initial usage]

              but

      Subjects in the <u>small</u> group [*Small* is not used as
      irony, slang, or coinage; it is underlined to prevent
      misreading—here it means a group designation, not the size
      of the group.]

- to set off the title of an article or chapter in a periodical or book when the title is mentioned in text (see Table 17 for the treatment of such titles in the reference list).

      Smith's (1983) article, "Children's Conceptions of
      Society,"

- to reproduce material from a test item or verbatim instructions to subjects.

      The first fill-in item was "could be expected to
      _____."

  If instructions are long, set them off from text in a block format without quotation marks. (See section 3.34 for discussion of block format.)

Do not use double quotation marks:
- to identify the anchors of a scale. Instead, underline them.

      We ranked the items on a scale ranging from
      <u>all of the time</u> (1) to <u>never</u> (5).

- to cite a letter, word, phrase, or sentence as a linguistic example. Instead, underline the term.

      He clarified the distinction between <u>farther</u> and
      <u>further</u>.

- to introduce a technical or key term. Instead, underline the term.

      The term <u>zero-base budgeting</u> appeared frequently
      in the speech.

      She compared it with <u>meta-analysis</u>, which is
      described in the next section.

- to hedge or to apologize for using a particular expression. Do not use any punctuation with such expressions.

      Incorrect: The teacher "rewarded" the class with
                tokens.
      Correct: The teacher rewarded the class with tokens.

3.07 Parentheses

Use parentheses:
- to set off structurally independent elements.

      The patterns were significant (see Figure 5).

      (When a complete sentence is enclosed in
      parentheses, place punctuation in the sentence
      inside the parentheses, like this.) If only part
      of a sentence is enclosed in parentheses (like
      this), place punctuation outside the parentheses
      (like this).

- to set off reference citations in text (see sections 3.86 to 3.95 for further discussion of reference citations in text).

      Smith and Jones (1979) reported

      is fully described elsewhere (James & Nelson,
      1980)

- to introduce an abbreviation.

      effect on the galvanic skin response (GSR)

- to set off letters that identify items in a series (see also section 3.31 on seriation).

      The three measures were (a) . . ., (b) . . ., and
      (c) . . . .

- to group mathematical expressions (see also section 3.57).

  $(\underline{k} - 1)/(\underline{q} - 2)$

- to enclose the citation or page number of a direct quotation (see also section 3.37).

  The author stated, "The effect disappeared within minutes" (Smith, 1981, p. 311), but he did not say which effect.

  Smith (1981) found that "the effect disappeared within minutes" (p. 311).

- to enclose numbers that identify displayed formulas and equations.

  $$\underline{U}_{\underline{x}}(\underline{p}) = (\underline{m}_1 - \underline{m}_0)\underline{p}'_{\underline{x}}(1 - \underline{p}'_{\underline{x}}) \tag{1}$$

3.08 Brackets

Use brackets:
- to enclose parenthetical material within parentheses.

  (The results for the control group [$\underline{n}$ = 8] are also presented in Figure 2.)

  Exception 1: Do not use brackets if the material can be set off easily with commas without confounding meaning:

  Poor: (as Smith [1970] later concluded)
  Better: (as Smith, 1970, later concluded)

  Exception 2: In mathematical material, the placement of brackets and parentheses is reversed; that is, parentheses appear within brackets. (See section 3.57 for further discussion of brackets in equations.)

- to enclose material inserted in a quotation by some person other than the original writer.

  "when [his own and others'] behaviors were studied" (Smith, 1981, p. 311)

Spelling

3.09 Preferred Spelling

Webster's New Collegiate Dictionary is the standard spelling reference for the APA journals. If a word is not in the *Collegiate*, consult the more comprehensive *Webster's Third New International Dictionary.* If the dictionary gives a choice, use the first spelling listed; for example, use *aging* and *canceled* rather than *ageing* and *cancelled.*

3.10 Hyphenation

Most spelling questions concern compound words, that is, two words that may be written as (a) one unbroken word, (b) a hyphenated word, or (c) two separate words. For example, is *followup, follow-up,* or *follow up* the form to be used? The dictionary answers many such questions, especially for nonscientific words (the term is *follow-up* in this case). But because the language is constantly expanding, especially in science, dictionaries may not provide an authoritative spelling for the new compounds common to science. If a compound is *not* in the dictionary, follow the general principles of hyphenation given here and in Table 2. When you are still in doubt, use hyphens for clarity rather than omit them.

TABLE 2

Guide to Hyphenating Psychological Terms

Rule	Example
Hyphenate:	
1. A compound with a participle when it precedes the noun it modifies	• role–playing technique • anxiety–arousing condition • water–deprived animals
2. A phrase used as an adjective when it precedes the noun it modifies	• trial–by–trial analysis • to–be–recalled items • all–or–none questionnaire
3. An adjective and noun compound when it precedes and modifies another noun	• high–anxiety group • middle–class families • low–frequency words
4. A compound with a number as the first element when the compound precedes a noun	• two–way analysis of variance • six–trial problem • 12th–grade students
Do not hyphenate:	
1. A compound using an adverb ending in *-ly*	• widely used test • relatively homogeneous sample • randomly assigned subjects
2. A compound using a comparative or superlative adjective	• better written paper • less informed interviewers • higher scoring students
3. Chemical terms	• sodium chloride solution • amino acid compound
4. Foreign phrases used as adjectives or adverbs	• a posteriori test • laissez faire policy • fed ad lib [*but* hyphenate the adjective form: ad–lib feeding; see *Webster's Third*]
5. A modifier using a letter or numeral as the second element	• Group B subjects • Type II error • Trial 1 performance

General principle 1. Do not use a hyphen unless it serves a purpose. If a compound adjective cannot be misread or, as with many psychological terms, its meaning is established, a hyphen is not necessary.

```
least squares solution
semantic differential technique
covert learning conditions
day treatment program
grade point average
sex role differences
constant stimulus method
rank order correlation coefficient
repeated measures design
heart rate scores
```

General principle 2. In an invented or temporary compound that is used as an adjective before a noun, use a hyphen if the term can be misread. For example, are *different word lists* (a) word lists that are different from other word lists (spelled *different word lists*) or (b) lists that present different words (spelled *different-word lists*). A properly placed hyphen helps the reader understand the intended meaning.

General principle 3. Most compound adjective rules are appropriate only when the compound adjective *precedes* the noun. If a compound adjective *follows* the noun, do not use a hyphen because relationships are sufficiently clear without one.

```
client-centered counseling, but the counseling was
client centered
t-test results, but results from t tests
same-sex children, but children of the same sex
```

General principle 4. Write most words formed with prefixes as one word (see Table 3). Some exceptions, as in Table 4, require hyphens.

General principle 5. When two or more compound modifiers have a common base, this base is sometimes omitted in all except the last modifier, but the hyphens are retained.

```
long- and short-term memory
2-, 3-, and 10-min trials
```

Capitalization

Capitalize words, that is, use an uppercase letter for the first letter of a word, according to the guidelines in the following sections.

3.11 Words Beginning a Sentence

Capitalize:
• the first word in a complete sentence.

- the first word after a colon that begins a complete sentence.

      The author made one main point: No explanation
      that has been suggested so far answers all
      questions.

3.12   Major Words in Titles and Headings

Capitalize:

- major words in titles of books and articles. Conjunctions, articles, and short prepositions are not considered major words; however, capitalize *all* words of four letters or more. When a capitalized word is a hyphenated compound, capitalize both words. Also, capitalize the first word after a colon or a dash.

      In her book, <u>History of Pathology</u>

      The criticism of the article, "Attitudes Toward
      Mental Health Workers"

      "Memory in Hearing—Impaired Children:
      Implications for Vocabulary Development"

  Exception: In titles of books and articles in reference lists, capitalize only the first word, the first word after a colon or a dash, and proper nouns. (See Table 17 for further discussion of reference style.)

      Smith, A. J. (1983). When too much is not enough:
      Reply to Jacob and Winston.

- major words in article headings and subheadings.

  Exception: In indented paragraph headings, capitalize only the first word and proper nouns (see section 3.29).

- major words in table titles and figure legends. In table *headings* and figure *captions*, capitalize only the first word and proper nouns (see sections 3.64 for headings and 3.80 for captions).

- references to titles of sections within the same article.

      as explained in the Method section

TABLE 3

Prefixes Not Requiring Hyphens

Prefix	Example	Prefix	Example
after	aftereffect	non	nonsignificant
anti	antisocial	over	overaggressive
bi	bilingual	post	posttest
co	coeducation	pre	preexperimental
counter	counterbalance	pro	prowar
extra	extracurricular	pseudo	pseudoscience
infra	infrared	re	reevaluate
inter	interstimulus	semi	semidarkness
intra	intraspecific	sub	subtest
macro	macrocosm	super	superordinate
micro	microcosm	supra	supraliminal
mid	midterm	ultra	ultrahigh
mini	minisession	un	unbiased
multi	multiphase	under	underdeveloped

3.13 Proper Nouns and Trade Names

Capitalize:
- proper nouns and adjectives and words used as proper nouns. Proper adjectives that have acquired a common meaning are not capitalized.

      Wilks's lambda
      Greco-Latin square
            but
      eustachian tube

- names of university departments if they refer to a specific department within a specific university and complete names of academic courses if they refer to a specific course.

      Department of Sociology, University of Washington
      Psychology 101
            but
      a sociology department
      an introductory psychology course

- trade and brand names of drugs, equipment, and food.

      Hunter Klockounter
      Plexiglas
      Purina Lab Chow
      Xerox

Do not capitalize names of laws, theories, and hypotheses.

      Gregory's theory of illusions
      the empirical law of effect

TABLE 4

Prefixed Words Requiring Hyphens

Occurrence	Example
Compounds in which the base word is	
capitalized	• pro-Freudian
a number	• post-1960
an abbreviation	• pre-UCS trial
more than one word	• non-achievement-oriented students
All *self-* compounds whether they are adjectives or nouns	• self-report technique • the test was self-paced • self-esteem
Words that could be misunderstood	• re-pair [pair again] • re-form [form again] • un-ionized
Words that could be misread	• anti-intellectual • co-occur • co-worker

3.14 Nouns Followed by Numerals or Letters

Capitalize nouns followed by numerals or letters that denote a specific place in a numbered series.

```
On Day 2 of Experiment 4
during Trial 5, Group B performed
as seen in Table 2 and Figure 3
```

Exception: Do not capitalize nouns that denote common parts of books or tables followed by numerals or letters.

```
chapter 4
page iv
row 3
column 5
```

Do not capitalize nouns that precede a variable.

```
trial n and item x
```
          but
```
Trial 3 and Item 4 [the numbers are not variables]
```

3.15 Titles of Tests

Capitalize exact, complete titles of published and unpublished tests. Words such as *test* or *scale* are not capitalized if they refer to subscales of tests.

```
Advanced Vocabulary Test
Minnesota Multiphasic Personality Inventory
Stroop Color-Word Interference Test
the authors' Mood Adjective Checklist
```
          but
```
MMPI Depression scale
```

Do not capitalize shortened, inexact, or generic titles of tests.

```
a vocabulary test          Stroop color test
```

3.16 Names of Conditions or Groups in an Experiment

Do not capitalize names of conditions or groups in an experiment.

```
experimental and control groups

subjects were divided into information and
no-information conditions
```
          but
```
Conditions A and B [see section 3.14]
```

3.17 Names of Factors, Variables, and Effects

Capitalize names of derived factors within a factor analysis. The word *factor* is not capitalized unless it is followed by a number (see section 3.14).

```
Mealtime Behavior (Factor 4)
Factors 6 and 7
the Activity factor
```

Do not capitalize effects or variables unless they appear with multiplication signs. (Take care that you do not use the term *factor* when you mean *effect* or *variable*, for example, in an interaction or analysis of variance.)

```
a significant age effect
the sex, age, and weight variables
              but
the Sex x Age x Weight interaction
a 3 x 3 x 2 (Group x Trial x Response) design
```

Italics

3.18 Underlining Words

Words underlined in a manuscript appear in italics when typeset. For specific use of italics in APA journals, see Table 5. In general, use italics infrequently. When in doubt, do not underline words in the manuscript because at the copy-editing stage adding underlines is easier than deleting them.

TABLE 5

Use of Italics

Typewritten example	Typeset example

Use italics for:

1. Titles of books, periodicals, and microfilm publications

The elements of style	*The elements of style*
American Psychologist	*American Psychologist*

2. Genera, species, and varieties

Macaca mulatta	*Macaca mulatta*

3. Introduction of new, technical, or key term or label [After a term has been used once, do not underline it.]

the term backward masking	the term *backward masking*
box labeled empty	box labeled *empty*

4. Letter, word, or phrase cited as a linguistic example

words such as big and little	words such as *big* and *little*
the letter a	the letter *a*

5. Letters used as statistical symbols or algebraic variables

$F(1, 53) = 10.03$	$F(1, 53) = 10.03$
t test	t test
trial n	trial n
$a/b = c/d$	$a/b = c/d$
SE_M	SE_M

continued

(Table 5 continued)

6. **Some test scores and scales**

Rorschach scores: F+%, <u>Z</u>	Rorschach scores: *F*+%, *Z*
MMPI scales: <u>Hs</u>, <u>Pd</u>	MMPI scales: *Hs, Pd*

7. **Volume numbers in reference lists**

<u>26</u>, 46–67.   *26*, 46–67.

Do not use italics for:

1. **Foreign words and abbreviations common in English**

a posteriori	a posteriori
a priori	a priori
ad lib	ad lib
et al.	et al.
per se	per se
vis–a–vis	vis-à-vis

2. **Chemical terms**

NaCl, LSD   NaCl, LSD

3. **Trigonometric terms**

sin, tan, log   sin, tan, log

4. **Nonstatistical subscripts to statistical symbols or mathematical expressions**

<u>MS</u>$_e$, <u>F</u>$_{max}$	*MS*$_e$, *F*$_{max}$
<u>S</u>$_A$ + <u>S</u>$_B$, where <u>S</u>$_A$ represents Group A's score and <u>S</u>$_B$ represents Group B's score	*S*$_A$ + *S*$_B$, where *S*$_A$ represents Group A's score and *S*$_B$ represents Group B's score

5. **Greek letters**

 χ   χ

6. **Mere emphasis [Italics are permissible if emphasis might otherwise be lost; in general, however, use syntax to provide emphasis.]**

It is <u>important</u> to bear in mind that <u>this</u> process is <u>not</u> proposed as a <u>stage</u> theory of development. [not acceptable]	It is *important* to bear in mind that *this* process is *not* proposed as a *stage* theory of development. [not acceptable]

7. **Letters used as abbreviations**

intertrial interval (ITI)   intertrial interval (ITI)

Abbreviations

3.19 Use of Abbreviations

The APA journals use abbreviations sparingly. Although abbreviations are sometimes useful for long, technical terms in scientific writing, communication is usually garbled rather than clarified if, for example, an abbreviation is unfamiliar to the reader. Consider whether the space saved by abbreviations in the following sentence justifies the time necessary to master the meaning:

```
The advantage of the LH was clear from the RT
data, which reflected high FP and FN rates for the
RH.
```

Without abbreviations the passage reads as follows:

```
The advantage of the left hand was clear from the
reaction time data, which reflected high false-
positive and false-negative rates for the right
hand.
```

Excessive use of abbreviations, whether standard or unique to one manuscript, can hinder reading comprehension. In the following example, however, a standard abbreviation for a long familiar term eases the reader's task:

```
The MMPI was administered to patients at seven
hospitals.
```

In all circumstances other than in the reference list (see section 3.98 and Table 16), you must decide (a) whether to spell out a given expression every time it is used in an article or (b) whether to spell it out initially and abbreviate it thereafter. For example, the abbreviations L for large and S for small in a paper discussing different sequences of reward (LLSS or LSLS) would be an effective and readily understood shortcut. In another paper, however, writing about the L reward and the S reward would be both unnecessary and confusing. In most instances, abbreviating experimental group names is ineffective because the abbreviations are not adequately informative or easily recognizable and may even be more cumbersome than the full name. In general, use abbreviations only (a) if the abbreviation is conventional and if the reader is more familiar with the abbreviation than with the complete form or (b) if considerable space can be saved and cumbersome repetition avoided (Reisman, 1962). In short, use only those abbreviations that will help you communicate with your readers.

3.20 Explanation of Abbreviations

Because the acronyms that psychologists use in their daily writing may not be familiar to students or to readers in other disciplines or other countries, authors must explain acronyms and abbreviations.

A term to be abbreviated must, on its first appearance, be spelled out completely and followed immediately by its abbreviation in parentheses. Thereafter, the abbreviation may be used in text without further explanation.

```
The results of studies of simple reaction time
(RT) to a visual target have shown a strong
negative relationship between RT and luminance.
```

Abbreviations in a figure or table must *always* be explained in the figure caption or table note. An abbreviation that is used in several figures or tables must be explained in each figure or table in which the abbreviation is used.

3.21   Abbreviations Accepted as Words

APA style permits the use of abbreviations that appear as word entries (i.e., that are not labeled *abbr*) in *Webster's New Collegiate Dictionary* (1981). Such abbreviations do not need explanation in text. Examples:

```
IQ  LSD  REM  ESP
```

3.22   Abbreviations Used Often in APA Journals

Some abbreviations are not in the dictionary but appear frequently in the journal for which you are writing. Although probably well understood by many readers, these abbreviations must always be explained when first used (see section 3.20). Examples:

```
Minnesota Multiphasic Personality Inventory (MMPI)
conditioned stimulus (CS)
conditioned avoidance (CA)
intertrial interval (ITI)
consonant-vowel-consonant (CVC)
short-term memory (STM)
reaction time (RT)
```

Do not use the abbreviations *S*, *E*, and *O* for subject, experimenter, and observer. (Note: If a generic term, such as *patients*, *children*, or *rats*, better describes the experimental group, use that term rather than *subjects*.)

3.23   Latin Abbreviations

Use the following standard Latin abbreviations only in parenthetical material; in nonparenthetical material, use the English translation of the Latin terms:

```
cf.       compare          i.e.,    that is,
e.g.,     for example,     viz.,    namely,
etc.      and so forth     vs.      versus, against
```

Exception: Use the abbreviation v (for "versus") in references and text citations to court cases, whether parenthetical or not (see sections 3.94 and 3.99).

Exception: In the reference list and in text, use the Latin abbreviation et al., which means "and others," in nonparenthetical as well as parenthetical material.

3.24   Abbreviations of Units of Measurement and Statistics

Use abbreviations for metric and nonmetric units that are accompanied by numeric values (e.g., 4 cm, 30 s, 12 lb).

Exception: To prevent misreading, do not abbreviate the following units of time, even when accompanied by numeric values: day, week, month, and year.

Do not use abbreviations for metric and nonmetric units that are not accompanied by numeric values (e.g., measured in centimeters, several pounds).

Use abbreviations for statistics as described in section 3.55.

3.25 Use of Periods With Abbreviations

Use the following guide for the use of periods with abbreviations.

Use periods with:
- initials of names (J. R. Smith).
- abbreviations of geographic names (U.S. Navy) *except* state names.
- Latin abbreviations (i.e.; vs.; a.m.).
- reference abbreviations (Vol. 1; 2nd ed.; p. 6).

Do not use periods with:
- abbreviations of state names (NY; OH; Washington, DC). Note: For reference list entries APA has adopted the two-letter U.S. Postal Service abbreviations for states. (See Table 16 for the official abbreviations.)
- capital letter abbreviations and acronyms (APA, NDA, UNESCO, IQ, PhD).
- metric and nonmetric measurement abbreviations (cm, kg, cd, s, ft, lb).

    Exception: The abbreviation for inch (in.) takes a period because without the period it could be misread.

3.26 Plurals of Abbreviations

To form the plural of most abbreviations and statistical symbols, add *s* alone, without an apostrophe.

IQs Eds. vols. M̲s p̲s n̲s

Exception: Do not make abbreviations of units of measurement plural (see section 3.48).

Exception: To form the plural of the reference abbreviation p. (page), write pp.; do not add an *s*.

3.27 Abbreviations Beginning a Sentence

Never begin a sentence with a lowercase abbreviation (e.g., lb) or a symbol (e.g., μ). Begin a sentence with a capitalized abbreviation or acronym (e.g., U.S. or APA) only when necessary to avoid indirect and awkward writing.

Headings and Series

3.28 Organizing a Manuscript With Headings

Headings indicate the organization of a manuscript and establish the importance of each topic. All topics of equal importance have the same level of heading throughout a manuscript. For example, in a multiexperiment paper, the headings for the Method and Results sections in Experiment 1 should be the same level as the headings for the Method and Results sections in Experiment 2.

In manuscripts submitted to APA journals, headings function

as an outline to reveal a manuscript's organization. In your manuscript, do not use a heading for the introduction because the introduction is identified by its position in the article.

Do not label headings with numbers or letters. The sections and headings in the *Manual* are labeled only to permit indexing and cross-referencing.

3.29 Levels of Headings

Articles in APA journals use from one to five levels of headings:

CENTERED UPPERCASE HEADING *(Level 1)*

Centered Uppercase and Lowercase Heading *(Level 2)*

Centered, Underlined, Uppercase and *(Level 3)*

Lowercase Heading

Flush Left, Underlined, Uppercase and Lowercase *(Level 4)*

Side Heading

Indented, underlined, lowercase paragraph *(Level 5)*

heading ending with a period.

For example,

EXPERIMENT 1: AN INTERVIEW VALIDATION STUDY

External Validation

Method

Subjects

The nonclinical group.

3.30 Selecting the Levels of Headings

Not every article requires all levels of headings. Use the following guidelines to determine the level, position, and arrangement of headings.

One level. For a short article, one level of heading may be sufficient. In such cases, use only centered uppercase and lowercase headings (Level 2).

Two levels. For many articles in APA journals, two levels of headings meet the requirements. Use Level 2 and Level 4 headings:

Method *(Level 2)*

Procedure *(Level 4)*

If the material subordinate to the Level 2 headings is short or if many Level 4 headings are necessary, indented, underlined paragraph headings (Level 5) may be more appropriate than Level 4 headings. (An indented, underlined paragraph heading—a Level 5 heading—should cover all material between it and the next heading, regardless of what level the next heading is.)

Three levels. For some articles, three levels of headings are needed. Use Level 2, Level 4, and Level 5 headings.

In a single-experiment study, these three levels of headings may look like this:

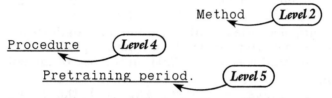

In a multiexperiment study, these three levels of headings may look like this:

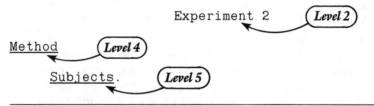

Four levels. For some articles, particularly multiexperiment studies, monographs, and lengthy literature reviews, four levels of headings are needed. Use Level 2, Level 3, Level 4, and Level 5 headings:

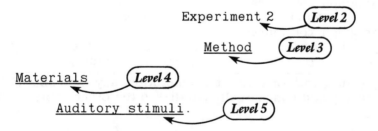

Five levels. If the article requires five levels of headings, subordinate all four levels above by introducing a Level 1 heading—A CENTERED UPPERCASE HEADING—above the other four (as shown in section 3.29).

3.31 Seriation

Enumerate elements in a series to prevent misreading or to clarify the sequence or relation between elements, particularly when they are lengthy or complex. Identify the elements by a letter (within a paragraph or sentence) or by a number (at the start of each paragraph in a series).

Within a paragraph or sentence, identify elements in a series by lowercase letters (not underlined) in parentheses.

```
The subject's three choices were (a) working with
one other subject, (b) working with a team, and
(c) working alone.
```

Within a sentence, use commas to separate three or more elements that do not have internal commas; use semicolons to separate three or more elements that have internal commas.

```
We tested three groups: (a) low scorers, who
scored fewer than 20 points; (b) moderate scorers,
who scored between 20 and 50 points; and (c) high
scorers, who scored more than 50 points.
```

If the elements of a series within a paragraph constitute a compound sentence and are preceded by a colon, capitalize the first word of the first item (see section 3.04 on the use of the colon).

```
In Frank and Yuler's (1982) analysis of this
study, two points were essential: (a) The original
authors never claimed that femininity and
socialization constituted a typology, and (b) the
original method of data analysis cannot be
obtained with the fixed general linear model.
```

Separate paragraphs in a series, such as itemized conclusions or steps in a procedure, are identified by an arabic numeral followed by a period but not enclosed or followed by parentheses.

```
Using the learned helplessness theory, we
predicted that the depressed and nondepressed
subjects would make the following judgments of
control:
     1. Individuals who . . . [paragraph continues].
     2. Nondepressed subjects exposed to . . .
[paragraph continues].
     3. Depressed subjects exposed to . . .
[paragraph continues].
     4. Depressed and nondepressed subjects in the
no-noise groups . . . [paragraph continues].
```

In any series, with or without enumeration, any item should be syntactically and conceptually parallel to the other items in the series.

Quotations

3.32 Quotation of Sources

Material quoted from another author's work or from one's own previously published work, material duplicated from a test item, and verbatim instructions to subjects should be reproduced word for word. Incorporate a short quotation (fewer than 40 words) in text and enclose the quotation with double quotation marks. (See section 3.06 for other uses of double quotation marks.)

Display a quotation of more than 40 words in a free-standing block of typewritten lines and omit the quotation marks. Start such a *block quotation* on a new line, indented five spaces from the left margin. Type the entire quotation double-spaced on the new margin and indent the first line of any subsequent paragraphs within the quotation five spaces from the new margin.

The following examples illustrate the application of APA style to direct quotation of a source. (See section 4.13 for typing instructions.) When quoting, always provide the author, year, and specific page citation in the text and include a complete reference in the reference list.

Quotation 1: (3.34) (3.36)

He stated, "The 'placebo effect,' . . .

disappeared when behaviors were studied in this

manner" (Smith, 1982, p. 276), but he did not

clarify which behaviors were studied.

Quotation 2: (3.35)

Smith (1982) found that "the 'placebo effect,'

which had been verified in previous studies, (3.36)

disappeared when [his own and others'] behaviors

were studied in this manner" (p. 276). (3.37)

Quotation 3:

Smith (1982) found the following:

(3.34) The "placebo effect," which had been verified

in previous studies, disappeared when

behaviors were studied in this manner. (3.36)

Furthermore, the behaviors, <u>were never</u>

<u>exhibited again</u> [italics added], even when

reel [<u>sic</u>] drugs were administered. Earlier

studies were clearly premature in attributing

the results to a placebo effect. (p. 276)

3.33 Accuracy

Direct quotations must be accurate. Except as noted in sections 3.35 to 3.36, the quotation must follow the wording, spelling, and interior punctuation of the original source, even if the source is incorrect.

If any incorrect spelling, punctuation, or grammar in the source might confuse readers, insert the word *sic*, underlined and bracketed (i.e., [<u>sic</u>]), immediately after the error in the quotation (see section 3.36 for the use of brackets). Always check the typed copy against the source to ensure that no discrepancies occur.

3.34 Double or Single Quotation Marks

In text. Use *double* quotation marks for quotations in text. Use *single* quotation marks within double quotation marks to set off material that in the original source was enclosed in double quotation marks (see Quotation 2).

In block quotations. Do not use *any* quotation marks to enclose block quotations. Use double quotation marks to enclose any quoted material within a block quotation (see Quotation 3).

With other punctuation. Place periods and commas within closing single or double quotation marks. Place other punctuation marks inside quotation marks only when they are part of the quoted material.

3.35 Changes From the Source Requiring No Explanation

The first letter of the first word in a quotation may be changed to a capital or lowercase letter. The punctuation mark at the end of a sentence may be changed to fit the syntax. Single quotation marks may be changed to double quotation marks and vice versa (see section 3.34). Any other changes (e.g., italicizing words for emphasis or omitting words) must be explicitly indicated (see section 3.36).

3.36 Changes From the Source Requiring Explanation

Omitting material. Use three ellipsis points (. . .) within a sentence to indicate that you have omitted material from the original source (see Quotation 1). Use four points to indicate any omission between two sentences (literally a period followed by three spaced dots. . . .). Do not use ellipsis points at the beginning or end of any quotation unless, in order to prevent misinterpretation, you need to emphasize that the quotation begins or ends in midsentence.

Inserting material. Use brackets, not parentheses, to enclose material (additions or explanations) inserted in a quotation by some person other than the original author (see Quotation 2).

Adding emphasis. If you want to emphasize a word or words in a quotation, underline the word or words (underlined manuscript copy will be set in italic type). Immediately after the underlined words, insert within brackets the words *italics added*, that is, [italics added] (see Quotation 3).

3.37 Citation of Sources

Always cite the source of a direct quotation along with the quotation. (For permission to quote, see section 3.38.) In text, give the author, year, and page number in parentheses. Include a complete reference in the reference list. Depending on where the quotation falls, punctuation differs.

In midsentence. End the passage with quotation marks, cite the source in parentheses immediately after the quotation marks, and continue the sentence. Use no other punctuation unless the meaning of the sentence requires such punctuation (see Quotation 1).

At the end of a sentence. Close the quoted passage with quotation marks, cite the source in parentheses immediately after the quotation marks, and end with the period or other punctuation outside the final parenthesis (see Quotation 2).

At the end of a block quote. Cite the quoted source in parentheses after the final punctuation mark (see Quotation 3).

3.38 Permission to Quote

Any direct quotation, regardless of length, must be accompanied by a reference citation that includes a page number. (For the form of the citation of a source, see section 3.37.) If you quote at length from a copyrighted work in material you intend to publish, you usually also need written permission from the owner of the copyright. Requirements for obtaining permission to quote copyrighted material vary from one copyright owner to another; for example, APA policy permits use of up to 500 words of APA-copyrighted journal text without explicit permission. It is the author's responsibility to determine whether permission is required from the copyright owner.

If you must obtain written permission from the copyright owner, footnote the quoted material with a superscript number and in the footnote acknowledge permission from the owner of the copyright. Format the footnote like the permission footnotes used for tables and figures (see section 3.69) but substitute the indented superscript number for the word *Note*. Enclose a copy of the letter of permission with the submitted manuscript.

Numbers

The general rule governing APA style on the use of numbers is to use figures to express numbers 10 and above and words to express numbers below 10. Sections 3.39 to 3.41 expand on this rule and state exceptions and special usages.

3.39 Numbers Expressed in Figures

Use figures to express:
- all numbers 10 and above. (*Exceptions:* See sections 3.40 and 3.41.)

```
12 cm wide                the 15th trial
the remaining 10%         13 lists
25 years old              105 stimulus words
10th-grade students
```

- all numbers below 10 that are grouped for comparison with numbers 10 and above (and appear in the same paragraph). (*Exceptions:* See sections 3.40 and 3.41.)

```
3 of 21 analyses
of 10 conditions . . . the 5th condition
5 and 13 lines
```

in the 2nd and 11th grades . . . the 2nd-grade
  students
on 2 trials . . . on the remaining 18 trials
4 of the 40 stimulus words
in 7 blocks . . . in 12 blocks
the 6th group . . . 12 groups
the 1st and 12th items of all 15 lists
2 of the 20 responses
toys included 14 balloons, 3 stuffed animals, and
  5 balls
25 words . . . 8 verbs, 12 nouns, and 5 adjectives

but

15 traits on each of four checklists [traits and
checklists are not being compared; they are different
categories of items]

- **numbers that immediately precede a unit of measurement.**
a 5-mg dose
with 10.54 cm of
- **numbers that represent statistical or mathematical functions, fractional or decimal quantities, percentages, ratios, and percentiles and quartiles.**
multiplied by 3
2 1/2 times as many
0.33 of the
more than 5% of the sample
the 1st quartile
a ratio of 16:1
- **numbers that represent time, dates, ages, sample or population size, scores and points on a scale, exact sums of money, and numerals as numerals.**
in about 3 years
2 weeks ago
3 hr 34 min
at 12:30 a.m.
June 5, 1982
2-year-olds
3 subjects
scored 4 on a 7-point scale
were paid $5 each
the numerals on the score card were 0-6
- **numbers that denote a specific place in a numbered series, parts of books and tables, each number in a list of four or more numbers.**
Grade 8 [*but* the eighth grade; see section 3.42]
Group 3
Table 3
page 71

```
chapter 5
row 5
1, 3, 4, and 7 words, respectively
```

3.40 Numbers Expressed in Words

Use words to express:
- numbers below 10 that do not represent precise measurements and that are not grouped for comparison with numbers 10 and above.

```
two or three times before
the only one who
two words that mean
five trials
three conditions
seven lists
one-tailed t test
nine words each
three-dimensional blocklike figures
eight items
four responses
six sessions
nine pages
three-way interaction
```

- the numbers *zero* and *one* when the words would be easier to comprehend than the figures or when the words do not appear in context with numbers 10 and above.

```
zero-base budgeting
one-line sentence
However, one response was valid. [but However, 1
   of 15 responses was valid.]
```

- any number that begins a sentence, title, or heading. (Whenever possible, reword the sentence to avoid beginning with a number.)

```
Ten subjects participated.
Forty-eight percent of the sample showed an
   increase; 2% showed no change.
Four subjects improved, and 4 subjects did not
   improve.
```

- common fractions.

```
one fifth of the class
two-thirds majority
reduced by three fourths
```

- universally accepted usage.

```
the Twelve Apostles
the Fourth of July
the Ten Commandments
```

3.41 Combining Figures and Words to Express Numbers

Use a combination of figures and words to express:
- rounded large numbers.

```
almost 3 million people
a budget of $2.5 billion
```

- back-to-back modifiers.

```
2 two-way interactions
ten 7-point scales
twenty 6-year-olds
the first 10 items
```

3.42 Ordinal Numbers

Treat ordinal numbers (except percentiles and quartiles) as you would cardinal numbers (see sections 3.39 to 3.41).

```
second-order factor
the fourth graders
the fifth list for the 12th-grade students
the first item of the 75th trial (Item 1
  of Trial 75)
the 2nd and 11th rows
the first and third groups
the third column
```

3.43 Decimal Fractions

Place the decimal point on the line, not above the line. Use a zero before the decimal point when numbers are less than 1.

```
0.23 cm, 0.48 s
```

Exception: Do *not* use a zero before a decimal fraction when the number cannot be greater than 1 (e.g., correlations, proportions, and levels of statistical significance).

```
r = -.96, p<.05
```

The number of places to which an infinite or very large decimal value is carried reflects the precision with which the quantity was measured. Carry more precisely measured quantities to more decimal places.

3.44 Arabic or Roman Numerals

Use arabic, not roman, numerals whenever possible.

Exception: If roman numerals are part of an established terminology, do not change to arabic numerals; for example, use Type II error.

3.45 Commas in Numbers

Use commas between groups of three digits in most figures of 1,000 or more.

Exceptions:

page numbers	page 1029
binary digits	00110010
serial numbers	290466960
degrees of temperature	3071 °F
acoustic frequency designations	2000 Hz
degrees of freedom	$F(24, 1000)$
numbers to the right of a decimal point	4,900.0744

3.46 Plurals of Numbers

To form the plurals of numbers, whether expressed as figures or as words, add *s* or *es* alone, without an apostrophe.

fours and sixes   1950s   10s and 20s

Metrication

3.47 Policy on Metrication

The APA uses the metric system in its journals. All references to physical measurements, where feasible, should be expressed in metric units. The metric system outlined in this section is based, with some exceptions, on the International System of Units (SI), an extension and refinement of the traditional metric system, which is supported by the national standardizing bodies in many countries, including the United States.

The transition to SI from the traditional nonmetric system is a long and complex task. In preparing manuscripts, authors should use metric units if possible. Experimenters who use instruments that record measurements in nonmetric units may report the nonmetric units but also must report the established SI equivalents in parentheses immediately following the nonmetric units.

The rods were spaced 19 mm apart. [Measurement was made in metric units.]

The rod was 3 ft (0.91 m) long. [Measurement was made in nonmetric units and converted to the rounded SI equivalent.]

Journal editors reserve the right to return manuscripts if measurements are not expressed properly. Tables 6–10 (see section 3.49) provide guidelines on the use of metric expressions.

3.48 Style for Metric Units

Abbreviation. Use the metric symbol (see Tables 6–10) to express a metric unit when it appears with a numeric value (e.g., 4 m). When a metric unit does not appear with a numeric value, spell out the unit in text (e.g., measured in meters) and use the metric symbol in table headings (e.g., lag in ms).

Capitalization. Start names of units with lowercase letters (e.g., meter) except in capitalized material or at the beginning of a sentence.

Use lowercase letters for symbols (e.g., cd) except when symbols are derived from the name of a person (e.g., Gy). *Exception:* Use the symbol L for liter because a lowercase el may be misread as the numeral 1.

Use lowercase letters for all symbols for prefixes that represent powers of 10 except the following, for which you would use uppercase letters: exa (E), peta (P), tera (T), giga (G), and mega (M). Use lowercase letters when writing out full names of units (e.g., nanometer) unless the name appears in capitalized material.

Plurals. Make full names of units plural when appropriate. Example: meters

Do not make symbols of units plural. Example: 3 cm, not 3 cms

Periods. Do not use a period after a symbol, except at the end of a sentence.

Spacing. Never use a space between a prefix and a base unit. Examples: kg, kilogram

Use a space between a symbol and the number to which it refers except for measures of angles (e.g., degrees, minutes, and seconds). Examples: 4.5 m, 12 °C, *but* 45° angle

Compound units. Use a centered dot between the symbols of a compound term formed by the multiplication of units. Example: Pa•s

Use a space between full names of units of a compound unit formed by the multiplication of units; do not use a centered dot. Example: pascal second

3.49 Metric Tables

Tables 6–10 are intended to assist authors in the conversion to the metric system. They are based on tables that appeared in the National Bureau of Standards' (1979) "Guidelines for Use of the Modernized Metric System." For more detailed information, consult the sources on metrication referenced in section 7.03.

TABLE 6

International System (SI) Base and Supplementary Units

Quantity	Name	Symbol
Base units		
amount of substance	mole	mol
electric current	ampere	A
length	meter	m
luminous intensity	candela	cd
mass	kilogram	kg
thermodynamic temperature[a]	kelvin	K
time	second	s
Supplementary units		
plane angle	radian	rad
solid angle	steradian	sr

[a]Celsius temperature is generally expressed in degrees Celsius (symbol: °C).

TABLE 7

International System (SI) Prefixes

Factor	Prefix	Symbol	Factor	Prefix	Symbol
10^{18}	exa	E	10^{-1}	deci	d
10^{15}	peta	P	10^{-2}	centi	c
10^{12}	tera	T	10^{-3}	milli	m
10^{9}	giga	G	10^{-6}	micro	μ
10^{6}	mega	M	10^{-9}	nano	n
10^{3}	kilo	k	10^{-12}	pico	p
10^{2}	hecto	h	10^{-15}	femto	f
10^{1}	deka	da	10^{-18}	atto	a

TABLE 8

International System (SI) Derived Units With Special Names

Quantity	Name	Symbol	Expression in terms of other units
absorbed dose, specific energy imparted, kerma, absorbed dose index	gray	Gy	J/kg
activity (of a radionuclide)	becquerel	Bq	s^{-1}
capacitance	farad	F	C/V
conductance	siemens	S	A/V
dose equivalent, dose equivalent index	sievert	Sv	J/kg
electric charge, quantity of electricity	coulomb	C	A·s
electric potential, potential difference, electromotive force, voltage	volt	V	W/A
electric resistance	ohm	Ω	V/A
energy, work, quantity of heat	joule	J	N·m
force	newton	N	$(kg \cdot m)/s^2$
frequency	hertz	Hz	s^{-1}
illuminance	lux	lx	lm/m^2
inductance	henry	H	Wb/A
luminous flux	lumen	lm	cd·sr
magnetic flux	weber	Wb	V·s
magnetic flux density	tesla	T	Wb/m^2
pressure, stress	pascal	Pa	N/m^2
radiant flux, power	watt	W	J/s
volume (capacity)	liter	L	dm^3

TABLE 9

Other International System (SI) Derived Units

Quantity	Name	Symbol
absorbed dose rate	gray per second	Gy/s
acceleration	meter per second squared	m/s^2
angular acceleration	radian per second squared	rad/s^2
angular velocity	radian per second	rad/s
area	square meter	m^2
concentration (amount of substance)	mole per cubic meter	mol/m^3
current density	ampere per square meter	A/m^2
density, mass density	kilogram per cubic meter	kg/m^3
electric charge density	coulomb per cubic meter	C/m^3
electric field strength	volt per meter	V/m
electric flux density	coulomb per square meter	C/m^2
energy density	joule per cubic meter	J/m^3
exposure (x and γ rays)	coulomb per kilogram	C/kg
heat capacity, entropy	joule per kelvin	J/K
luminance	candela per square meter	cd/m^2
magnetic field strength	ampere per meter	A/m
molar energy	joule per mole	J/mol
molar entropy, molar heat capacity	joule per mole kelvin	J/(mol·K)
moment of force	newton meter	N·m
permeability	henry per meter	H/m
permittivity	farad per meter	F/m
power density, heat flux density, irradiance	watt per square meter	W/m^2
radiance	watt per square meter steradian	$W/(m^2 \cdot sr)$
radiant intensity	watt per steradian	W/sr
specific energy	joule per kilogram	J/kg
specific heat capacity, specific entropy	joule per kilogram kelvin	J/(kg·K)
specific volume	cubic meter per kilogram	m^3/kg
surface tension	newton per meter	N/m
thermal conductivity	watt per meter kelvin	W/(m·K)
velocity, speed	meter per second	m/s
viscosity (dynamic)	pascal second	Pa·s
viscosity (kinematic)	square meter per second	m^2/s
volume	cubic meter	m^3
wave number	one per meter	m^{-1}

TABLE 10

Examples of Conversions to International System (SI) Equivalents

Physical quantity	Traditional U.S. unit	SI equivalent
Area	acre	4,046.873 m^2
	square foot[a]	0.09290304 m^2
	square inch[a]	645.16 mm^2
	square mile (statute)	2.589998 km^2
	square yard	0.8361274 m^2
Energy	British thermal unit (IT)	1,055.056 J
	calorie (IT), thermochemical[a]	4.186800 J
	erg	10^{-7} J
	kilowatt hour[a]	3.6×10^6 J
Force	dyne	10^{-5} N
	kilogram force[a]	9.80665 N
	poundal	0.138255 N
Length	angstrom (Å)[a]	0.1 nm
	foot (international)[a]	0.3048 m
	inch[a]	2.54 cm
	micron[a]	1.0 μm
	mile (U.S. statute)	1.609347 km
	nautical mile (international; nmi)[a]	1,852.0 m
	yard[a]	0.9144 m
Light	footcandle	10.76391 lx
	footlambert	3.426359 cd/m^2
Mass	grain[a]	64.79891 mg
	ounce	28.34952 g
	pound (U.S.)[a]	0.45359237 kg
Power	horsepower (electric)[a]	0.746 kW
Pressure	atmosphere (normal)[a]	101,325.0 Pa
	pound per square inch (psi)	6,894.757 N/m^2
	torr[a]	(101,325/760) Pa
	sound pressure level (SPL; 0.0002 dynes/cm^2)[b]	20 μN/m^2
Volume	cubic foot	0.02831685 m^3
	cubic inch	16.38706 cm^3
	fluid ounce	29.57353 mL
	quart (liquid)	0.9463529 L

Note. IT = International Table.
[a] Conversion factors for these units are exact. (For conversion factors that are not exact, the precision with which the quantity was measured determines the number of decimal places.)
[b] A decibel value is a measure of the power of sound relative to a specific reference level. The most common reference level on which decibel values are based is at 20 μN/m^2. If decibel values are based on another reference level, specify the level. Also, always indicate how frequencies were weighted: If frequencies were equally weighted, write SPL (i.e., sound pressure level) in parentheses after the decibel value; if frequencies were unequally weighted, specify the standard weighting used (e.g., A, B, or C) in parentheses after the decibel value.

Statistical and Mathematical Copy

APA style for presenting statistical and mathematical copy reflects both standards of content and form agreed upon in the field and requirements of the printing process.

3.50 Selecting the Method of Analysis and Retaining Data

Authors are responsible for the statistical method selected and for all supporting data. Access to computer analyses of data does not relieve the author of responsibility for selecting the appropriate statistic. To permit interested readers to challenge the statistical analysis, an author should retain the raw data after publication of the research. The usual practice is to keep the data for at least 5 years.

3.51 Selecting Effective Presentation

Statistical and mathematical copy can be presented in text, in tables, and in figures. Read sections 3.54, 3.59, and 3.71 to compare methods of presentation and to decide how best to present your data. When you are in doubt about the clearest and most effective method of presentation, prepare tables or figures with the understanding that if the manuscript is accepted, they are to be published at the editor's discretion. In any case, be prepared to submit tables and figures of complex statistical and mathematical material if an editor requests them.

3.52 References for Statistics

Do not give a reference for statistics in common use; this convention applies to most statistics used in journal articles. Do give a reference for (a) less common statistics, especially those that have appeared in journals but that are not yet incorporated in textbooks; or (b) a statistic used in a controversial way (e.g., to justify a test of significance when the data do not meet the assumptions of the test). When the statistic itself is the focus of the article, give supporting references.

3.53 Formulas

When deciding whether to include formulas, use the guidelines in section 3.52 (when to give a reference for a statistic). That is, do not give a formula for a statistic in common use; do give a formula when the statistic or mathematical expression is new, rare, or essential to the paper. Presentation of equations is described in sections 3.57 and 3.58.

3.54 Statistics in Text

To present an inferential statistic in text, give the symbol, degrees of freedom, value, and probability level. (Do not use a zero before the decimal in probability levels; see section 3.43.) In addition, give the mean, standard deviation, or other descriptive statistic to clarify the nature of the effect. Use a form like that in the following examples (see section 4.14 on typing statistical and mathematical copy):

> As predicted, the first-grade girls reported a significantly greater liking for school ($\underline{M}$ = 4.63) than did the first-grade boys ($\underline{M}$ = 1.38), $\underline{t}$(22) = 2.62, $\underline{p}$<.01.

> The mean score for the long retention interval was 1.38, and the mean score for the short retention interval was 28.90. The analysis of variance indicated a significant retention interval effect, $\underline{F}$(1, 34) = 123.07, $\underline{p}$<.001.

With chi-square, report degrees of freedom and sample size in the parentheses:

> (chi)→ χ^2(4, $\underline{N}$ = 90) = 10.51, $\underline{p}$<.05

When enumerating a series of similar statistics, be certain that the relation between the statistics and their referents is clear. Words such as *respectively* and *in order* can clarify this relation.

> Means for Trials 1 through 4 were 2.43, 2.59, 2.68, and 2.86, respectively.

> In order, means for Trials 1 through 4 were 2.43, 2.59, 2.68, and 2.86.

3.55 Statistical Symbols

When using a statistical term in the narrative, use the term, not the symbol. For example, use The means were, **not** The $\underline{M}$s were.

Symbols for population versus sample statistics. Population (i.e., theoretical) statistics, sometimes called parameters, are usually represented by lowercase Greek letters. A few sample (i.e., observed) statistics are also expressed by Greek letters (e.g., χ^2), but most sample statistics are expressed by italicized Latin letters (e.g., *SD*).

Symbol for numbers of subjects. Use an uppercase underlined *N* to designate the number of members in a total sample (e.g., $\underline{N}$ = 135) and a lowercase underlined *n* to designate the number of members in a limited portion of the total sample (e.g., $\underline{n}$ = 30).

Symbol for percent (%). Use the symbol for percent only when it is preceded by a numeral. Use the word *percentage* when a number is not given.

> found that 18% of the rats

> determined the percentage of rats

> *Exception:* In table headings and figure legends, use the symbol % to conserve space.

Roman, boldface, and italic type. Statistical symbols and mathematical copy are typeset in three different typefaces: roman, **boldface,** and *italic.* The same typeface is used for a symbol whether the symbol appears in text, tables, or figures.

Greek letters, subscripts and superscripts that function as

identifiers (i.e., that are not variables), and abbreviations that are not variables (e.g., sin, log) are typeset in a roman typeface. On the manuscript, do *not* underline them.

μ_{girls} (μ_{girls}), α (α), ϵ (ϵ), β (β), sin px (sin px)

Symbols for vectors are set in a bold typeface. In the manuscript, underline these symbols with a wavy line. Example: $\underset{\sim}{V}$ (**V**)

All other statistical symbols are set in italic type. On the manuscript underline them.

$\underline{N}$ (N), $\underline{M}_X$ (M_X), $\underline{df}$ (df), $\underline{p}$ (p), $\underline{SS}_b$ (SS_b), $\underline{SE}$ (SE), $\underline{MS}_e$ (MS_e), $\underline{t}$ (t), $\underline{F}$ (F), $\underline{a}$ (a), $\underline{b}$ (b)

Identifying letters and symbols. Some letters, numerals, and other characters may be ambiguous to the printer (see Equation 1 in section 3.58). The following characters, for example, may be misread in typewritten and handwritten copy: 1 (one or the letter el), 0 (zero or the letter oh), X (multiplication sign or the letter ex), Greek letters (the letter bee or beta), and some letters whose capital and lowercase forms may be confused, especially in subscripts and superscripts (e.g., c, s, and x). Identify ambiguous characters, when they first appear in the manuscript, with penciled notations (e.g., "lowercase el throughout").

In general, remember that the copy editor and the printer, who will convert the manuscript to a printed version, usually do not have mathematical backgrounds and will reproduce what they see, not what a mathematician knows. Avoid misunderstandings and corrections by preparing mathematical copy carefully.

3.56 Spacing, Alignment, and Punctuation

Space mathematical copy as you would space words: $\underline{a}+\underline{b}=\underline{c}$ is as difficult to read as wordswithoutspacing; $\underline{a} + \underline{b} = \underline{c}$ is much better. Align mathematical copy carefully. Subscripts usually precede superscripts ($\underline{x}_a{}^2$), but a prime is set next to a letter or symbol ($\underline{x}'_a$).

Punctuate all equations, whether they are in the line of text or displayed (i.e., typed on a new line), to conform to their place in the syntax of the sentence (see Equation 1 in section 3.58). If an equation exceeds the column width of a journal page, the printer will decide how to break it.

3.57 Equations in Text

Place short and simple equations, such as $\underline{a} = [(1 + \underline{b})/\underline{x}]^{1/2}$ in the line of text. Equations in the line of text should not project above or below the line; for example, the equation above would be difficult to set in the line of text if it were in this form:

$$\underline{a} = \sqrt{\frac{1 + \underline{b}}{\underline{x}}}.$$

To present fractions in the line of text, use a slanted line (/) and appropriate parentheses and brackets: Use ( ) first, then [( )], and finally {[( )]}. Use parentheses and brackets to avoid ambiguity: Does $a/b + c$ mean $(a/b) + c$ or $a/(b + c)$?

3.58 Displayed Equations

To display equations, start them on a new line and double-space twice above and twice below the equation. Simple equations should be displayed if they must be numbered for later reference. Display all complex equations.

Number displayed equations consecutively, with the number in parentheses near the right margin of the page:

$$\chi = -2\sum a_x^2 + a_0 + \frac{\cos x - 5ab}{1/n + a_x}. \tag{1}$$

(annotations: chi, sigma, zero, one, lc ex)

When referring to numbered equations, spell out the reference; for example, write Equation 1 (do not abbreviate as Eq. 1) or write the first equation.

Tables

3.59 Tabular Versus Textual Presentation

Tables are complicated to set in type and, therefore, are more expensive to publish than text. For this reason, they are best reserved for important data directly related to the content. However, a well-constructed table can be economical in that the author, by isolating the data from the text, enables the reader to quickly see patterns and relationships of the data not readily discernible in text. Compare the following presentation with Table 11.

Poor:

The mean numbers of words reported for the 3

subjects were, in order, 2.6, 2.8, and 1.6 at the

25-ms interstimulus interval; 3.0, 1.8, and 2.2 at

the 50-ms interstimulus interval; 2.6, 2.0, and

2.8 at the 75-ms interstimulus interval; and 3.0,

3.0, and 3.0 at the 100-ms interstimulus interval.

Better:

The reader can more easily comprehend and compare these data when they are presented in tabular form; however, the data in unusually short and simple tables (e.g., a table with only two columns and two rows) are more efficiently presented in text.

Determine the amount of data the reader needs to understand the discussion and then decide whether those data are best presented in text or tabular form. Peripherally related or extremely detailed data should be omitted or, depending on their nature, deposited in a national retrieval center (see the discussion of NAPS in the Appendix).

Table 11

Mean Numbers of Words Reported as a Function of

Interstimulus Interval

Subject	Interstimulus interval (in ms)			
	25	50	75	100
1	2.6	3.0	2.6	3.0
2	2.8	1.8	2.0	3.0
3	1.6	2.2	2.8	3.0

Tables usually present quantitative data. Occasionally, however, a table that consists of words is used to present qualitative comparisons. For additional information on word tables, see section 3.65.

Tables that communicate the quantitative aspects of data are effective only when the data are arranged so that their significance is obvious at a glance (Ehrenberg, 1977). After deciding what data to present but before constructing a table, you should consider that (a) rounded-off values may display patterns and exceptions more clearly than precise values, (b) a reader can compare numbers down a column more easily than across a row, (c) column and row averages can provide a visual focus that allows the reader to inspect the data easily, and (d) ample spacing between rows and columns can improve a table because white space creates a perceptual order to the data. (For a discussion on how to improve the presentation of data in a table, see Ehrenberg, 1977.) An author's thoughtful preparation makes the difference between a table that confuses and one that informs the reader.

Tables 12, 13, and 14 are examples of different kinds of tables as they would appear in a manuscript, that is, as prepared on a typewriter. These tables show the proper form and arrangement of titles, headings, data in the body of the table, footnotes, and rules. Detailed information on the preparation of tables is presented in sections 3.60–3.70.

3.60 Relation of Tables and Text

An informative table supplements—it does not duplicate—the text. In the text, refer to every table and its data. Although in text you should tell the reader what to look for in the table, discuss

APA Editorial Style • 85

Table 12

Mean Attribution Scores for Experiment 1

		Attribution	
Condition	n	Causality	Responsibility
High situational similarity/ high personal similarity	21		
M		1.49	0.94
SD		0.51	0.36
High situational similarity/ low personal similarity	25		
M		2.01	1.92
SD		1.14	1.74
Low situational similarity/ high personal similarity	23		
M		1.56	1.59
SD		1.13	0.84
Low situational similarity/ low personal similarity	22		
M		3.25	3.79
SD		1.21	1.39

Note. The higher the score, the greater the attribution.

Table 14

Intercorrelations Between Subscales for Students and Older Adults

Subscale	2	3	4
University students (n = 200)			
1. Tranquility	.93	−.09	.73
2. Goodwill	—	−.34	.62
3. Happiness		—	.14
4. Elation			—
Older adults (n = 189)			
1. Tranquility	.42	−.07	.52
2. Goodwill	—	.43	.62
3. Happiness		—	.47
4. Elation			—

Table 13

Recognition Memory for Words and Nonwords as a Function of Age and Viewing Condition

	Viewing condition		
Stimulus	1	2	3
Children[a]			
Words			
M	75.0	63.0	45.0
SD	16.0	15.0	14.0
Nonwords			
M	58.0	62.0	51.0
SD	15.0	17.0	15.0
Adults[b]			
Words			
M	91.0	88.0	61.0
SD	10.0	19.0	11.0
Nonwords			
M	78.0	65.0	80.0
SD	17.0	12.0	13.0

Note. The values represent mean percentages of correctly recognized words or nonwords.
[a]Children were 12–14 years old.
[b]Adults were 18–21 years old.

only the table's highlights. If you discuss every item of the table in text, the table is unnecessary.

Each table should be an integral part of the text and also should be intelligible without reference to the text. Explain all abbreviations (except such standard statistical abbreviations as *M, SD,* and *df*) and use of underlining and parentheses and always identify units of measurement (see Table 11).

In the text, refer to tables by their numbers:

```
as shown in Table 8, the responses
to children with pretraining (see Table 8)
```

Do not write "the table above/below" or "the table on page 32" because the position and page number of a table cannot be determined until the printer makes up the typeset pages. Do, however, indicate to the printer the approximate placement of each table in the text (see section 4.21 for typing instructions).

3.61 Relation Between Tables

Ordinarily an identical column of figures should not appear in two tables. When two tables overlap, consider combining them.

To facilitate comparison between tables in a paper, be consistent in the presentation of all tables. For example, use the same terminology (response time or reaction time, but not both) and similar formats, that is, similar titles and headings.

3.62 Table Numbers

Number all tables with arabic numerals in the order in which the tables are first mentioned in text. Do not use suffix letters to indicate relations between tables; that is, do not number separate tables as, for example, Tables 5, 5a, and 5b. Instead, label them as Tables 5, 6, and 7 or combine the related tables into one table. If the manuscript includes an appendix with tables, identify the tables of the appendix with capital letters and arabic numerals (e.g., Table A-1 is the first table of Appendix A, Table C-2 is the second table of Appendix C).

3.63 Table Titles

Give every table a brief but clear and explanatory title.
Too telegraphic:

```
Relation Between College Majors and Performance
```

[unclear as to what data are presented in the table]
Too detailed:

```
Mean Performance Scores on Test A, Test B, and
Test C of Students With Psychology, Physics,
English, and Engineering Majors [duplicates
```

information in the headings of the table]

Good title:

Mean Performance Scores of Students With Different

College Majors

Abbreviations that appear in the headings or the body of a table sometimes can be parenthetically explained in the table title. For example,

Table 2

Hit and False Alarm (FA) Proportions in

Experiment 2

Abbreviations that require longer explanations or that do not relate to the table title are explained in a general note to the table (see section 3.66).

3.64 Headings

A table compares and classifies related items. Data form the body of the table. Correct headings, which belong at the top of the table, establish the logic of your organization of the data. Headings, like table titles, should be telegraphic and should not be many more characters in length than the widest entry of the column beneath it. For example,

Poor: *Better:*

Grade level	Grade
3	3
4	4
5	5

You may use standard abbreviations for nontechnical terms (e.g., *no.* for *number*, % for *percent*) in table headings without explanation. Abbreviations of technical terms, group names, and the like must be explained in a note to the table (see section 3.66).

Depending on the complexity of the table, headings may be stubheads, column heads, column spanners, or table spanners. The left-hand column (called the *stub*) usually lists the major independent variables. The stub always has a heading (the *stubhead*), which describes the elements listed in that column. In Table 15, for example, the stub lists the groups. Number elements only when they appear in a correlation matrix (see Table 14) or if the text refers to them by number.

Subordination within the stub is better indicated by indenting stub items than by creating an additional column (see Table 15):

Poor:

Sex	Pretraining
Girls	With
	Without
Boys	With
	Without

Better:

Group
Girls
With
Without
Boys
With
Without

The headings just above the body of the table (called *column heads* and *column spanners*) identify the entries in the vertical columns in the body of the table. A column head covers just one column; a column spanner covers two or more columns, each with its own column head. Headings stacked in this way are called *decked heads*. Often decked heads can be used to avoid repetition of words in column headings (see Table 15). If possible, do not use more than two levels of decked heads.

Poor:

Grade 3	Grade 4

Better:

Grade		
3	4	5

A few tables may require table spanners in the body of the table. These table spanners cover the entire width of the body of the table, allowing for further divisions within the table (see Table 15). Also, table spanners can be used to combine two tables into one.

Any item within a column should be syntactically as well as conceptually comparable to the other items in that column, and all items should be described by the heading:

Poor:

Condition
Functional psychotic
Drinks to excess
Character disorder

Better:

Condition
Functional psychosis
Alcoholism
Character disorder

Table 15

Mean Numbers of Correct Responses by Children With and
Without Pretraining

decked heads *column spanner*

column heads

stubhead

Group	n^a	3	4	5
Verbal tests *(table spanner)*				
Girls				
With	18	280	297	301
Without	19	240	251	260
Boys				
With	19	281	290	306
Without	20	232	264	221
Mathematical tests *(table spanner)*				
Girls				
With	20	201	214	221
Without	17	189	194	216^b
Boys				
With	19	210	236	239
Without	18	199	210	213

Grade *(column spanner)*

stub

cell

body

Note to table gives
total score for
comparison with
table entries.

Note. Maximum score = 320.

[a]Numbers of children out of 20 in each group who
completed all tests. [b]One girl in this group gave only two
correct responses.

Stubheads, column heads, and column spanners are singular, and table spanners may be plural. Capitalize only the first word (and any proper names) of headings and column entries.

3.65 Body of a Table

The body of a table contains the data. Express numerical values in the number of decimal places that the precision of measurement justifies and, if possible, carry all comparable values to the same number of decimal places. In any case, do not change the unit of measurement or the number of decimal places within a column.

If the point of intersection between a row and a column (called a *cell*) cannot be filled because data are unavailable, unreported, or inapplicable, insert a dash in that cell and explain in the general note to the table the use of the dash. By convention, a dash in a correlation matrix (see Table 14) usually indicates that the correlation of an item with itself was not performed. No explanation of the dash in a correlation matrix is needed. If you need to explain that data in a correlation matrix are unavailable, unreported, or inapplicable, use a specific note (see section 3.66) rather than a dash.

Do not include columns of data that can be calculated easily from other columns:

Poor:

| Subject | No. responses | | | |
	First trial	Second trial	Total	Mean
1	5	7	12	6

Better:

Be selective in your presentation. For example, (a) give either the number of responses per trial or the total number of responses, whichever is important to the discussion, and (b) do not include a row or column of averages if their calculation is simple.

Unlike most tables, which present quantitative data, some tables consist mainly of words. Such word tables present qualitative comparisons or descriptive information. For example, a word table can compare characteristics of studies in an article that reviews many studies, or it can present questions and responses from a survey or briefly outline the elements of a theory. Word tables illustrate the discussion in the text; they should not repeat the discussion.

The format of word tables is like the format of other tables in terms of table numbers and title, headings, notes, and rules. Keep column entries brief and simple. Indent any runover lines in entries. *Double-space all parts of a word table.*

3.66 Notes to a Table

Tables have three kinds of notes, which are placed below the table: general notes, specific notes, and probability notes.

A general note qualifies, explains, or provides information relating to the table as a whole, including an explanation of abbreviations, symbols, and the like.

General notes are designated by the word <u>Note</u> (underlined) followed by a period. (See section 3.69 for examples of general notes indicating that a table is reprinted from another source.)

<u>Note</u>. All nonsignificant three-way interactions

were omitted. M = match process; N = nonmatch

process.

A specific note refers to a particular column or to an individual entry. Specific notes are indicated by superscript lowercase letters ([a], [b], [c],). Within the headings and table body, order the superscripts horizontally from left to right across the table by rows, starting at the top left. Specific notes to a table are independent of any other table and begin with a superscript lowercase *a* in each table. (See Tables 13 and 15 for examples of this kind of note.)

[a]<u>n</u> = 25. [b]This subject did not complete the

trials.

A probability level note indicates the results of tests of significance. Asterisks indicate the probability levels of tests of significance. When more than one level appears in a table, use one asterisk for the lowest level, two for the next level, and so on. Probability levels and the number of asterisks need not be consistent from table to table.

<u>F</u>

2.80*

4.38**

*<u>p</u> $<$ .05.   **<u>p</u> $<$ .01.

To distinguish between one-tailed and two-tailed tests in the same table, use asterisks for the one-tailed *p* values and an alternate symbol (e.g., daggers) for the two-tailed *p* values.

*<u>p</u> $<$ .05, one-tailed. **<u>p</u> $<$ .01, one-tailed. †<u>p</u> $<$ .05,

two-tailed. ††<u>p</u> $<$ .01, two-tailed.

Asterisks attached to a table entry indicate the significance level of a particular table value. To indicate significance *between* two or more table entries, use lowercase *su*bscripts, brackets, braces, or a column of *p* values. Explain the use of these devices in the table note (see the following sample table notes). Lowercase *su*bscripts are appropriate when an author has used Duncan's multiple-range test to compare differences (significant or nonsignificant) between means. The table note would read as follows:

<u>Note</u>. Means having the same subscript are not

significantly different at $\underline{p} < .01$.

        or

<u>Note</u>. Means with different subscripts differ

significantly at $\underline{p} < .01$.

Order the notes to a table in the following sequence: *general* note, *specific* note, *probability level* note.

<u>Note</u>. The subjects . . . responses.

$^a\underline{n}$ = 25. $^b\underline{n}$ = 42.

$^*\underline{p} < .05$. $^{**}\underline{p} < .01$.

Each type of note begins flush left (i.e., no paragraph indention) on a new line, below the table. The first *specific* note begins flush left on a new line under the *general* note; subsequent specific notes follow one after the other on the same line (i.e., they are run in). The first *probability level* note begins flush left on a new line; subsequent probability level notes are run in.

Certain types of information may be appropriate either in the table or in a note. To determine the placement of such material, remember that clearly and efficiently organized data enable the reader to focus on the significance of the data. Thus, if *p*s or *n*s are numerous, use a column rather than many notes. Conversely, if a row or a column contains few entries (or the same entry), eliminate the column by adding a note to the table:

Poor: *Better:*

Group	$\underline{n}$
1	15
2	15
3	15

Group^a
1
2
3

$^a\underline{n}$ = 15 for each

group.

3.67 Ruling of Tables

Printing requirements restrict the use of rules in a table. Limit the rules to those that are necessary for clarity, and use horizontal rather than vertical rules. (Vertical rules are almost never used in APA journals.) Appropriately positioned white space can be an effective substitute for rules; for example, long, uninterrupted columns of numbers or words are more readable if a horizontal line of space is inserted after every fourth or fifth entry.

In the typewritten manuscript, use generous spacing between columns and rows and strict alignment to clarify relationships within a table. *Draw all rules in pencil* so that they may be changed if necessary for printing requirements.

3.68 Size of Tables

Turning a journal sideways to read a table is an inconvenience to readers. You can design a table to fit the width of a journal page or column if you count characters (i.e., letters, numbers, and spaces). Count characters in the widest entry in each column (whether in the table body or in a heading) and allow 3 characters for spaces between columns. If the count exceeds 50, the table will not fit across the width of most APA journal columns. If the count exceeds 100, the table will not fit across the width of most APA journal pages. To determine exact fit, count the characters in the journal for which you are writing and adjust your table if necessary.

3.69 Tables From Another Source

Authors must obtain permission to reproduce or adapt all or part of a table (or figure) from a copyrighted source. It is not necessary to obtain permission from APA to reproduce a single table (or figure) from an APA article provided you obtain the author's permission and give full credit to APA as copyright holder and to the author through a complete and accurate citation. When you wish to reproduce material from sources not copyrighted by APA, contact the copyright holders to determine their requirements. If you have any doubt about the policy of the copyright holder, you should request permission. Always enclose the letter of permission when submitting the manuscript.

Any reproduced table (or figure) must be accompanied by a note at the bottom of the reprinted table (or in the figure caption) giving credit to the original author and to the copyright holder. Use the following form for tables or figures. (For copyright permission footnotes in text [see section 3.38 for permission to quote], use the following form, but substitute the indented superscript footnote number for the word *Note.*)

Material reprinted from a journal article:

Note. From [*or* The data in column 1 are from]

"Title of Article" by A. N. Author and

C. O. Author, 1982, Title of Journal, 50,

```
p. 22. Copyright 1982 by the Name of Copyright

Holder. Reprinted [or Adapted] by permission.
```

Material reprinted from a book:
```
Note. From [or The data in column 1 are from]

Title of Book (p. 103) by A. N. Author and C. O.

Author, 1982, Place of Publication: Publisher.

Copyright 1982 by the Name of Copyright Holder.

Reprinted [or Adapted] by permission.
```

3.70 Table Checklist

- Is the table necessary?
- Is the entire table—including the title and headings—double-spaced?
- Are all comparable tables in the manuscript consistent in presentation?
- Is the title brief but explanatory?
- Does every column have a column heading?
- Are all abbreviations, underlines, parentheses, and special symbols explained?
- Are all probability level values correctly identified, and are asterisks attached to the appropriate table entries?
- Are the notes in the following order: general note, specific note, probability level note?
- Are all vertical rules eliminated?
- Are horizontal rules drawn in pencil only?
- Will the table fit across the width of a journal column or page?
- If all or part of a copyrighted table is reproduced, do the table notes give full credit to the copyright owner? Is a letter of permission included with the submitted manuscript?
- Is the table referred to in text? Does the manuscript include an indication for the printer of the approximate placement in text of each table?

Figures

3.71 Deciding to Use Figures

In APA journals any type of illustration other than a table is called a *figure*. (Because tables are typeset rather than photographed from artwork supplied by the author, they are not considered figures.) A figure may be a chart, graph, photograph, drawing, or other depiction.

Consider carefully whether to use a figure. On the one hand, a well-prepared figure can convey the qualitative aspects of data, such as comparisons, relationships, and structural or pictorial concepts, more efficiently than can text or tables. On the other hand, a figure is usually more time-consuming and more expensive than text or tables to prepare and reproduce.

During the process of drafting a manuscript, and *before* deciding to use a figure, ask yourself these questions:
- Is the figure necessary? If it duplicates text, it is not necessary. If it complements text or eliminates lengthy discussion, it may be the most efficient way to present the information.
- What idea do you need to convey?
- What type of figure (e.g., graph, chart, diagram, drawing, map, or photograph) is most suited to your purpose? Will a simple, relatively inexpensive figure convey the point as well as an elaborate, expensive figure?

3.72 Standards for Figures

The standards for good figures are simplicity, clarity, and continuity. A good figure
- augments rather than duplicates the text;
- conveys only essential facts;
- omits visually distracting detail;
- is easy to read—its elements (type, lines, labels, etc.) are large enough to be read with ease in the printed form;
- is easy to understand—its purpose is readily apparent;
- is consistent with and is prepared in the same style as similar figures in the same article; that is, the lettering is of the same size and typeface, lines are of the same weight, and so forth;
- is carefully planned and prepared.

Types of figures and figure preparation guidelines are described in some detail in sections 3.73–3.80 so that you can select the figure most appropriate to the information being presented and ensure the preparation of a figure of professional quality. If you engage a professional artist, supply the artist with the guidelines in this section so that the artist is aware of the requirements for figures published in APA journals. (See the references in section 7.03 for more on the preparation of figures.)

3.73 Types of Figures

Graphs show relationships—comparisons and distributions—in a set of data and may show, for example, absolute values, percentages, or index numbers. Keep the lines clean and simple and eliminate all extraneous detail. The presentation of information on the horizontal and vertical axes should be orderly (e.g., small to large) and consistent (e.g., in comparable units of measurement).
- **Line graphs** are most often used to show continuous change (e.g., time series). The independent variable is plotted on the horizontal (or x) axis, and the dependent variable is plotted on the vertical (or y) axis (see Figure 1). The length of the vertical axis should be approximately two thirds the length of the horizontal axis. Grid marks on the axes demarcate units of measurement. A change in the proportionate sizes of the x units to the y units changes the slant of the line. Thus, for example, disproportionately large units on the vertical axis will distort differences. Be sure the curve or slant of the line accurately reflects the data. If the graph could be misinterpreted because the origin of the coordinates is not zero, break the axes with a double slash.

FIGURE 1

Sample Line Graph

From "Cortical Substrates of Taste Aversion Learning: Dorsal Prepiriform (Insular) Lesions Disrupt Taste Aversion Learning" by P. S. Lasiter and D. L. Glanzman, 1982, *Journal of Comparative and Physiological Psychology, 96,* p. 387. Copyright 1982 by the American Psychological Association. Adapted by permission.

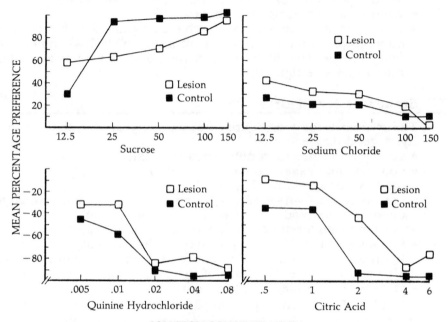

FIGURE 2

Sample Bar Graph

From "Prolactin-Steroid Influences on the Thermal Basis for Mother–Young Contact in Norway Rats" by B. Woodside et al., 1981, *Journal of Comparative and Physiological Psychology, 95,* p. 776. Copyright 1981 by the American Psychological Association. Adapted by permission.

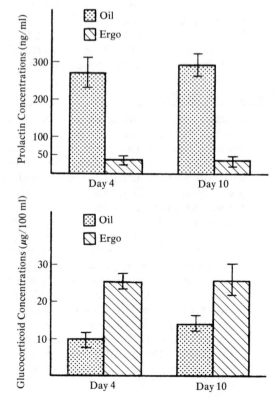

FIGURE 3

Sample Scatter Graph

From "Stimulus Processing During Eye Fixations" by T. A. Salthouse, C. L. Ellis, D. C. Diener, and B. L. Somberg, 1981, *Journal of Experimental Psychology: Human Perception and Performance, 7,* p. 616. Copyright 1981 by the American Psychological Association. Adapted by permission.

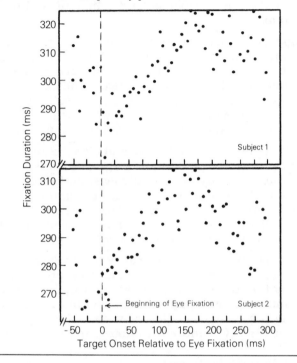

- **Bar graphs** are simple, adaptable, and telegraphic (see Figure 2). Solid horizontal or vertical bars each represent one kind of datum. In a subdivided bar graph, each bar shows two or more divisions of data. Other bar graphs include multiple bar graphs (in which whole bars represent different single variables in one set of data) and sliding bar graphs (in which bars are split by a vertical line that serves as the reference for each bar, e.g., in order to show less-than-zero and greater-than-zero relationships).
- **Circle (or pie) graphs,** by nature 100% graphs, are used to show percentages and proportions. The number of items compared should be kept to five or fewer. Order the segments from large to small, beginning the largest segment at 12 o'clock. A good way to highlight differences is to shade the segments from light to dark, making the smallest segment the darkest. Use patterns of lines and dots to shade the segments.
- **Scatter graphs** consist of single dots plotted on a line graph; the dots are not joined by lines (see Figure 3). Each dot represents the intersection of two variables. A cluster of dots along a diagonal indicates a correlation.
- **Pictorial graphs** are used to represent simple quantitative differences between groups. All symbols representing equal values should be the same size. Keep in mind that if you double the height of a symbol, you quadruple its area.

Charts can describe the relationships between parts of a group or object or the sequence of operations in a process; charts are usually boxes connected with lines. For example, organizational charts show the hierarchy in a group, flow charts show the sequence of steps in a process, and schematics show components in a system.

Dot maps can show population density, and **shaded maps** can show averages or percentages. In these cases, plotted data are superimposed on a map. Maps should always be prepared by a professional artist, who should clearly indicate the compass orientation (e.g., north–south) of the map, fully identify the map's location, and provide the scale to which the map is drawn. Use arrows to help readers focus on reference points.

Drawings are by nature selective and give the author the flexibility to emphasize any aspect of an image or idea (see Figure 4). They can be done from any of several views, for instance, a two-dimensional view of any side of an object or a view of an object rotated and tipped forward to show several sides at once. Drawings should be prepared by a professional artist and should use the least amount of detail necessary to convey the point.

Photographs have excellent eye appeal (see Figure 5). They should be of professional quality and should be prepared with a background that produces the greatest amount of contrast. A photographer can highlight a particular aspect of the photograph by manipulating the camera angle or by choosing a particular type of lighting or film. (For more on photographs, see section 3.78.)

3.74 Line Art Versus Halftone

Although there are many types of figures, usually only two printing processes are involved in reproducing them: line art processing and halftone processing. Line art is any material that will reproduce only in black and white, for example, type, lines, boxes, dots, and so on. Halftones are figures that have shades of gray, for example, photographs or graphs with shaded bars. Halftones require a complicated printing process, which makes them more expensive than line drawings to reproduce.

3.75 Size and Proportion

When planning a figure, take into consideration that
- All published figures must fit the dimensions of a journal page; if your figure is larger than a journal page, it will be reduced to the width of a journal page or column.
- Reducing the width of a figure will reduce the length by the same percentage. For example, reducing a figure's width by 50% will simultaneously reduce its length by 50%.
- Parallel figures or figures of equal importance should be of equal size; that is, they should be prepared according to the same scale.
- Combining like figures (e.g., two line graphs with identical axes) saves preparation time, production expense, and journal space. You can either place like figures next to each other on one page

FIGURE 4

Sample Drawing

From "Processing of Formational, Semantic, and Iconic Information in American Sign Language" by H. Poizner, U. Bellugi, and R. D. Tweney, 1981, *Journal of Experimental Psychology: Human Perception and Performance, 7*, p. 1152. Copyright 1981 by the American Psychological Association. Reprinted by permission.

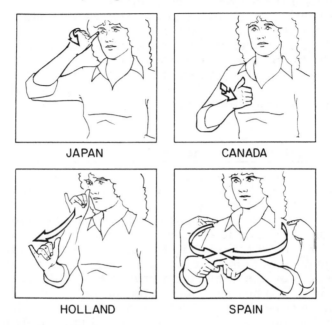

FIGURE 5

Sample Photograph

From "Face Scanning and Responsiveness to Social Cues in Infant Rhesus Monkeys" by M. J. Mendelson, M. M. Haith, P. S. Goldman-Rakic, 1982, *Developmental Psychology, 18,* p. 224. Copyright 1982 by the American Psychological Association. Reprinted by permission.

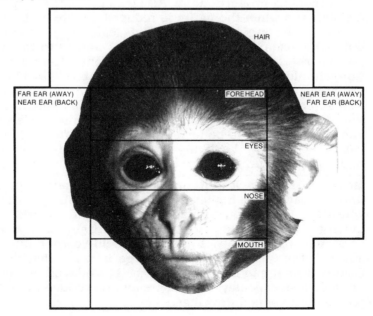

and treat the whole as a single figure (see Figures 1, 2, and 3) or plot several curves on one pair of axes (see Figure 1). Use legibility as a guide in determining the number of curves to place on a figure. A good general rule is no more than four curves per figure. Allow adequate space between and within curves, particularly if the figure is to be reduced.

- All elements of a figure must be large enough to be legible, even when the figure is reduced.
- A figure legend, unlike a caption, should be positioned within the figure itself. Place labels for parts of a figure as close as possible to the components being identified. If a legend is outside the axis area, the figure will have to be reduced more to accommodate the extra width.

3.76 Mechanical Preparation of Figures

Usually professional drafting services are used to produce a finished figure because most authors do not have the technical skill to produce a figure that meets printing requirements. However, the glossy print (see the end of this section) of any figure of professional quality is acceptable, whether drawn by a professional or by a person skilled in the use of press-on letters or other graphic aids. Computer-generated figures are usually unacceptable because the lines and lettering are often light and broken and therefore do not reproduce satisfactorily.

In any case, all figures must adhere to the following mechanical specifications and must be in finished form ready for reproduction (camera ready).

Size and proportion. As you construct a figure, consider what will happen to its various elements—the letters, numbers, lines, plot points, subtle shading, and spaces between and within curves—when reduced proportionally. All elements of the figure must be legible, even when the figure is reduced. Figure 6 shows how reduction of the original artwork affects legibility of letters and symbols. The size of lettering on a figure reduced to the width of a journal page or column (i.e., the height of the lettering *after reduction*) should be no smaller than approximately $\frac{1}{16}$ in. (1.6 mm) and no larger than approximately $\frac{1}{8}$ in. (3.2 mm). Also consider the weight (i.e., size, density) of each element in a figure in relation to that of every other element. Each element must be large enough and sharp enough to be legible if reduced to fit the journal page (see section 3.75). Legibility is ensured if the glossy print of a figure requires no further reduction.

Materials. Use black india ink and a good grade of bright white drawing paper. The higher the contrast, the sharper the detail. If you draw a graph on tracing paper over a dark grid, use high-quality tracing paper. Professional artists also use pencil, scratchboard (white lines on a black field), carbon dust (to show shades of gray), and ink wash. Keep in mind that pen-and-ink figures, which can almost always be reproduced as line art, will often be less expensive to prepare and reproduce than, for example, halftone pencil drawings.

Shading. Drawings and graphs can be shaded and still be reproduced as line art rather than as more expensive halftones. For example, instead of using pencil shading or a different shade of gray for each bar in a bar graph, use a pattern of lines or dots. Patterns of lines or dots on pressure-sensitive adhesive paper (e.g., Zipatone, Letraset, Formatt) are available from art supply stores.

Lettering. Nonprofessional-freehand or typewritten lettering is not acceptable. Three methods of lettering are acceptable: professional lettering, stencil, or dry-transfer sheets. Professional lettering includes typeset or hand lettering. A stencil (e.g., Chartpack, Leroy, Wrico, or Ames lettering devices) provides a guide to the size and proportion of all lettering on the figure. (Remember that to be legible, the lettering must be no less than $\frac{1}{16}$ in. [1.6 mm] high after reduction.) Align letters from dry-transfer or pressure-sensitive sheets carefully and press the letters securely on the original figure so that they do not rub off. You can protect the lettering until you photograph the figure to make a glossy print by applying a light coat of a spray fixative.

Use a simple typeface with enough space between letters to avoid compression after reduction. Letters should be clear, sharp, and uniformly black and should be as consistent a size as possible throughout the figure so that even the smallest lettering is legible after reduction. Style of type also affects legibility: For example, a roman type font is more legible when reduced than is a boldface font. Uppercase and lowercase letters generally are easier to read than all uppercase letters, but if the figure requires several distinctions (i.e., levels) of lettering, the use of all uppercase letters is acceptable.

FIGURE 6

Effects of Reducing Letters and Symbols Frequently Used in Figures

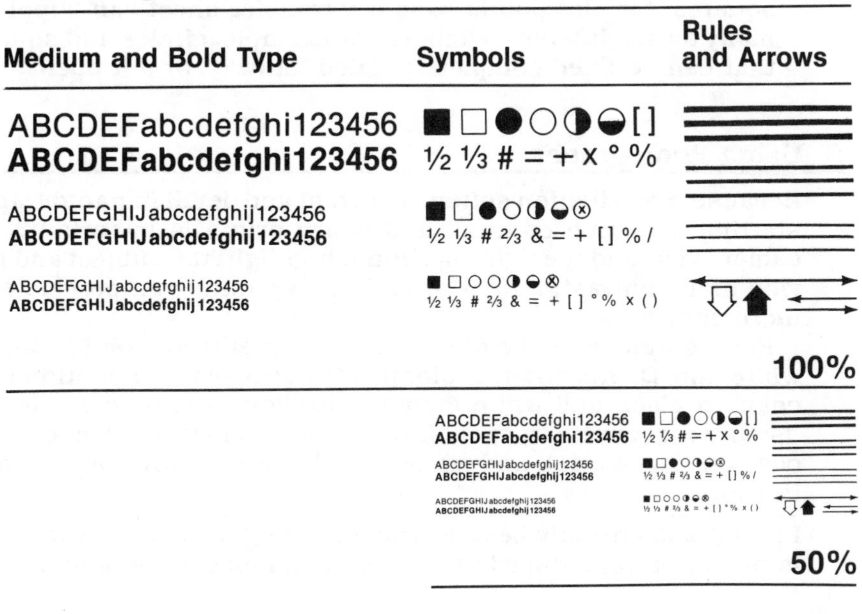

Medium and Bold Type	Symbols	Rules and Arrows

Glossy prints. After the figure has been prepared, have a photographic proof of the figure made on gloss-coated paper. Because glossy paper is higher in contrast than mat (nonglossy) paper, it reproduces detail more sharply. Submit the resulting proof, called a glossy print, with the original manuscript. (For additional information on glossy prints, see section 3.81.)

3.77 Drawing Graphs

To draw a graph, follow these steps:
- Use high-quality white drawing paper.
- Ink in or use press-on tape to make heavy lines for the vertical and horizontal axes. The length of the vertical axis (on which the dependent variable is plotted) should be approximately two thirds the length of the horizontal axis (on which the independent variable is plotted).
- Choose the appropriate grid scale. Consider the range and scale separation to be used on both axes and the overall dimensions of the figure so that plotted curves span the entire illustration.
- Indicate units of measurement by placing grid marks on each axis at the appropriate intervals.
- Clearly label each axis with both the quantity measured and the units in which the quantity is measured.
- Place the axis labels parallel to the proper axes. The numbering and lettering of grid points should be horizontal on both axes.
- Use legibility as a guide in determining the number of curves to place on a figure—usually no more than four curves per figure. It is best to use a continuous line for all functions, identifying each line with a symbol, because the combination of several solid and dotted lines can be hard to read and because dotted lines are difficult to draw. Allow adequate space between and within curves, particularly if the figure is to be reduced.
- Use distinct, simple geometric forms, such as circles or squares, for plot points. One dry-transfer sheet can supply as many as six different symbols, for example, circles and squares that can be filled completely, filled halfway, or left open.

3.78 Using Photographs

Because reproduction softens contrast and detail in photographs, starting with rich contrast and sharp prints is important. The camera view and the lighting should highlight the subject and provide high contrast; a light or dark background can provide even more contrast.

Photographs must be of professional quality and on black-and-white film. Do not submit color prints because the transition from color to black and white for reproduction is unpredictable and usually inaccurate in tone. Have a color negative, slide, or print developed as a black-and-white print before submitting it for publication.

Photographs usually benefit from cropping (i.e., eliminating what is not to be reproduced). Cropping recomposes the photograph, eliminates extraneous detail, and recenters the image. Cropping can also remove blemishes.

To prepare for cropping a photograph, first determine the ideal area to be reproduced, that is, the part of the photograph that you want to appear on the printed page. The area to be reproduced need not be the same shape as the larger photograph, but the edges should be straight lines at right angles to each other.

Next, mark the area to be reproduced. One way to indicate the area is to outline it on a piece of tissue paper covering the photograph. Write lightly in pencil. Never write directly on the face of the photograph.

Finally, have a print made of the outlined area of the photograph and submit the new print with the manuscript.

If you group photographs for purposes of comparison or to save space, place the photographs right next to each other. The printer can insert a thin white or black line between the photographs to separate them.

Photomicrographs are produced with specialized equipment. Indicate the degree of magnification by including a scale line on the photograph. Also, indicate in the figure caption the type of staining materials and any unusual lighting used.

If you photograph a person, get a signed release from that person to use the photograph. If you use a photograph from another source, try to obtain the original photograph, because photographs of photographs do not print clearly. Obtain written permission to reprint from the copyright holder and acknowledge the copyright holder in the figure caption (see section 3.69).

3.79 Identifying and Citing Figures

Number all figures consecutively with arabic numerals throughout an article in the order in which they are first mentioned in text (i.e., Figure 1, Figure 2). This number should be written *lightly* with a pencil or pen (but do not use ballpoint) on the back of the glossy print of the figure. Always write as close to the edge of the figure as possible and never write on the face of the figure. Also on the back of the glossy print, write the article's short title and write the word *TOP* to designate the top of the figure.

In the text, refer to figures by their numbers:

```
as shown in Figure 2, the relationships are

data are related (see Figure 5)
```

Never write "the figure above/below" or "the figure on page 12" because the position and page number of a figure cannot be determined until the printer makes up the typeset pages. However, indicate to the printer the approximate placement of each figure in text (see section 4.22 for typing instructions).

3.80 Figure Captions and Legends

In APA journals, a caption is a concise explanation of the figure; on the typeset journal page, it is placed below the figure. A legend is a key to symbols used in the figure; it is placed within the figure and photographed as part of the figure.

The caption serves both as an explanation of the figure and as a figure title; therefore, it should describe the contents of the figure in a brief sentence or phrase. Compare the following captions for Figure 3:

Poor:

<u>Figure 3</u>. Fixation duration.

Better:

<u>Figure 3</u>. Fixation duration as a function of the

delay between the beginning of eye fixation and

the onset of the stimulus in Experiment 1.

In parentheses after the figure caption, add any information needed to clarify the figure and always explain units of measurement and abbreviations that are not included in the legend. A reader should not have to refer to the text to decipher the figure. Make certain that the symbols, abbreviations, and terminology in the caption agree with the symbols, abbreviations, and terminology in the figure, in other figures in the article, and in the text. Compare the caption with the figure; proofread all lettering and make sure no labels are missing.

Unlike the figure and figure legend, which are reproduced from the glossy print, the caption is typeset and is placed outside the figure. Therefore, type all figure captions, with their numbers, double-spaced on a separate sheet (see section 4.22 for typing instructions).

An author must obtain permission to reproduce or adapt a figure from a copyrighted source and must give credit in the figure caption to the original author and copyright holder (see section 3.69).

The legend is an integral part of the figure; therefore, it should have the same kind and proportion of lettering that appear in the rest of the figure. Because it is photographed as part of the figure, the legend must appear on the glossy print.

3.81 Submitting Figures

Submit the same number of copies of figures as of the typed text of the manuscript. All original figures must be photographed and submitted as 8 x 10 in. (20 x 25 cm) glossy prints. If it is necessary to submit smaller glossy prints, mount them on 8½ x 11 in. (22 x 28 cm) paper. Duplicate figures can be photocopies (i.e., copies made with a copier machine).

To reproduce the figure, the printer photographs the glossy print submitted with the manuscript. Flaws in the glossy print will appear in the published figure. Therefore do not attach anything to the print with staples or paper clips and avoid pressing down on the print when you write the identification information on the back. If it is necessary to retouch a figure or to apply letterpress to the glossy print, protect the figure by putting a piece of tissue paper over it. Placing the prints between pieces of cardboard will also help protect them.

3.82 Figure Checklist

- Is the figure necessary?
- Is the figure simple, clean, and free of extraneous detail?
- Are the data plotted accurately?
- Is the grid scale correctly proportioned?
- Is the lettering large and black enough to read, especially if the figure must be reduced? Is the lettering compatible in size with the rest of the figure? (Freehand or typewritten lettering is not acceptable.)
- What will be the effects of reduction on detail and on lettering?
- Are parallel figures or equally important figures prepared according to the same scale?
- Are terms spelled correctly?
- Are all abbreviations and symbols explained in a figure legend or figure caption? Are the symbols, abbreviations, and terminology in the figure consistent with those in the figure caption? in other figures? in the text?
- Are all figure captions typed on a separate page?
- Are the figures numbered consecutively with arabic numerals?
- Are all figures mentioned in text?
- Is each figure an 8 x 10 in. (20 x 25 cm) glossy print?
- Are all figures identified lightly in pencil or nonballpoint pen on the back by figure number and short article title?
- Is *TOP* written on the back of figures to show orientation?
- Is written permission enclosed for figures that are being used from another source?

Footnotes and Notes

Notes may be substantive or explanatory or may identify sources, according to where they are used and what needs to be conveyed. Sections 3.83 to 3.85 define the kinds of notes in APA journals.

3.83 Footnotes in Text

Footnotes in text are of two kinds: content footnotes and copyright permission footnotes.

Content footnotes supplement or amplify substantive information in the text and should not include irrelevant or nonessential information. Because they are distracting to readers and expensive to include in printed material, such footnotes should be included only if they strengthen the discussion. In most cases, an author integrates an article best by presenting important information in the text, not in a footnote.

Rather than reproducing in a footnote long or complicated material, such as proofs or derivations unnecessary to the text, consider (a) indicating in a short footnote that the material is available from the author, (b) depositing the material in a national retrieval center and including an appropriate footnote (see the Appendix, A.06), or (c) adding an appendix (see section 1.14 and, for typing instructions, section 4.19). If appendixes are used, the reference in text reads as follows:

```
the same results for both studies (see Appendixes A and
B for complete proofs)
```

Copyright permission footnotes acknowledge the source of quotations (see section 3.38 on permission to quote). Use the suggested wording for reprinted tables or figures (see section 3.69). All other kinds of reference citations, including legal citations and citations to material of limited availability, should appear in the reference list (see section 3.99 and Table 17).

Number content and copyright permission footnotes consecutively throughout an article with superscript arabic numerals. Type these footnotes on a separate page (see section 4.20 for typing instructions). Subsequent references to a footnote are by parenthetical note:

```
the same results (see Footnote 3)
```

3.84 Notes to Tables

Table notes, which are placed below the bottom rule of a table, explain the table data or provide additional information (see section 3.66 on notes to a table). They also acknowledge the source of a table if the table is reprinted (see section 3.69 for form of acknowledgment).

3.85 Author Identification Notes

Author identification notes appear with each printed article. These notes should

- acknowledge (a) the basis of a study (e.g., doctoral dissertation or paper presented at a meeting), (b) a grant or other financial support, and (c) any scholarly review or assistance in conducting the study or preparing the manuscript;
- elaborate on the author's affiliation or note a change in affiliation;
- designate the address of the author to whom requests for reprints or inquiries should be sent.

For example,

```
        Preparation of this article was supported in

part by National Institute of Mental Health Grant

MH00000 to David Yusi.

        We gratefully acknowledge the assistance of

Charles Cooper and Anne Domino in the data

collection and of Virginia Adams, Paul Bergren,

Susan Locke, and two anonymous reviewers for
```

comments on a draft of this article.

Requests for reprints should be sent to David

Yusi, who is now at the Department of Psychology,

University of Maryland, College Park, Maryland

20742.

Do not number author identification notes, which are typed on a separate page. If the manuscript is to be blind reviewed, type the author identification notes on the title page (see section 4.20 for typing instructions).

Reference Citations in Text

Citation of an author's work in text documents your work, briefly identifies the source for readers, and enables readers to locate the source of information in the alphabetical reference list at the end of an article. (See sections 3.98 to 3.101 and Table 17 on the preparation of the reference list.)

3.86 One Work by a Single Author

APA journals use the author-date method of citation; that is, the surname of the author and the year of publication are inserted in the text at the appropriate point:

Smith (1983) compared reaction times

In a recent study of reaction times (Smith, 1983)

If the name of the author appears as part of the narrative, as in the first example, cite only the year of publication in parentheses. Otherwise, place both the name and the date, separated by a comma (as in the second example), in parentheses. In the rare case in which both the year and the author are given as part of the textual discussion, do not add parenthetical information:

In 1983, Smith compared

Within a paragraph, you need not include the year in subsequent references to a study as long as the study cannot be confused with other studies cited in the article:

In a recent study of reaction times, Smith (1983) described the method . . . Smith also found

3.87 One Work by Two or More Authors

When a work has two authors, always cite both names every time the reference occurs in text.

When a work has more than two authors and fewer than six authors, cite all authors the first time the reference occurs; in subsequent citations include only the surname of the first author followed by "et al." (not underlined and with no period after "et") and the year:

```
Williams, Jones, Smith, Bradner, and Torrington
(1983) found [first citation]
Williams et al. (1983) found [subsequent citations]
```

Exceptions: If two references with the same year shorten to the same form (e.g., both Bradley, Ramirez, & Soo, 1983, and Bradley, Soo, Ramirez, & Brown, 1983, shorten to Bradley et al., 1983), always cite both references in full to avoid confusion. Also, all multiple-author citations in footnotes, tables, and figures should include the surnames of all authors every time the citations occur.

When a work has six or more authors, cite only the surname of the first author followed by "et al." (not underlined and with no period after "et") and the year for the first and subsequent citations. (In the reference list, the surnames in references with six or more authors are spelled out.)

Exception: If two references with six or more authors shorten to the same form, cite the surnames of the first authors and of as many of the subsequent authors as are necessary to distinguish the two references, followed by "et al." For example, the references Takac, Schaefer, Bryant, Wood, Maloney, and Cron (1982) and Takac, Schaefer, Maloney, Bryant, Cron, and Wang (1982) in text would be cited, respectively, as Takac, Schaefer, Bryant, et al. (1982) and as Takac, Schaefer, Maloney, et al. (1982).

Join the names in a multiple-author citation in running text by the word *and.* In parenthetical material, in tables, and in the reference list, join the names by an ampersand (&):

```
as James and Ryerson (1983) demonstrated

as has been shown (James & Ryerson, 1983)
```

3.88 Corporate Authors

The names of corporate authors are usually spelled out each time they appear in a text citation. The names of some corporate authors are spelled out in the first citation and abbreviated thereafter. In deciding whether to abbreviate the name of a corporate author, use the general rule that you need to give enough information in the text citation for the reader to locate the entry in the reference list without difficulty. If the name of the corporate author is long and cumbersome and if the abbreviation is familiar or readily understandable, you may abbreviate the name in the second and subsequent citations. If the name is short or if the abbreviation would not be readily understandable, spell out the name each time it occurs.

Example of the name of a corporate author (e.g., association, government agency) that may be abbreviated:
Entry in reference list:

```
National Institute of Mental Health. (1981).
```

First text citation:

```
(National Institute of Mental Health [NIMH], 1981)
```

Subsequent text citations:

```
(NIMH, 1981)
```

Example of the name of a corporate author that is spelled out:
Entry in reference list:
    University of Pittsburgh. (1983).
All text citations:
    (University of Pittsburgh, 1983)

3.89 Works With No Author or With an Anonymous Author

When a work has no author, cite in text the first two or three words of the reference list entry (usually the title) and the year. Use double quotation marks around the title of an article or chapter and underline the title of a periodical or book:

    on free care ("Study Finds," 1982)

    the book <u>College Bound Seniors</u> (1979)

(See Examples 8 and 25 in Table 17 for the reference list entries of these text citations.) Treat references to legal materials like references to works with no author; that is, in text cite materials such as court cases and statutes by the first few words of the reference and the year (see sections 3.94 and 3.99 for the format of text citations and references for legal materials).

When a work's author is designated as "Anonymous" (see section 3.100), cite in text the word *Anonymous* followed by a comma and the date:

    (Anonymous, 1983)

In the reference list, an anonymous work is alphabetized by the word *Anonymous*.

3.90 Authors With the Same Surname

If a reference list includes publications by two or more authors with the same surname, include the authors' initials in all text citations to avoid confusion, even if the year of publication differs (see section 3.100 for the order of appearance in the reference list):

    S. E. Dykes (1983) and B. A. Dykes (1980) also found

    S. E. Dykes et al. (1983) and B. A. Dykes (1980) studied

3.91 Two or More Works Within the Same Parentheses

Order the citations of two or more works within the same parentheses in the same order in which they appear in the reference list (see section 3.100), according to the following guidelines.

Arrange two or more works by the same authors in the same order by year of publication. Place in-press citations last. Give the authors' surnames once; for each subsequent work, give only the date.

    Past research (Hassam & Grammick, 1981, 1982)

    Past research (Zalichin, 1978, 1979, in press)

Identify works by the same author (or by the same two or more authors in the same order) with the same publication date by the suffixes a, b, c, and so forth after the year; repeat the year. The suffixes are assigned in the reference list, where these kinds of references are ordered alphabetically by title.

> Several studies (Farrell & Hammond, 1977a, 1977b, in press-a, in press-b)

> Several studies (Bruce, 1980a, 1980b, 1980c; Wolman, 1983, in press-a, in press-b)

List two or more works by different authors who are cited within the same parentheses in alphabetical order by the first author's surname. Separate the citations by semicolons.

> Several studies (Dorow & O'Neal, 1979; Mullaney, 1978; Talpers, 1981)

3.92 Specific Parts of a Source

To cite a specific part of a source, indicate the page, chapter, figure, table, or equation at the appropriate point in text. Always give page numbers for quotations (see section 3.37). Note that the words *page* and *chapter* are abbreviated in such text citations:

> (Czapiewski & Ruby, 1978, p. 10)

> (Wilmarth, 1980, chap. 3)

3.93 Personal Communications

Personal communications may be letters, memos, telephone conversations, and the like. Because they do not provide recoverable data, personal communications are not included in the reference list. Cite personal communications in text only. Give the initials as well as the surname of the communicator and provide as exact a date as possible:

> J. O. Reiss (personal communication, April 18, 1983)

> (J. O. Reiss, personal communication, April 18, 1983)

3.94 References to Legal Materials

Legal materials include court cases, statutes, and other legislative materials. In APA journals, references for legal materials are prepared according to *A Uniform System of Citation* (1981) (see section 3.99 of the *Manual* for guidelines and examples). Although the reference format for these legal materials differs from that of other kinds of works cited in APA journals, the text citations are formed in the same way and serve the same purpose: Give the first few words of the reference list entry and the date; that is, give enough information in the text citation to enable the reader to locate the reference list entry quickly and easily. Examples of text citations for specific kinds of legal materials are given below.

Court cases. In text, give the name of the case (underlined) and the year of the decision. If two years are given, give the year of the most recent decision.

Reference list entry:

> Lessard v. Schmidt, 349 F. Supp. 1078
> (E.D. Wisc. 1972).

Text citation:

> Lessard v. Schmidt (1972) *or*
> (Lessard v. Schmidt, 1972)

Statutes. In text, give the name of the act and the year of the act. In some cases the year the act was codified differs from the year the act was introduced; give the year the act was introduced, not the year it was codified.

Reference list entry:

> National Environmental Policy Act of 1969, § 102,
> 42 U.S.C. § 4332 (1976).

Text citation:

> National Environmental Policy Act (1969) *or*
> National Environmental Policy Act of 1969 [No
> additional parenthetical information is necessary.]

3.95 References in Parenthetical Material

In a citation that appears in parenthetical text, use commas (not brackets) to set off the date:

> (see Table 2.of Philips & Ross, 1983, for complete
> data)

Reference List

The reference list at the end of a journal article documents the article and provides the information necessary to identify and retrieve each source. Authors should choose references judiciously and must include only the sources that were used in the research and preparation of the article. Note that a reference list cites works that specifically support a particular article. In contrast, a bibliography cites works for background or for further reading. APA journals require reference lists, not bibliographies.

3.96 Agreement of Text and Reference List

References cited in text must appear in the reference list; conversely, each entry in the reference list must be cited in text (see sections 3.86–3.95 for citation of references in text). The author must make certain that each source referenced appears in both places and that the text citation and reference list entry are identical. Failure to do so can result in expensive changes after a manuscript is set in type. The author bears the cost of these changes.

3.97 Construction of an Accurate and Complete Reference List

Because one purpose of listing references is to enable readers to retrieve and use the sources, reference data must be correct and complete. Each entry usually contains the following elements: author, year of publication, title, and publishing data, all the information necessary for unique identification and library search. The best way to ensure that information is accurate and complete is to check each reference carefully against the original publication. Give special attention to spelling of proper names and of words in foreign languages, including accents or other special marks, and to completeness of journal titles, years, volume numbers, and page numbers. Authors are responsible for all information in a reference. Accurately prepared references help establish your credibility as a careful researcher. An inaccurate or incomplete reference "will stand in print as an annoyance to future investigators and a monument to the writer's carelessness" (Bruner, 1942, p. 68).

3.98 APA Style

APA style for the preparation of references is detailed in Table 17. The style for the preparation of legal references is detailed in section 3.99 (in APA journals, legal materials are given in the reference list, not in text footnotes). Because a reference list includes only references that document the article and provide recoverable data, do not include personal communications. Instead, cite personal communications only in text (see section 3.93 for format).

Following APA reference style meticulously is a good way to catch omissions and oversights. Remember that the reference list must be double-spaced. Because journal editors and copy editors cannot make major adjustments in reference format or complete incomplete references, they will return to authors improperly prepared or incomplete references for corrections.

Abbreviations. Acceptable abbreviations in the reference list for parts of books and other publications include:

chap.	chapter
ed.	edition
rev. ed.	revised edition
2nd ed.	second edition
Ed. (Eds.)	Editor (Editors)
Trans.	Translator(s)
p. (pp.)	page (pages)
Vol.	Volume (as in Vol. 4)
vols.	volumes (as in 4 vols.)
No.	Number
Pt.	Part
Tech. Rep.	Technical Report
Suppl.	Supplement

The names of states and territories in the reference list are abbreviated. Use official two-letter U.S. Postal Service abbreviations listed in Table 16.

Arabic numerals. Although some volume numbers of books and journals are given in roman numerals, APA journals use arabic numerals for all numbers in reference lists (e.g., Vol. 3, not Vol. III). *Exception:* A roman numeral that is part of a title should remain roman.

TABLE 16

Abbreviations for States and Territories

Alabama	AL	Missouri	MO
Alaska	AK	Montana	MT
American Samoa	AS	Nebraska	NE
Arizona	AZ	Nevada	NV
Arkansas	AR	New Hampshire	NH
California	CA	New Jersey	NJ
Canal Zone	CZ	New Mexico	NM
Colorado	CO	New York	NY
Connecticut	CT	North Carolina	NC
Delaware	DE	North Dakota	ND
District of Columbia	DC	Ohio	OH
Florida	FL	Oklahoma	OK
Georgia	GA	Oregon	OR
Guam	GU	Pennsylvania	PA
Hawaii	HI	Puerto Rico	PR
Idaho	ID	Rhode Island	RI
Illinois	IL	South Carolina	SC
Indiana	IN	South Dakota	SD
Iowa	IA	Tennessee	TN
Kansas	KS	Texas	TX
Kentucky	KY	Utah	UT
Louisiana	LA	Vermont	VT
Maine	ME	Virginia	VA
Maryland	MD	Virgin Islands	VI
Massachusetts	MA	Washington	WA
Michigan	MI	West Virginia	WV
Minnesota	MN	Wisconsin	WI
Mississippi	MS	Wyoming	WY

3.99 References to Legal Materials

Legal periodicals and APA journals differ in the placement and format of references. The main difference is that legal periodicals cite references in footnotes, whereas APA journals locate all references, including legal references, in the reference list. For most references, you should use APA format as described in Table 17. However, references to legal materials will be more useful to the reader if they include the information usually contained in legal citations. References to court cases and statutes are the most frequently used legal references. Therefore, some examples of references to cases and statutes and guidelines for their preparation appear in this section (see section 3.94 for citation of legal references in text). For more information on preparing these and other kinds of legal references, consult *A Uniform System of Citation* (1981).

Court cases at the trial level

• *Sample reference to a state trial court opinion:*

In re Lee, No. 68 C.J.D. 13.62 (Cook County Cir. Court, Juv. Div., Ill. Feb. 29, 1972).

Explanation: This case was tried in the Juvenile Division of the Cook County Circuit Court in Illinois. The case was decided on February 29, 1972. *In re* means "in the matter of" or "petition of."

- *Sample reference to a federal district court opinion:*

Lessard v. Schmidt, 349 F. Supp. 1078 (E.D. Wisc. 1972).

Explanation: The case was tried in the federal district court for the Eastern District of Wisconsin and was decided in 1972. It appears in volume 349 of the *Federal Supplement* and starts on page 1078 of that volume.

Court cases at the appellate level

- *Sample reference to a case appealed to a state supreme court:*

Carter v. General Motors, 361 Mich. 577, 106 N.W.2d. 105 (1960).

Explanation: This case was decided by the Michigan Supreme Court in 1960. It can be found in volume 361 of the *Michigan Reports* starting on page 577 or in volume 106 of the second series of the *North Western Reporter.* A reporter prints cases; the *North Western Reporter* is a regional reporter containing cases from several states in the northwest section of the country.

- *Sample reference to a case appealed to a U.S. court of appeals:*

Rouse v. Cameron, 373 F.2d 451 (D.C. Cir. 1966).

Explanation: This case was decided by the U.S. Court of Appeals for the District of Columbia and can be found in the second series, volume 373, of the *Federal Reporter* starting on page 451.

- *Sample references to cases appealed to the U.S. Supreme Court:*

O'Connor v. Donaldson, 422 U.S. 563 (1975).

Youngberg v. Romeo, 102 S.Ct. 2452 (1982).

Explanation: These cases were both decided by the U.S. Supreme Court. The first citation is to the *United States Reports.* Such a citation is given when the appropriate volume of the *United States Reports* is available. The second citation is to the *Supreme Court Reporter.* Use this source when the volume of the *United States Reports* in which the case will appear has not yet been published.

Statutes

- *Sample reference to a statute in a state code:*

Ervin Act, D.C. Code Ann. §§ 21-501-592 (1981).

Explanation: This District of Columbia act can be found in chapter 21 of the 1981 edition of the *District of Columbia Code Annotated.* Sections 501 to 592 are the whole act. If you are discussing a particular provision of the law, cite that particular section in which the provision appeared (e.g., § 21-503). *Ann.* stands for *Annotated*, which means that the code contains summarized cases interpreting particular sections of the statute.

- *Sample reference to a statute in a federal code:*

  ```
  National Environmental Policy Act of 1969, § 102,
     42 U.S.C. § 4332 (1976).
  ```

  Explanation: This act is codified in title 42 of the *United States Code* in section 4332. The act was proposed in 1969 and codified in 1976. If you are discussing a particular section of the original act, give that section number (in this example, section 102).

3.100 Order of References in the Reference List

Alphabetizing names. Arrange entries in alphabetical order by the surname of the first author, using the following rules for special cases.
- **Alphabetize letter by letter.** Remember, however, that "nothing precedes something": Brown, J. R. precedes Browning, A. R., even though *i* precedes *j* in the alphabet.
- **Alphabetize the prefixes M', Mc, and Mac literally,** not as if they were all spelled Mac. Disregard the apostrophe: MacArthur precedes McAllister, and MacNeil precedes M'Carthy.
- **Surnames that use articles and prepositions** (de, la, du, von, etc.) are alphabetized according to different rules for different languages. If you know that the prefix is commonly part of the surname (e.g., De Vries), treat the prefix as part of the last name and alphabetize by the prefix (e.g., DeBase precedes De Vries). If the prefix is not customarily used (e.g., Helmholtz rather than von Helmholtz), disregard it in alphabetization and treat the prefix as part of the middle name (e.g., Helmholtz, H. L. F. von). The biographical section of *Webster's New Collegiate Dictionary* (1981) is a helpful guide on surnames with articles or prepositions.

Order of several works by the same first author. When ordering several works by the same first author, give the author's name in the first and all subsequent references and use the following rules to arrange the entries:
- **Single-author entries precede multiple-author entries beginning with the same surname:**

  ```
  Kaufman, J. R. (1981).
  Kaufman, J. R., & Cochran, D. F. (1978).
  ```
- **References with the same first author and different second or third authors** are arranged alphabetically by the surname of the second author, and so on:

  ```
  Kaufman, J. R., Jones, K., & Cochran, D. F.
     (1982).
  Kaufman, J. R., & Wong, D. F. (1978).
  ```

- **References with the same authors in the same order** are arrranged by year of publication, the earliest first:

  Kaufman, J. R., & Jones, K. (1977).

  Kaufman, J. R., & Jones, K. (1980).

- **References by the same author (or by the same two or more authors in the same order) with the same publication date** are arranged alphabetically by title (excluding A or The).

  Exception: If references with the same authors published in the same year are identified as articles in a series (e.g., Part 1 and Part 2), order the references in the series order, not alphabetically by title.

  Lowercase letters—a, b, c, and so on—are placed immediately after the year, within the parentheses:

  Kaufman, J. R. (1980a). Control . . . .

  Kaufman, J. R. (1980b). Roles of . . . .

Order of several works by different authors with the same surname. Works by different authors with the same surname are arranged alphabetically by the first initial:

  Eliot, A. L. (1983).

  Eliot, G. E. (1980).

Order of works with corporate authors or with no authors. Occasionally a work will have as its author an agency, association, or institution, or it will have no author at all.

Alphabetize corporate authors, such as associations or government agencies, by the first significant word of the name. Full official names should be used (e.g., American Psychological Association, not APA). A parent body precedes a subdivision (e.g., University of Michigan, Department of Psychology).

If, and only if, the work is signed "Anonymous," the entry begins with the word *Anonymous* spelled out, and the entry is alphabetized as if Anonymous were a true name.

If there is no author, the title moves to the author position, and the entry is alphabetized by the first significant word of the title.

Include legal materials in the reference list. Treat legal references like references with no author; that is, alphabetize legal references by the first significant word in the entry (see section 3.99 for the format of reference entries and section 3.94 for text citations of legal materials).

3.101 Application of APA Reference Style

Table 17 contains elements and examples of references in APA style. The examples of references are grouped into the following categories: Periodicals, Books, Technical and Research Reports, Proceedings of Meetings and Symposia, Doctoral Dissertations and Master's Theses, Unpublished Manuscripts and Publications of Limited Circulation, Reviews and Interviews, and Nonprint Media.

For periodicals, books, and technical and research reports, the most common kinds of references, Table 17 provides a model reference and describes the elements of the reference, such as the author and the date of publication. The elements are described in the order in which they appear in the reference. Detailed notes on style and punctuation accompany the description of each element. Sample references follow.

Table 17 also provides examples for the remaining categories of references. Notes on style, if needed, follow each example.

An index of reference examples precedes the examples in Table 17. By category, the index lists types of works referenced and then variations in specific elements. The numbers after each index entry refer to the numbered examples in the table.

The most common kinds of references found in APA journals are illustrated in Table 17. However, you may need to use a reference for a source for which Table 17 does not provide a specific example. In such a case, choose the example in the table that is most like your source and follow that format. When in doubt, provide more information rather than less.

Table 17 begins on page 118.

TABLE 17

Elements and Examples of References in APA Style

Index to Table 17 (numbers after each entry refer to numbered examples)

Type of Work Referenced

Periodicals
abstract or synopsis, 15, 21
annually published, 17
document deposit service, manuscript
    from, 21
edited issue of a journal, 11
in-press article, 5
issue of a journal, entire, 11
journal article, 1–5
letter to the editor, 10
magazine article, 6
monograph, 12–14
newsletter article, 7
newspaper article, 8–10
non-English article, 18
paginated by issue, 2
secondary source, 20
special issue, 11
supplement, 16
supplement, monograph, 13
synopsis or abstract, 15, 21
translated article, 19

Books
article in an edited book, 30–32
book, entire, 22–23
chapter in an edited book, 30–32
edited book, 24, 27
in-press book, 31
multivolume work, 27, 31–32, 34
no author, 25
non-English article in an edited book,
    33
non-English book, 28
reprinted work, 35
republished work, 34
review of, 57
revised or subsequent edition, 22–23,
    26
translated article in an edited book,
    34–35
translated book, 29

Technical and Research Reports
document deposit service, report from,
    37–38
edited report, 42
edited work, report in, 40
ERIC report, 38
government report, 36, 39–40
GPO report, 36
monograph, 42
NTIS report, 37
private organization, report from, 43
university, report from, 41–42

**Proceedings of Meetings and
    Symposia**
annually published proceedings, 45
paper in an edited proceedings, 44
paper presented at a meeting,
    unpublished, 47
proceedings, published, 44–45
summary of a paper in a proceedings,
    45
symposium, contribution to:
        published, 44
        unpublished, 46

**Doctoral Dissertations and Master's
    Theses**
abstract:
        in *Dissertation Abstracts
            International*, 48–49
        in *Masters Abstracts*, 48–49
dissertation, unpublished, 50
thesis, unpublished, 51
university:
        dissertation obtained from, 49–50
        thesis obtained from, 49, 51
university microfilm:
        dissertation on, 48
        thesis on, 48

**Unpublished Manuscripts and
    Publications of Limited Circulation**
accepted for publication, in-press work,
    5, 31
data from study, unpublished, 55
document deposit service, manuscript
    from, 21, 37–38
limited circulation work, 56
not submitted for publication, 52
secondary source, unpublished
    manuscript in, 20
submitted for publication, 54
university cited, 53

Reviews and Interviews
book review, 57
film review, 58
interview, 59
titled review, 57–58
untitled review, 57–58

Nonprint Media
cassette recording, 61
computer program, 63
computer program manual, 63
film, 60
machine-readable data file, 62
nonprint media, general, 60

Elements of a Reference

Author Variations

author modified (e.g., as editor), 11, 24, 42, 60–61
author as publisher, 23, 43
corporate author, 7, 23, 36, 43
initials and surname, order of:
    for the specific work referenced, 1–2
    for the book or collection in which the specific work is found, 30–31
Jr. in name, 22
no author, 8, 25
number of authors:
    one, 1
    two, 2
    more than two, 3
    six or more, 4
number of editors:
    one, 32
    two, 30
    more than two, 40
    six or more, 31

Title Variations

non-English title (with translation), 18, 28, 33
proper name in title, 13, 24, 43–44, 56
revised or new edition, 22–23, 26
subtitle (see two-part title)
title within a title, 58
translated work, title of, 19, 29, 34–35
translation of title into English, 18, 28, 33
three-part title, 32
two-part title, 3, 9, 24, 31, 36, 63
untitled work, 55, 59
volume number(s) of a book, 27, 31–32, 34
volume number appearing with page numbers, 34

Publication Information Variations

author as publisher, 23, 43
in-press book, 31
in-press journal article, 5
letter to the editor, 10
monograph, 12–14, 42
pages discontinuous, 9, 59
pagination by issue.rather than volume, 2, 19
publication outside the United States, 44
publication over more than 1 year, 27
publisher name abbreviated, 22, 24
publisher name not abbreviated, 25–26
reprinted or republished work, 34–35
unpublished work, 46–47, 50–53, 55

Periodicals

Elements of a reference to a periodical

Spetch, M. L., & Wilkie, D. M. (1983). Subjective shortening: A model of pigeons' memory for event duration. <u>Journal of Experimental Psychology: Animal Behavior Processes</u>, <u>9</u>, 14–30.

Article authors: Spetch, M. L., & Wilkie, D. M.

- Invert all authors' names; give surnames and initials for *all* authors, regardless of the number of authors. (However, *in text*, when authors number six or more, abbreviate second and subsequent authors as "et al." [not underlined and with no period after "et"].)
- Use commas to separate authors and to separate surnames and initials; with two or more authors, use an ampersand (&) before the last author.
- Spell out the full name of a corporate author.
- In a reference to a work with no author, move the title to the author position, before the date of publication, and treat the title like a book title (see elements of a reference to an entire book).
- Finish the element with a period. In a reference to a work with a corporate author, the period follows the corporate author. In a reference to a work with no author, the period follows the title, which is moved to the author position. (When an author's initial with a period ends the element, do not add an extra period.)

continued

(Table 17 continued)

Date of publication: (1983).

- Give the year the work was copyrighted (for unpublished works, this is the year the work was produced). For magazines and newspapers, give the year followed by the month and day, if any (see Examples 6–10).
- Enclose the date in parentheses.
- Write "in press" in parentheses for articles that have been accepted for publication but that have not yet been published. Do not give a date until the article has actually been published. (See Examples 52–55 for references to unpublished manuscripts.)
- Finish the element with a period after the closing parenthesis.

Article title: Subjective shortening: A model of pigeons' memory for event duration.

- Capitalize only the first word of the title and of the subtitle, if any, and any proper names; do not underline the title or place quotation marks around it.
- Use arabic numerals, not roman numerals, in two-part titles unless the roman numeral is part of the published title (see Example 3).
- Enclose nonroutine information that is important for identification and retrieval in brackets immediately after the article title (e.g., [Letter to the editor], see Example 10). Brackets indicate a description of form, not a title.
- Finish the element with a period.

Journal title and publication information: Journal of Experimental Psychology: Animal Behavior Processes, 9, 14–30.

- Give the journal title in full, in uppercase and lowercase letters; underline the title.
- Give the volume number and underline it. Do not use "Vol." before the number. If, and *only* if, each issue begins on page 1, give the issue number in parentheses immediately after the volume number (see Example 2).
- Give inclusive page numbers. Use "pp." before the page numbers in references to newspapers and magazines, but not in references to journal articles.
- Use commas to separate the parts of this element.
- Finish the element with a period.

Examples of references to periodicals

1. Journal article, one author

Paivio, A. (1975). Perceptual comparisons through the mind's eye. Memory & Cognition, 3, 635–647.

2. Journal article, two authors, journal paginated by issue

Becker, L. J., & Seligman, C. (1981). Welcome to the energy crisis. Journal of Social Issues, 37(2), 1–7.

3. Journal article, more than two authors

Horowitz, L. M., Post, D. L., French, R. S., Wallis, K. D., & Siegelman, E. Y. (1981). The prototype as a construct in abnormal psychology: 2. Clarifying disagreement in psychiatric judgments. Journal of Abnormal Psychology, 90, 575–585.

4. Journal article, six or more authors

Winston, B. L., Reinhart, M. L., Sacker, J. R., Gottlieb, W., Oscar, B. B., & Harris, D. P. (1983). Effect of intertrial delays on retardation of learning. Journal of Experimental Psychology: Animal Behavior Processes, 9, 581–593.

- In text, use the following parenthetical citation each time the work is cited: (Winston et al., 1983).

5. Journal article in press

Corcoran, D. L., & Williamson, E. M. (in press). Unlearning
learned helplessness. <u>Journal of Personality and Social
Psychology</u>.

- Do not give either the year or the volume and page numbers until the article is published. In text, use the following parenthetical citation: (Corcoran & Williamson, in press).

6. Magazine article

Gardner, H. (1981, December). Do babies sing a universal song?
<u>Psychology Today</u>, pp. 70–76.

7. Newsletter article, corporate author

Staff. (1980, September 1). Professionals face tax rises as IRS
targets personal-service corporations. <u>Behavior Today</u>, p. 5.

- Alphabetize corporate authors by the first significant word of the name (i.e., disregard words such as *A* and *The*).

8. Newspaper article, no author

Study finds free care used more. (1982, April). <u>APA Monitor</u>,
p. 14.

- Alphabetize works with no author by the first significant word in the title.
- In text, use a short title for the parenthetical citation: ("Study Finds," 1982).

9. Newspaper article, discontinuous pages

Lublin, J. S. (1980, December 5). On idle: The unemployed shun
much mundane work, at least for a while. <u>The Wall Street Journal</u>,
pp. 1, 25.

- If an article appears on discontinuous pages, give all page numbers and separate the numbers with a comma.

10. Newspaper article, letter to the editor

O'Neill, G. W. (1982, January). In support of DSM-III [Letter to
the editor]. <u>APA Monitor</u>, p. 4.

11. Entire issue of a journal

Glaser, R., & Bond, L. (Eds.). (1981). Testing: Concepts, policy,
practice, and research [Special issue]. <u>American Psychologist</u>,
<u>36</u>(10).

- To cite an entire issue of a journal (in this example, a special issue), give the editors of the issue and the title of the issue.
- If the issue has no editors, move the issue title to the author position, before the year of publication, and end the title with a period. Alphabetize the reference entry by the first significant word in the title. In text, use a short title for the parenthetical citation, for example: ("Testing," 1981).

continued

(Table 17 continued)

12. Monograph with issue number and serial (or whole) number

Hood, L., & Bloom, L. (1979). What, when, and how about why: A longitudinal study of early expressions of causality. <u>Monographs of the Society for Research in Child Development</u>, <u>44</u>(6, Serial No. 181).

- Give the volume number and, immediately after in parentheses, the issue and serial (or whole) numbers. Use the word *Whole* instead of *Serial* if the monograph is identified by whole number.
- For a monograph that is not treated as a periodical, see Example 42.

13. Monograph bound separately as a supplement to a journal

Battig, W. F., & Montague, W. E. (1969). Category norms of verbal items in 56 categories: A replication and extension of the Connecticut category norms. <u>Journal of Experimental Psychology Monographs</u>, <u>80</u>(3, Pt. 2).

- Give the issue number and supplement or part number in parentheses immediately after the volume number.

14. Monograph bound into journal with continuous pagination

Corrigan, J. D., Dell, D. M., Lewis, K. N., & Schmidt, L. D. (1980). Counseling as a social influence process: A review [Monograph]. <u>Journal of Counseling Psychology</u>, <u>27</u>, 395–441.

15. Citing an abstract only

Misumi, J., & Fujita, M. (1982). Effects of PM organizational development in supermarket organization. <u>Japanese Journal of Experimental Social Psychology</u>, <u>21</u>, 93–111. (From <u>Psychological Abstracts</u>, 1982, <u>68</u>, Abstract No. 11474)

- If only the abstract and not the entire article is used as the source, cite the collection of abstracts in parentheses at the end of the entry.
- If the date of the secondary source is different from the date of the original publication, cite both dates (separated by a slash) with the original date first.

16. Journal supplement

Koczkas, S., Holmberg, G., & Wedin, L. (1981). A pilot study of the effect of the 5-HT uptake inhibitor, zimelidine, on phobic anxiety. <u>Acta Psychiatrica Scandinavica</u>, <u>63</u>(Suppl. 290), 328–341.

- Give the supplement number in parentheses immediately after the volume number.

17. Periodical published annually

Cialdini, R. B., Petty, R. E., & Cacioppo, J. T. (1981). Attitude and attitude change. <u>Annual Review of Psychology</u>, <u>32</u>, 357–404.

- Treat annually published series, like the *Annual Review of Psychology*, that have specified, regular publication dates as periodicals, not books.

18. Non-English journal article, title translated into English

```
Assink, E. M. H., & Verloop, N. (1977). Het aanleren van
    deel-geheel relaties in het aanvankelijk rekenonderwijs
    [Teaching part-whole relations in elementary mathematics
    instruction]. Pedagogische Studiën, 54, 130-142.
```

• If the original version of a non-English article is used as the source, cite the original version: Give the original title and, in brackets, the English translation.
• Punctuate non-English words as they are punctuated in the original language (in this example, *Studiën*).

19. English translation of a journal article, journal paginated by issue

```
Stutte, H. (1972). Transcultural child psychiatry.
    Acta Paedopsychiatrica, 38(9), 229-231.
```

• If the English translation of a non-English article is used as the source, cite the English translation: Give the English title without brackets (for use of brackets with non-English works, see Examples 18, 28, and 33).

20. Citation of a work discussed in a secondary source

```
Beatty, J. (1982). Task-evoked pupillary responses, processing
    load, and the structure of processing resources. Psychological
    Bulletin, 91, 276-292.
```

• Give the secondary source in the reference list and cite the original work with the secondary source in text. For example, if Johnson's unpublished manuscript is cited in Beatty, cite Beatty in the reference list. In text, use the following citation: Johnson's study (cited in Beatty, 1982).

21. Synopsis appearing in the *Psychological Documents* catalog, article available from the APA Psychological Documents service

```
Ree, M. J., Mullins, C. J., Mathews, J. J., & Massey, R. H. (1983).
    Vocational aptitude battery: Item and factor analyses.
    Psychological Documents, 13, 3. (Ms. No. 2469)
```

• Reference the synopsis of the article published in the catalog of synopses, *Psychological Documents* (formerly JSAS: *Catalog of Selected Documents in Psychology*).
• Use this citation whether the synopsis or the full document was used as the source.

Books

Elements of a reference to an entire book

```
Bernstein, T. M. (1965). The careful writer: A modern guide to

    English usage. New York: Atheneum.
```

Book authors or editors: Bernstein, T. M.
• See elements of a reference to a periodical.
• In a reference to an edited book, place the editors' names in the author position and enclose the abbreviation "Ed." or "Eds." in parentheses after the last editor.
• Finish the element with a period. In a reference to an edited book, the period follows the parenthetical abbreviation "(Eds.)." (When an author's initial with a period ends the element, do not add an extra period.)

continued

(Table 17 continued)

Date of publication: (1965).
• See elements of a reference to a periodical.

Book title: The careful writer: A modern guide to English usage.
• Capitalize only the first word of the title and of the subtitle, if any, and any proper names; underline the title.
• Enclose additional information necessary for identification and retrieval (e.g., 3rd ed. or Vol. 2) in parentheses immediately after the title. Do not use a period between the title and the parenthetical information.
• In two-part titles, use arabic numerals, not roman numerals, unless the roman numeral is part of the published title.
• Finish the element with a period.

Publication information: New York: Atheneum.
• Give the city and, if the city is not well known for publishing or could be confused with another location, the state (or country) where the publisher is located. Use U.S. Postal Service abbreviations for states (see Table 16). Use a colon after the location.
• Give the name of the publisher in as brief a form as is intelligible. Spell out the names of associations and university presses, but omit superfluous terms such as *Publishers*, *Co.*, or *Inc.* that are not required for easy identification of the publisher.
• If two or more publisher locations are given, give the location listed first in the book or, if specified, the location of the publisher's home office.
• Finish the element with a period.

Examples of references to entire books

22. Book, third edition, Jr. in name

Strunk, W., Jr., & White, E. B. (1979). The elements of style (3rd ed.). New York: Macmillan.

23. Book, corporate author, third edition, author as publisher

American Psychiatric Association. (1980). Diagnostic and statistical manual of mental disorders (3rd ed.). Washington, DC: Author.

• Alphabetize corporate authors by the first significant word of the name.
• When the author and publisher are identical, use the word *Author* as the name of the publisher.

24. Edited book

Letheridge, S., & Cannon, C. R. (Eds.). (1980). Bilingual education: Teaching English as a second language. New York: Praeger.

25. Book, no author or editor

College bound seniors. (1979). Princeton, NJ: College Board Publications.

• Alphabetize books with no author or editor by the first significant word in the title.
• In text, use the following parenthetical citation: (College Bound Seniors, 1979).

26. Book, revised edition

Cohen, J. (1977). <u>Statistical power analysis for the behavioral sciences</u> (rev. ed.). New York: Academic Press.

27. Several volumes in a multivolume edited work, publication over more than 1 year

Wilson, J. G., & Fraser, F. C. (Eds.). (1977–1978). <u>Handbook of teratology</u> (Vols. 1–4). New York: Plenum Press.

• In text, use the following parenthetical citation: (Wilson & Fraser, 1977–1978).

28. Non-English book

Piaget, J., & Inhelder, B. (1951). <u>La genèse de l'idée de hasard chez l'enfant</u> [The origin of the idea of danger in the child]. Paris: Presses Universitaires de France.

• If the original version of a non-English book is used as the source, cite the original version: Give the original title and, in brackets, the English translation.

29. English translation of a book

Luria, A. R. (1969). <u>The mind of a mnemonist</u> (L. Solotaroff, Trans.). New York: Avon Books. (Original work published 1965)

• If the English translation of a non-English work is used as the source, cite the English translation: Give the English title without brackets (for use of brackets with non-English works, see Examples 18, 28, and 33).
• In text, use the following parenthetical citation: (Luria, 1965/1969).

Elements of a reference to an article or chapter in an edited book

Hartley, J. T., Harker, J. O., & Walsh, D. A. (1980).

Contemporary issues and new directions in adult

development of learning and memory. In L. W. Poon (Ed.),

<u>Aging in the 1980s: Psychological issues</u> (pp. 239–252).

Washington, DC: American Psychological Association.

Article or chapter authors: Hartley, J. T., Harker, J. O., & Walsh, D. A.
• See elements of a reference to a periodical.

Date of publication: (1980).
• See elements of a reference to a periodical.

Article or chapter title: Contemporary issues and new directions in adult development of learning and memory.
• See elements of a reference to a periodical.

Book editor: In L. W. Poon (Ed.),
• When an editor's name is not in the author position, do not invert the name; use initials and surname.
• Give initials and surnames for *all* editors, regardless of the number of editors.

continued

(Table 17 continued)

- With two names, use an ampersand (&) before the last name and do not use commas to separate the names. With three or more names, use an ampersand before the last name and use commas to separate the names.
- Identify the editor by the abbreviation "Ed." in parentheses after the surname. To identify a translator, use "Trans."
- Finish the element with a comma.

Book title and article or chapter page numbers: Aging in the 1980s: Psychological issues (pp. 239–252).
- See elements of a reference to an entire book.
- Give inclusive page numbers of the article or chapter in parentheses after the title.
- Finish the element with a period.

Publication information: Washington, DC: American Psychological Association.
- See elements of a reference to an entire book.

Examples of references to articles or chapters in edited books

30. Article or chapter in an edited book, two editors

Gurman, A. S., & Kniskern, D. P. (1981). Family therapy outcome research: Knowns and unknowns. In A. S. Gurman & D. P. Kniskern (Eds.), Handbook of family therapy (pp. 742–775). New York: Brunner/Mazel.

31. Article or chapter in an edited book, book in press, six or more editors, separately titled volume in a multivolume work (two-part title)

Woodward, J. T. (in press). Children's learning systems. In J. T. Woodward, A. Pimm, S. S. Keenan, M. N. Blum, H. A. Hamner, & P. Sellzner (Eds.), Research in cognitive development: Vol. 1. Logical cognition in children. New York: Springer.

- Do not give the year unless the book is published. In text, use the following parenthetical citation: (Woodward, in press).
- Page numbers are not available until a work is published; therefore, you cannot give inclusive page numbers for articles or chapters in books that are in press.

32. Article or chapter in an edited book, one editor, volume in a section in a series (three-part title)

Epstein, A. N. (1967). Oropharyngeal factors in feeding and drinking. In C. F. Code (Ed.), Handbook of physiology: Sec. 6. Alimentary canal: Vol. 1. Control of food and water intake (pp. 197–218). Bethesda, MD: American Physiological Society.

- Give the editor of the section (not of the volume or series).

33. Non-English article or chapter in an edited book, title translated into English

Davydov, V. V. (1972). De introductie van het begrip grootheid in de eerste klas van de basisschool: Een experimenteel onderzoek [The introduction of the concept of quantity in the first grade of the primary school: An experimental study]. In C. F. Van Parreren & J. A. M. Carpay (Eds.), Sovjetpsychologen aan het

woord (pp. 227–289). Groningen, The Netherlands: Woleters–
Noordhoff.

- If the original version of a non-English article or non-English book is used as the source, cite the original version: Give the original title and, in brackets, the English translation.

34. English translation of an article or chapter in an edited book, volume in a multivolume work, republished work

Freud, S. (1961). The ego and the id. In J. Strachey (Ed. and
Trans.), The standard edition of the complete psychological works
of Sigmund Freud (Vol. 19, pp. 3–66). London: Hogarth Press.
(Original work published 1923)

- If the English translation of a non-English work is used as the source, cite the English translation: Give the English title without brackets (for use of brackets with non-English works, see Examples 18, 28, and 33).
- In text, use the following parenthetical citation: (Freud, 1923/1961).

35. English translation of an article or chapter in an edited book, reprint from another source

Sluzki, C. E., & Beavin, J. (1977). Symmetry and complementarity:
An operational definition and a typology of dyads. In P.
Watzlawick & J. H. Weakland (Eds. and Trans.), The interactional
view (pp. 71–87). New York: Norton. (Reprinted from Acta
Psiquiátrica y Psicológica de America Latina, 1965, 11, 321–330)

- If the English translation of a non-English work is used as the source, cite the English translation: Give the English title without brackets (for use of brackets with non-English works, see Examples 18, 28, and 33).
- In text, use the following parenthetical citation: (Sluzki & Beavin, 1965/1977).

Technical and Research Reports

Elements of a reference to a report

Birney, A. J., & Hall, M. M. (1981). Early identification

of children with written language disabilities (Report

No. 81–1502). Washington, DC: National Education

Association.

Report authors: Birney, A. J., & Hall, M. M.
- See elements of a reference to a periodical.

Date of publication: (1981).
- See elements of a reference to a periodical.

Report title: Early identification of children with written language
disabilities (Report No. 81–1502).
- See elements of a reference to an entire book.
- If the issuing organization assigned a number (e.g., report number, contract number, monograph number) to the report, give that number in parentheses immediately after the title. Do not use a period between the report title and the parenthetical material. If the report carries two numbers, give the number that best aids identification and retrieval.

continued

(Table 17 continued)

Publication information: Washington, DC: National Education Association.

- See elements of a reference to an entire book. Give the name, exactly as it appears on the publication, of the specific department, office, agency, or institute that published or produced the report. Give the higher department, office, agency, or institute also only if the office that produced the report is not well known. For example, if the National Institute on Drug Abuse, an institute of the U.S. Department of Health and Human Services, produced the report, give only the institute as publisher (see Example 40). Because this institute is well known, it is not necessary to give the higher department as well. If you include the higher department, give the higher department first, then the specific department (see Examples 41–42).
- For reports from a document deposit service (e.g., NTIS or ERIC), enclose the document number in parentheses at the end of the entry (see Examples 37 and 38). Do not use a period after the document number.

Examples of references to reports

36. Report available from the Government Printing Office (GPO), corporate author

National Institute of Mental Health. (1982). <u>Television and behavior: Ten years of scientific progress and implications for the eighties</u> (DHHS Publication No. ADM 82–1195). Washington, DC: U.S. Government Printing Office.

37. Report available from the National Technical Information Service (NTIS)

Tandy, S. (1980). <u>Development of behavioral techniques to control hyperaggressiveness in young children</u> (CYC Report No. 80–3562). Washington, DC: Council on Young Children. (NTIS No. P880–143282)

- Give the NTIS number in parentheses at the end of the entry.

38. Report available from the Educational Resources Information Center (ERIC)

Gottfredson, L. S. (1980). <u>How valid are occupational reinforcer pattern scores</u>? (Report No. CSOS–R–292). Baltimore, MD: Johns Hopkins University, Center for Social Organization of Schools. (ERIC Document Reproduction Service No. ED 182 465)

- Give the ERIC number in parentheses at the end of the entry.

39. Government report not available from the GPO or a document deposit service such as the NTIS or ERIC

Brush, L. (1979). <u>Why women avoid the study of mathematics: A longitudinal study</u> (Contract No. 400–77–0099). Washington, DC: National Institute of Education.

40. Government report not available from the GPO or a document deposit service such as the NTIS or ERIC, article or chapter in an edited collection

Kandel, D. (1976). Study of high school students: Student questionnaire, Wave 1, Fall 1971. In A. Nehemkis, M. A. Macari, & D. J. Lettieri (Eds.), <u>Drug abuse instrument handbook</u> (Research Issues No. 12, pp. 259–260). Rockville, MD: National Institute on Drug Abuse.

- In parentheses immediately after the title of the collection, give the inclusive page numbers of the article or chapter as well as the number of the report.

41. Report from a university

Newport, E. L. (1975). <u>Motherese: The speech of mothers to young children</u> (Tech. Rep. No. 52). San Diego: University of California, Center for Human Information Processing.

- If the name of the state is included in the name of the university, do not repeat the name of the state in the publisher location.
- Give the name of the university first, then the name of the specific department or organization within the university that produced the report.

42. Report from a university, edited report, monograph

Ben—Yishay, Y. (Ed.). (1981). <u>Working approaches to remediation of cognitive deficits in brain damaged persons</u> (Rehabilitation Monograph No. 62). New York: New York University Medical Center, Institute of Rehabilitation Medicine.

- For monographs that are treated as periodicals, see Examples 12, 13, and 14.

43. Report from a private organization, corporate author, author as publisher

Life Insurance Marketing and Research Association. (1978). <u>Profits and the AIB in United States ordinary companies</u> (Research Rep. No. 1978—6). Hartford, CT: Author.

Proceedings of Meetings and Symposia

44. Published proceedings, published contribution to a symposium, article or chapter in an edited book, work published outside the United States

Chaddock, T. E., Carlson, G. M., & Hamilton, C. L. (1974). Gastric emptying of a nutritionally balanced liquid diet in the rhesus monkey. In E. E. Daniel (Ed.), <u>Proceedings of the Fourth International Symposium on Gastrointestinal Motility</u> (pp. 83—92). Vancouver, British Columbia, Canada: Mitchell Press.

- Capitalize the name of the symposium, which is a proper name.

45. Proceedings published annually, summary

Thumin, F. J., Craddick, R. A., & Barclay, A. G. (1973). Meaning and compatibility of a proposed corporate name and symbol [Summary]. <u>Proceedings of the 81st Annual Convention of the American Psychological Association</u>, <u>8</u>, 835—836.

- Treat regularly published proceedings as periodicals.
- Indicate if only a summary or abstract of a paper appears in the proceedings. Use brackets to show that the material is a description of form, not a title.
- Note that the APA did not publish proceedings after 1973.

46. Unpublished contribution to a symposium

Singh, R. (1980, February). Multiplying versus differential—weight averaging as integration rule in attribution of gift size. In C. M. Bhatia (Chair), <u>Dimensions of information processing</u>. Symposium conducted at the meeting of the Indian Science Congress Association, Calcutta.

- Give the month of the symposium if it is available.

continued

(Table 17 continued)

47. Unpublished paper presented at a meeting

Brener, J. (1979, October). <u>Energy, information, and the control of heart rate</u>. Paper presented at the meeting of the Society for Psychophysiological Research, Cincinnati, OH.

- Give the month of the meeting if it is available.
- Give the state name if the city may not be well known.

Doctoral Dissertations and Master's Theses

48. Doctoral dissertation abstracted in *Dissertation Abstracts International* (*DAI*) and obtained on university microfilm

Pendar, J. E. (1982). Undergraduate psychology majors: Factors influencing decisions about college, curriculum and career. <u>Dissertation Abstracts International</u>, <u>42</u>, 4370A–4371A. (University Microfilms No. 82–06,181)

- If the microfilm of the dissertation is used as the source, give the university microfilms number as well as the volume and page numbers of *DAI*.
- Beginning with Volume 27, *Dissertation Abstracts* paginates in two series, A for humanities and B for sciences.
- Beginning with Volume 30, the title of *Dissertation Abstracts* is *Dissertation Abstracts International*.
- For a master's thesis abstracted in *Masters Abstracts* and obtained on university microfilm, use the format shown here and give as publication information the title, volume number, and page number of *Masters Abstracts* as well as the University Microfilms number (see Example 51 for an unpublished master's thesis).

49. Doctoral dissertation abstracted in *Dissertation Abstracts International* (*DAI*) and obtained from the university

Foster–Havercamp, M. E. (1982). An analysis of the relationship between preservice teacher training and directed teaching performance (Doctoral dissertation, University of Chicago, 1981). <u>Dissertation Abstracts International</u>, <u>42</u>, 4409A.

- If a manuscript copy of the dissertation from the university was used as the source, give the university and year of the dissertation as well as the volume and page numbers of *DAI*. If the years are different, give both years in text. For this example, use the following parenthetical citation: (Foster–Havercamp, 1981/1982).
- For a master's thesis abstracted in *Masters Abstracts* and obtained from the university, use the format shown here and give as publication information the title, volume number, and page number of *Masters Abstracts* as well as the university and year of the thesis (see Example 51 for an unpublished master's thesis).

50. Unpublished doctoral dissertation, university outside the United States

Devins, G. M. (1981). <u>Helplessness, depression, and mood in end-stage renal disease</u>. Unpublished doctoral dissertation, McGill University, Montreal.

- If a dissertation does not appear in *Dissertation Abstracts International (DAI)*, use the format shown here. (For dissertations that appear in *DAI*, see Examples 48 and 49.)

- Give the city (and country if the city may not be well known) of a university outside the United States.

51. Unpublished master's thesis

Ryerson, J. F. (1983). <u>Effective management training: Two models</u>. Unpublished master's thesis, Clarkson College of Technology, Potsdam, NY.

- Give the name of the city and, if the city may not be well known, the name of the state. (Do not give the name of the state if it is included in the name of the university.)

Unpublished Manuscripts and Publications of Limited Circulation

52. Unpublished manuscript not submitted for publication

Cameron, S. E. (1981). <u>Educational level as a predictor of success</u>. Unpublished manuscript.

- For an unpublished manuscript with a university cited, see Example 53.

53. Unpublished manuscript with a university cited

Gottfredson, G. D. (1978). <u>Why don't vocational interests predict job satisfaction better than they do</u>? Unpublished manuscript, Johns Hopkins University, Center for Social Organization of Schools, Baltimore.

54. Manuscript submitted for publication but not yet accepted

Palm, E. J. (1981). <u>Associative learning and recognition</u>. Manuscript submitted for publication.

- Do not give the name of the journal or publisher to which the manuscript has been submitted.
- Treat a manuscript *accepted* for publication but not yet published as an in-press reference (see Examples 5 and 31).

55. Unpublished raw data from study, untitled work

Herbert, C. A. (1983). [Facilitating learning efficiency: Assessment scores]. Unpublished raw data.

- Do not underline the topic; use brackets to indicate that the material is a description of content, not a title.

56. Publication of limited circulation

Bailey, A. C. (Ed.). (1980, May). <u>Newsletter of the Committee on Women in Athletics</u>. (Available from [name and address])

- For a publication of limited circulation, give in parentheses immediately after the title a name and address from which the publication can be obtained.

continued

(Table 17 continued)

Reviews and Interviews

57. Review of a book

Carmody, T. P. (1982). A new look at medicine from the social perspective [Review of Social contexts of health, illness, and patient care]. Contemporary Psychology, 27, 208–209.

- If the review is untitled, use the material in brackets as the title; retain the brackets to indicate that the material is a description of form and content, not a title.

58. Review of a film

Bowers, K. S. (1982). Deeper into "Deeper into hypnosis" [Review of Deeper into hypnosis]. Contemporary Psychology, 27, 223–224.

- If the review is untitled, use the material in brackets as the title; retain the brackets to indicate that the material is a description of form and content, not a title.
- See Example 60 for the citation of this film.

59. Published interview, untitled work, discontinuous pages

Newman, P. (1982, January). [Interview with William Epstein, editor of JEP: Human Perception and Performance]. APA Monitor, pp. 7, 39.

- Use the format appropriate for the published source of the interview (in this example, a newspaper; see Examples 8, 9, and 10).
- Use brackets to indicate that the material is a description of form and content, not a title.

Nonprint Media

60. Film

Maas, J. B. (Producer), & Gluck, D. H. (Director). (1979). Deeper into hypnosis [Film]. Englewood Cliffs, NJ: Prentice–Hall.

- Give the name and, in parentheses, the function of the originator or primary contributors (in this example, Maas and Gluck, who are, respectively, the producer and the director).
- Specify the medium in brackets immediately after the title (in this example, the medium is film; other nonprint media include videotapes, audiotapes, slides, charts, and art work).
- See Example 58 for the citation of a review of this film.
- Give the location and name of the distributor (in this example, Prentice-Hall).

61. Cassette recording

Clark, K. B. (Speaker). (1976). Problems of freedom and behavior modification (Cassette Recording No. 7612). Washington, DC: American Psychological Association.

- Give the name and function of the originators or primary contributors (in this example, Clark, who is the speaker).

- Specify the medium in brackets immediately after the title (in this example, the medium is cassette recording). Give a number for the recording if it is necessary for identification and retrieval. Use parentheses if a number is necessary. If no number is necessary, use brackets (see Example 60).
- Give the location and name of the distributor (in this example, American Psychological Association).

---

62. Machine-readable data file

Miller, W., Miller, A., & Kline, G. (1975). <u>The CPS 1974 American national election study</u> [Machine-readable data file]. Ann Arbor: University of Michigan, Center for Political Studies (Producer). Ann Arbor: Inter-University Consortium for Political and Social Research (Distributor).

- Give as the authors the primary contributors (e.g., the designers of the survey or study).
- Give as the date of publication the year copies of the data file were first made generally available.
- Give the title and, in brackets immediately after the title, identify the source as a machine-readable data file. Do not use a period between the title and the bracketed material. (If the data file has no title, in brackets provide a complete description of content, including the year the data were collected.)
- Give the location and name of the producer (the person or organization that encoded the data) and the location and name of the distributor (the person or organization from which copies of the file can be obtained). In parentheses immediately after the names, write Producer and Distributor, respectively.

---

63. Computer program

Fernandes, F. D. (1972). <u>Theoretical prediction of interference loading on aircraft stores: Part 1. Subsonic speeds</u> [Computer program]. Pomona, CA: General Dynamics, Electro Dynamics Division. (National Aeronautics and Space Administration Report No. NASA CR-112065-1; Acquisition No. LAR-11249)

- Give as the author the primary contributor.
- In brackets immediately after the title of the program, identify the source as a computer program. Do not use a period between the title and the bracketed material.
- Give the location and the name of the organization that produced the program.
- Enclose any additional information necessary for identification and retrieval (in this example, the report number and acquisition number) in parentheses at the end of the entry.
- To reference a manual for a computer program, give the same information provided for a computer program. However, in the brackets after the title, identify the source as a computer program manual.

4 Typing Instructions and Sample Paper

The physical appearance of a manuscript can enhance the manuscript's impact or detract from it. On one hand, a well-prepared manuscript looks professional to editors and reviewers and may influence their decisions in a positive manner. On the other hand, mechanical flaws can sometimes lead reviewers to misinterpret content. A properly prepared manuscript, once accepted for publication, facilitates the work of the copy editor and the typesetter (hereinafter called printer*), minimizes the possibility of errors, and is more accurate and more economical to publish.*

This chapter describes the mechanical details of typing a typical manuscript. In many instances, however, typing has been replaced by keyboarding, and the typewriter has been replaced by a video display terminal. The impact of new technology on the writing, editing, and publishing process is substantial. Nonetheless, the Manual *defines the physical preparation of manuscripts in terms of typing because the development of uniform specifications for diverse kinds of word-processing and computerized electronic typesetting systems is beyond the scope of the* Manual. *Users of equipment more sophisticated than an electronic typewriter are likely to find that the typing specifications described in this chapter are adaptable to individual systems; indeed, the new technology makes it easier than ever to produce a manuscript in the form specified in this chapter.*

The sample paper and paper outlines at the end of this chapter show how a properly typed manuscript should look. The sample paper and outlines also serve as models of the typical structure of manuscripts. The typing requirements for some kinds of manuscripts (e.g., brief reports) may differ from the requirements described here. For information, refer to the Instructions to Authors in a recent issue of the journal to which the manuscript will be submitted.

Author's Responsibilities

The author is responsible for the quality of presentation of all aspects of the paper: correct spelling and punctuation, accurate quotations with page numbers, complete and accurate references, relevant content, coherent organization, legible appearance, and so forth. If the manuscript is to be blind reviewed, authors are responsible for preparing the manuscript to conceal their identities. Therefore, authors must

- prepare the material for the typist *exactly* as it is to be typed. The typist should not be expected to edit. The author should not hand the typist the *Manual* and expect the typist to transform a poorly prepared draft into a manuscript prepared according to APA style. For example, the author must prepare a running head of no more than 50 characters and not leave the selection of a running head to the typist.
- proofread the manuscript after it is typed, making all corrections and changes before submitting the manuscript for consideration (see sections 4.07 and 5.03).
- examine the manuscript using the checklist on the inside front and back covers of the *Manual* to ensure that the manuscript has been prepared according to APA style.
- prepare a cover letter to accompany the submitted manuscript (see section 5.02).

Typist's Responsibilities

The typist is responsible only for accurate transcription of the manuscript. Before typing, the typist should review the manuscript in order to prepare for unusual terms and treatments and should resolve any problems with the author. The typist should not be expected to edit but should type only what appears in the author's draft except for minor technical errors, such as an occasional misspelled word.

General Instructions

4.01 Paper

Type the manuscript on one side of standard-sized ($8\frac{1}{2}$ x 11 in. [22 x 28 cm]), heavy white bond paper. All pages of one manuscript must be the same size. Do not use half sheets or strips of paper glued, taped, or stapled to the pages; these are often torn off or lost in shipment and handling. Do not use onionskin or erasable paper because these papers do not withstand handling.

4.02 Type Element

Use a typeface that is similar to one of the following examples:

Acceptable typefaces:

```
that the probability of      that the probability of

aggressive acts is high      aggressive acts is high

(all things being equal)     (all things being equal)
```

The type must be dark, clear, and readable. A typeface that is made up of dots or that is unusual in appearance (such as that generated by some word-processing systems) is acceptable only if it is clear and legible. In the following example, some words could be misread; therefore, the type is unacceptable.

Unacceptable typeface:

> that the probability of
>
> aggressive acts is high
>
> (all things being equal)

The dots make reading the letters difficult. Also, the lack of descenders makes this typeface hard to read. For example, the letter *g* looks like the letter *s*, and a capital *Q* is used for a lowercase *q*.

When the printer cannot read a word and consequently makes an error, the author and APA must pay for that correction.

4.03 Double-Spacing

Double-space between *all* lines of the manuscript. Double-space after every line in the title, headings, footnotes, quotations, references, figure captions, and all parts of tables. Although you may apply triple- or quadruple-spacing in special circumstances, such as immediately before and after a displayed equation, never use single-spacing or one-and-a-half spacing.

4.04 Margins

Leave uniform margins of $1\frac{1}{2}$ in. (4 cm) at the top, bottom, right, and left of every page. The APA copy editor uses the margin space to write instructions and queries. Uniform margins also help copy editors estimate the length of the printed article from the manuscript.

Line length. The length of each typed line is $5\frac{1}{2}$ in. (14 cm). Set a pica typewriter for 55 characters and an elite machine for 66 characters. Do not justify lines; that is, do not adjust spacing between words to make all lines the same length. Instead, leave the right margin uneven. Do not divide words at the end of a line. Let a line run short or long rather than break a word at the end of a line.

Number of lines. Type no more than 25 lines of text (i.e., not counting the short title and the page number) on an $8\frac{1}{2}$ x 11 in. (22 x 28 cm) page with $1\frac{1}{2}$-in. (4-cm) margins.

4.05 Order of the Manuscript Pages

Number all pages except the figures consecutively. Arrange the pages of the manuscript as follows:
- title page with title, author's name and affiliation, and running head (separate page, numbered page 1)
- abstract (separate page, numbered page 2)
- text (start on a new page, numbered page 3)
- references (start on a new page)

- appendixes (start each on a separate page)
- author identification notes (start on a new page)
- footnotes (start on a new page)
- tables (start each on a separate page)
- figure captions (start on a new page)
- figures (place each on a separate page)

This arrangement is not the way the printed article will appear; it is necessary for handling by the copy editor and the printer.

4.06 Page Numbers and Short Titles

Page numbers. After the manuscript pages are arranged in the correct order, number them consecutively, beginning with the title page. Number *all* pages except the figures. Type the numbers in the upper right-hand corner using arabic numerals. If a page must be inserted or removed after numbering is completed, *renumber the pages*; do not number inserted pages with, for example, "6a" or make other repairs.

Short title. Pages occasionally are separated during the editorial process, so identify each manuscript page (except the figures) by typing the first two or three words from the title in the upper right-hand corner above the page number. (Do *not* use the author's name to identify each page because the name will have to be removed if the manuscript is blind reviewed.) Use this *short title* to identify manuscript pages. The short title should not be confused with the running head (see section 4.15), which goes only on the bottom of the title page and appears in the printed article.

4.07 Corrections

Keep corrections to a minimum and make them neatly.

Do:
- use correction paper, fluid, or tape to cover and type over an error;
- insert a typed correction directly above the word or line to be corrected (not in the margin); and
- retype the page if it has many corrections.

Do not:
- type vertically in the margin;
- strike over a letter;
- type inserts on slips and attach them to pages; or
- write on the manuscript.

4.08 Paragraphs and Indentation

Indent the first line of every paragraph and the first line of every footnote five spaces. Type the remaining lines of the manuscript to a uniform left-hand margin. The only exceptions to these requirements are (a) the abstract (see section 4.16); (b) block quotations (see section 4.13); (c) titles and headings (see section 4.10); (d) entries in the reference list (see section 4.18); and (e) table titles and notes and figure captions (see sections 4.21 and 4.22).

4.09 Uppercase and Lowercase Letters

The instruction "type in uppercase and lowercase letters" means to capitalize initial letters of important words. The parts of a manuscript typed in uppercase and lowercase letters are

- most elements on the title page (i.e., the title and the author and affiliation, but not the running head; see section 4.15),
- page identifiers (e.g., Abstract, Footnotes, etc.),
- most headings (see section 4.10),
- table titles (see section 4.21), and
- some elements of the reference list (see Table 17, Elements and Examples of References in APA Style).

4.10 Headings

Articles in APA journals use from one to five levels of headings. For most articles, three or four levels of headings are sufficient.

Three levels:

Centered Uppercase and Lowercase Heading

<u>Flush Left, Underlined, Uppercase and</u>

<u>Lowercase Side Heading</u>

    <u>Indented, underlined, lowercase paragraph</u>

<u>heading ending with a period</u>.

Four levels:

Centered Uppercase and Lowercase Heading

<u>Centered, Underlined, Uppercase</u>

<u>and Lowercase Heading</u>

<u>Flush Left, Underlined, Uppercase and</u>

<u>Lowercase Side Heading</u>

    <u>Indented, underlined, lowercase paragraph</u>

<u>heading ending with a period</u>.

One or two levels:
Some short articles may require only one or two levels of headings:

Centered Uppercase and Lowercase Heading

<u>Flush Left, Underlined, Uppercase and</u>

<u>Lowercase Side Heading</u>

Five levels of headings may be required for some long articles. Subordinate all four levels (previously described) by introducing a CENTERED UPPERCASE HEADING as the first level of heading. (For more on headings, see section 3.29.)

4.11 Spacing and Punctuation

Space after punctuation as follows:
- after commas and semicolons: one space
- after colons: two spaces
  Exceptions: no space after the colon in ratios (e.g., 6:1), one space after the colon in two-part titles (e.g., Measuring response empathy: Developing a multicomponent rating scale), and one space after the colon that follows the publisher location in the reference list (e.g., New York: Academic Press)
- after punctuation marks at the ends of sentences: two spaces
- after periods that separate parts of a reference citation: two spaces
- after the periods of the initials in personal names: one space (e.g., J. R. Jones)
- after internal periods in abbreviations: no space (e.g., a.m., i.e., U.S.).

Hyphens, dashes, and minus signs are each typed differently.
- hyphen: no space before or after (e.g., trial-by-trial analysis)
- dash: type as two hyphens with no space before or after (e.g., Studies--published and unpublished--are)
- minus: type as a hyphen with space on both sides (e.g., a − b).

Placement of punctuation with parentheses depends on the context. If the context requires a comma (as this does), the comma follows the closing parenthesis. If a complete sentence ends with a parenthesis, the period follows the closing parenthesis (like this). (If a complete sentence, like this one, is enclosed in parentheses, the period is placed inside the closing parenthesis.) See section 4.13 for use of punctuation with quotations.

4.12 Seriation

To show seriation *within a paragraph or sentence,* use lowercase letters (not underlined) in parentheses:

Subjects considered (a) some alternative courses

of action, (b) the factors influencing the

decision, and (c) the probability of success.

To indicate seriation *of separate paragraphs* (e.g., itemized conclusions or successive steps in a procedure), number each paragraph with an arabic numeral, followed by a period but not enclosed in or followed by parentheses:

1. Begin with paragraph indentation. Type second

and succeeding lines flush left.

2. The second item begins a new paragraph.

4.13 Quotations

Short quotations. Quotations of 40 words or fewer should be incorporated into the text and enclosed by double quotation marks (") .

Long quotations. Display quotations of more than 40 words in a double-spaced block of typewritten lines with no quotation marks. Do *not* single-space. Indent five spaces from the left margin and type the entire quotation on the indented margin without the usual opening paragraph indentation. If the quotation is more than one paragraph, indent the first line of second and additional paragraphs five spaces from the new margin. (See section 3.32 for typed examples of quotations in text and of block quotations.)

Quoted material within quotations. Enclose direct quotations within a block quotation in double quotation marks. In a quotation in running text that is already enclosed in double quotation marks, use single quotation marks to enclose quoted material. (See section 3.32 for examples.)

Ellipsis points. An author uses ellipses to indicate omitted material. Type three periods with a space before and after each period to indicate any omission within a sentence. Type four periods to indicate any omission between two sentences (a period for the sentence followed by three spaced periods. . . .). (See also section 3.36.)

Brackets. Use brackets, not parentheses, to enclose material inserted in a quotation by some person other than the original writer (see section 3.36). Hand-drawn brackets are acceptable in the typed manuscript.

Quotation marks and other punctuation. When a period or comma occurs with closing quotation marks, place the period or comma before rather than after the quotation marks. Put other punctuation outside quotation marks unless it is part of the quoted material.

```
At the beginning of each trial, the experimenter

said, "This is a new trial."

After the experimenter said, "This is a new

trial," a new trial began.

Did the experimenter forget to say, "This is a

new trial"?
```

(See section 3.32 for additional examples.)

4.14 Statistical and Mathematical Copy

Type all signs and symbols in mathematical copy that you can. If you do not have a typewriter with special mathematical characters, type a character that resembles the symbol or draw the symbol in by hand (or ask the author to draw in the symbol). Follow the author's copy exactly. Type fences (i.e., parentheses, brackets, and braces), uppercase and lowercase letters, underlines, punctuation, and all other elements exactly as they appear in the author's copy.

Identify symbols, whether handwritten or typewritten, that may be hard to read or ambiguous to the printer. The first time the ambiguous symbol appears in the manuscript, spell out and circle the name right next to the symbol. Symbols that may be misread include 1 (one or the letter el), 0 (zero or the letter oh), X (multiplication sign or the letter ex), and Greek letters (beta or the letter bee, chi or the letter ex). Some letters (e.g., c, s, and x) have lowercase forms that are similar to their uppercase forms and, especially in subscripts and superscripts, might be misread. Labeling such letters as uppercase or lowercase will help the printer distinguish them.

Space mathematical copy as you would space words: $\underline{a}+\underline{b}=\underline{c}$ is as difficult to read as wordswithoutspacing. Instead, type $\underline{a} + \underline{b} = \underline{c}$.

Align signs and symbols carefully. Type subscripts half a line below the symbol and superscripts half a line above the symbol. In most cases, type subscripts first, then superscripts ($\underline{x}_a^2$). However, place a superscript such as the symbol for prime right next to its letter or symbol ($\underline{x}'{}_a$). Follow the alignment in the author's copy.

The following examples show how symbols in mathematical copy are aligned and spaced and how symbols are identified:

(chi) →

$\underline{F}(2, 78) = 7.12, \underline{p} < .01$

$\chi^2(4, \underline{N} = 90) = 10.51, \underline{p} < .05$

$\underline{t}(49) = 2.11, \underline{p} < .05$

$(\underline{z} = 1.92, \underline{p} < .05, \text{one-tailed})$

Girls scored significantly higher on the first

three dimensions: $\underline{F}(1, 751) = 52.84, \underline{p} < .0001;$

$\underline{F}(1, 751) = 61.00, \underline{p} < .0001;$ and $\underline{F}(1, 751) =$

$34.24, \underline{p} < .0001.$

(mult)

a 3 x 2 x 3 (Age x Sex x Weight) analysis

$(\underline{r} = -.24)$

(Kappa) → (alpha) → $k\alpha = E[\underline{MS}(A)]/E[\underline{MS}(AB)]$

(omega) → $(\omega^2 = 0)$

Display a mathematical expression, that is, set it off from the text, by double-spacing twice above and below the expression. If the expression is identified by a number, type the number in parentheses flush against the right margin. Pay particular attention to the spacing and alignment of elements in a displayed expression. Follow the author's copy exactly. If the expression is too long to fit on one line, break before signs of operation (e.g., plus, minus, or equal signs). The following are examples of expressions that may be displayed:

$$\delta_{\underline{i}} = \frac{\mu_{\underline{i}}E - \mu_{\underline{i}}C}{\sigma_{\underline{i}}} \ . \tag{1}$$

$$y_{\underline{i}} = \sum_{\underline{j}=1}^{p} x_{\underline{i}\underline{j}}\,\beta_{\underline{j}} + e_{\underline{i}} \ , \tag{2}$$

$$Y = X\,\beta + E.$$

$$\Pr\left[H_{\underline{t}+\underline{k}} = 1 \,\middle|\, W_{\underline{t}} = 1\right]$$
$$- \Pr\left[H_{\underline{t}+\underline{k}} = 1 \,\middle|\, W_{\underline{t}} = 0\right],$$

$$z_{1} = \frac{z_{\underline{s}}}{\sqrt{1 - p_{\underline{W}}}}$$

(handwritten annotations: delta, mu, sigma, summation, beta, one, brackets, vertical bar, Re es, cap W)

Instructions for Typing the Parts of a Manuscript

4.15 Title Page

The title page includes three elements: title, author and affiliation, and running head. (If the paper is to be blind reviewed, place author identification notes on the title page. The title page is removed by the editor before the manuscript is reviewed.) Identify the title page with a short article title and the number 1, typed in the upper right-hand corner of the page (see section 4.06).

Title. Type the title in uppercase and lowercase letters, centered on the page. If the title is two or more lines, double-space between the lines.

Author and affiliation. Type the name of the author in uppercase and lowercase letters, centered on the page, one double-spaced line below the title. Type the institutional affiliation, centered under the author's name, on the next double-spaced line. If the author's department is *not* a department of psychology, include the name of the department. If the affiliation is not a college or university, include the city and state:

John C. Jones

Educational Testing Service, Princeton, New Jersey

If two or more authors are at the same institution, type the authors' names one right after the other, on one line if space permits. Separate the names of three or more authors with commas. The institutional affiliation appears on the next double-spaced line, just as it would for one author:

Nancy Smith, Paul Dykes, and Susan Brown

University of Colorado

If several authors are from different institutions or from different departments at the same institution, type the names on separate lines. Double-space between lines. Examples of such settings follow:

Two authors, two affiliations	*Three authors, two affiliations*
Paul Dykes	Roger Jones and Nancy Smith
University of Maryland	Department of Education
William Brown	University of Colorado
American University	Susan Brown
	University of Colorado

Three authors, three affiliations

Paul Dykes	William Brown
University of Maryland	American University

Nancy Smith

Department of Education

University of Colorado

Running head. Check that the author has supplied an abbreviated title to be used as a running head for the printed article. Type the running head centered at the bottom of the title page in all-upper-case letters. (See section 1.06 for a description of running heads.)

4.16 Abstract

Begin the abstract on a new page, and identify the abstract page with the short title and the number 2 typed in the upper right-hand corner of the page. Type the word Abstract in uppercase and lower-case letters, centered, at the top of the page. Type the abstract itself as a single paragraph in block format (i.e., without paragraph in-dentation).

4.17 Text

Begin the text on a new page and identify the first text page with the short title and the number 3 typed in the upper right-hand corner of the page. Type the title of the paper centered at the top of the page, double-space, and then type the text. The sections of the text follow each other without a break. Do not start a new page when a new heading occurs; for instance, do not begin the Method section on a new page. Each remaining manuscript page should also carry the short title and the page number.

4.18 References

Start the reference list on a new page. Type the word References (Reference, in the case of only one) in uppercase and lowercase letters, centered, at the top of the page.

Double-space all reference entries. (Although some theses and dissertations use single-spaced reference lists, single-spacing is *not* acceptable for manuscripts submitted to journals because it does not allow space for copy editing and printer's marks.) Type the first line of each entry flush left; indent the second and succeeding lines three spaces. (See Table 17, Elements and Examples of References in APA Style.)

4.19 Appendixes

Double-space the appendixes and begin each one on a separate page. Type the word Appendix and the identifying capital letters (A, B, etc., in the order in which they are mentioned in text) centered at the top of the page. If there is only one appendix, do not use an identifying letter; the word Appendix is sufficient. Double-space and type the title of the appendix, centered and underlined, in uppercase and lowercase letters. Double-space, indent the first line five spaces, and begin the text of the appendix.

4.20 Footnotes and Notes

Four types of notes appear in APA journals: author identification, content, copyright permission, and table notes.

Author identification notes are not numbered or cited in the text. Type these notes double-spaced on a separate page or, if the paper is to be blind reviewed, on the title page. If these notes are on a separate page, center the words Author Notes in uppercase and lowercase letters at the top of the page. Start each note with a paragraph indentation and type the acknowledgments first, if any, and then the author identification (e.g., change of affiliation, address).

Content footnotes and copyright permission footnotes that are mentioned in text are numbered consecutively throughout the article. (Copyright permission footnotes to tables and figures are typed as part of the table note or figure caption; see section 3.69 for sample permission notes.) To indicate in text the position of a footnote, use superscript arabic numerals, for example:

Type the footnote numbers slightly above the line, like this,[1] _following_ any punctuation mark except a dash. A footnote number that appears with a dash--like this[2]--always precedes the dash. (The number falls inside a closing parenthesis if it applies only to matter within the parentheses.[3])

Double-space all content and text copyright permission footnotes on a separate sheet. Center the word Footnotes in uppercase and lowercase letters at the top of the page. Indent the first line of each footnote five spaces, like the first line of a paragraph, and type the footnotes in the order in which they are mentioned in text. Number the footnotes to correspond with their numbers in text.

Table notes. For directions for typing table notes, see section 4.21.

4.21 Tables and Table Titles, Notes, and Rules

Tables are numbered consecutively in the order in which they are first mentioned in the text and are identified by the word Table and an arabic numeral. Double-space each table, regardless of length, and begin each table on a separate page. Type the short title of the manuscript and the page number in the upper right-hand corner of every page of a table.

In text, indicate the position of each table by a clear break in the text, with the instructions set off by lines above and below:

Insert Table 2 about here

Table titles and headings. Type the word Table and its arabic numeral flush left at the top of the table. Double-space and begin the table title flush left, capitalizing the initial letters of the principal words. If the title is longer than one line, double-space between lines and begin subsequent lines flush left under the first line. Center column heads and subheads over the appropriate columns within the table, capitalizing only the initial letter of the first word of each heading. Allow at least three spaces between the longest word in one column head and the longest word in another and align material in each column (e.g., align decimal points). Allow at least three spaces between columns. Center table spanner heads over the entire width of the table (see section 3.64 for more on table spanners). If a table is longer than a manuscript page, type (table continues) at the bottom right-hand corner of the page. Begin the second and subsequent pages by repeating the column heads.

Table notes. Double-space all notes at the end of the table. Begin the general note, the first specific note, and the first probability note flush left. (For more detailed information on the three kinds of table notes, see section 3.66.)

Table rules. Rule each table only if necessary to clarify divisions and only in light pencil. Use horizontal, not vertical rules. Make *no* heavy or typewritten rules. (See Tables 12, 13, and 14 for examples of correctly typed tables.)

4.22 Figures and Figure Captions

Figures are also numbered consecutively in the order in which they are first mentioned in the text. Use the word Figure and an arabic numeral. Indicate the location of each figure by a clear break in the text, in the same manner as for tables:

Insert Figure 1 about here

Make certain that the author (a) has identified the figures by labeling the back of each with the short article title (not the author's name) and the figure number and (b) has indicated how the figure should be placed on the printed page by placing the word *TOP* at the top of the figure.

Captions. Each figure must have a caption that includes the figure number:

Figure 1. A clear, brief description of the

figure.

Do not put the captions for figures on the figures themselves. Type all figure captions on a single separate sheet. Center the words Figure Captions, in uppercase and lowercase letters, at the top of the page. Begin each caption flush left, and type the word Figure (underlined), followed by the appropriate number (underlined), a period, and the caption (not underlined). Capitalize only the first word and any proper names in the caption. If the caption takes up more than one line, double-space between lines and type the second and subsequent lines of the caption flush left.

Sample Paper and Outlines

The sample paper and sample paper outlines in Figures 7, 8, and 9 were prepared especially for the *Publication Manual* in order to illustrate some applications of APA style in typed form. These are not actual manuscripts, and they have not been reviewed for content. Numbers and captions refer to sections of the *Manual*.

FIGURE 7

Sample One-Experiment Paper
The circled numbers refer to numbered sections in the *Manual*.

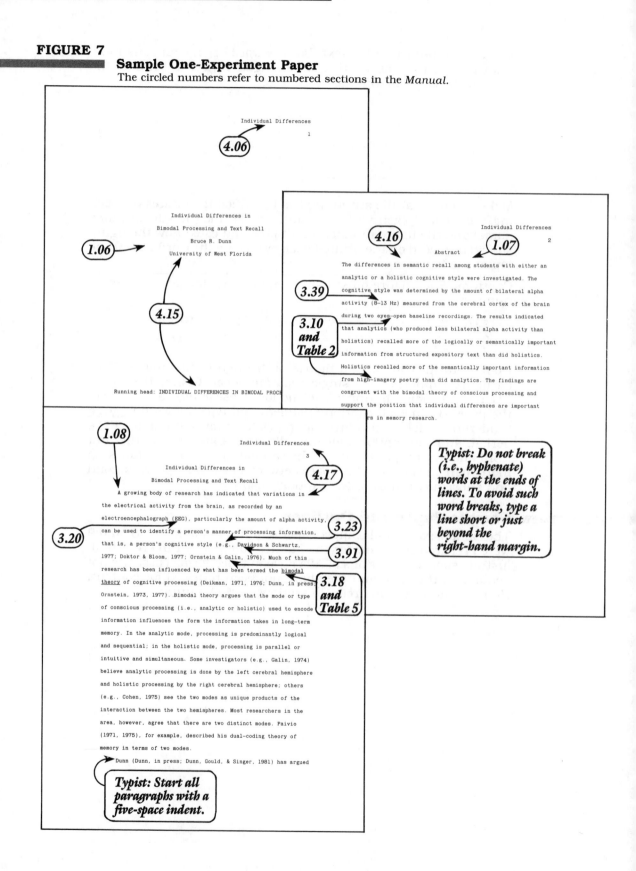

Individual Differences
1

(4.06)

(1.06)

Individual Differences in
Bimodal Processing and Text Recall
Bruce R. Dunn
University of West Florida

(4.15)

Running head: INDIVIDUAL DIFFERENCES IN BIMODAL PROCE

(4.16)   Individual Differences
2

Abstract   (1.07)

(3.39)

(3.10 and Table 2)

The differences in semantic recall among students with either an analytic or a holistic cognitive style were investigated. The cognitive style was determined by the amount of bilateral alpha activity (8-13 Hz) measured from the cerebral cortex of the brain during two eyes-open baseline recordings. The results indicated that analytics (who produced less bilateral alpha activity than holistics) recalled more of the logically or semantically important information from structured expository text than did holistics. Holistics recalled more of the semantically important information from high-imagery poetry than did analytics. The findings are congruent with the bimodal theory of conscious processing and support the position that individual differences are important ...rs in memory research.

Typist: Do not break (i.e., hyphenate) words at the ends of lines. To avoid such word breaks, type a line short or just beyond the right-hand margin.

(1.08)

Individual Differences
3

Individual Differences in
Bimodal Processing and Text Recall   (4.17)

(3.20)

(3.23)

(3.91)

(3.18 and Table 5)

A growing body of research has indicated that variations in the electrical activity from the brain, as recorded by an electroencephalograph (EEG), particularly the amount of alpha activity, can be used to identify a person's manner of processing information, that is, a person's cognitive style (e.g., Davidson & Schwartz, 1977; Doktor & Bloom, 1977; Ornstein & Galin, 1976). Much of this research has been influenced by what has been termed the bimodal theory of cognitive processing (Deikman, 1971, 1976; Dunn, in press; Ornstein, 1973, 1977). Bimodal theory argues that the mode or type of conscious processing (i.e., analytic or holistic) used to encode information influences the form the information takes in long-term memory. In the analytic mode, processing is predominantly logical and sequential; in the holistic mode, processing is parallel or intuitive and simultaneous. Some investigators (e.g., Galin, 1974) believe analytic processing is done by the left cerebral hemisphere and holistic processing by the right cerebral hemisphere; others (e.g., Cohen, 1975) see the two modes as unique products of the interaction between the two hemispheres. Most researchers in the area, however, agree that there are two distinct modes. Paivio (1971, 1975), for example, described his dual-coding theory of memory in terms of two modes.

Dunn (Dunn, in press; Dunn, Gould, & Singer, 1981) has argued

Typist: Start all paragraphs with a five-space indent.

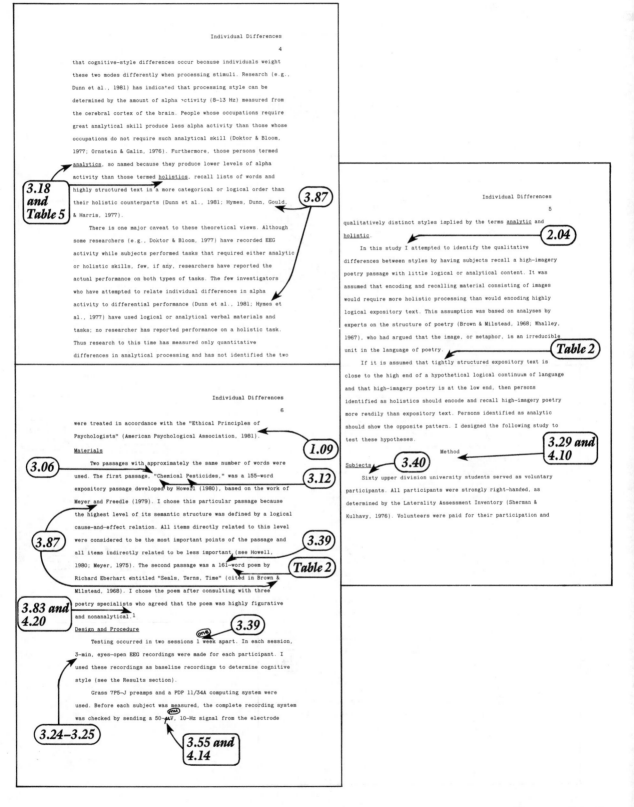

3.18 and Table 5

3.87

Individual Differences

4

that cognitive-style differences occur because individuals weight these two modes differently when processing stimuli. Research (e.g., Dunn et al., 1981) has indicated that processing style can be determined by the amount of alpha activity (8-13 Hz) measured from the cerebral cortex of the brain. People whose occupations require great analytical skill produce less alpha activity than those whose occupations do not require such analytical skill (Doktor & Bloom, 1977; Ornstein & Galin, 1976). Furthermore, those persons termed analytics, so named because they produce lower levels of alpha activity than those termed holistics, recall lists of words and highly structured text in a more categorical or logical order than their holistic counterparts (Dunn et al., 1981; Hymes, Dunn, Gould, & Harris, 1977).

There is one major caveat to these theoretical views. Although some researchers (e.g., Doktor & Bloom, 1977) have recorded EEG activity while subjects performed tasks that required either analytic or holistic skills, few, if any, researchers have reported the actual performance on both types of tasks. The few investigators who have attempted to relate individual differences in alpha activity to differential performance (Dunn et al., 1981; Hymes et al., 1977) have used logical or analytical verbal materials and tasks; no researcher has reported performance on a holistic task. Thus research to this time has measured only quantitative differences in analytical processing and has not identified the two

Individual Differences

5

qualitatively distinct styles implied by the terms analytic and holistic.

2.04

In this study I attempted to identify the qualitative differences between styles by having subjects recall a high-imagery poetry passage with little logical or analytical content. It was assumed that encoding and recalling material consisting of images would require more holistic processing than would encoding highly logical expository text. This assumption was based on analyses by experts on the structure of poetry (Brown & Milstead, 1968; Whalley, 1967), who had argued that the image, or metaphor, is an irreducible unit in the language of poetry.

Table 2

If it is assumed that tightly structured expository text is close to the high end of a hypothetical logical continuum of language and that high-imagery poetry is at the low end, then persons identified as holistics should encode and recall high-imagery poetry more readily than expository text. Persons identified as analytic should show the opposite pattern. I designed the following study to test these hypotheses.

3.29 and 4.10

Method

Subjects

3.40

Sixty upper division university students served as voluntary participants. All participants were strongly right-handed, as determined by the Laterality Assessment Inventory (Sherman & Kulhavy, 1976). Volunteers were paid for their participation and

Individual Differences

6

were treated in accordance with the "Ethical Principles of Psychologists" (American Psychological Association, 1981).

1.09

Materials

3.06

Two passages with approximately the same number of words were used. The first passage, "Chemical Pesticides," was a 155-word expository passage developed by Howell (1980), based on the work of Meyer and Freedle (1979). I chose this particular passage because the highest level of its semantic structure was defined by a logical cause-and-effect relation. All items directly related to this level were considered to be the most important points of the passage and all items indirectly related to be less important (see Howell, 1980; Meyer, 1975). The second passage was a 161-word poem by Richard Eberhart entitled "Seals, Terns, Time" (cited in Brown & Milstead, 1968). I chose the poem after consulting with three poetry specialists who agreed that the poem was highly figurative and nonanalytical.[1]

3.12

3.87

3.39

Table 2

3.83 and 4.20

Design and Procedure

one **3.39**

Testing occurred in two sessions 1 week apart. In each session, 3-min, eyes-open EEG recordings were made for each participant. I used these recordings as baseline recordings to determine cognitive style (see the Results section).

Grass 7P5-J preamps and a PDP 11/34A computing system were used. Before each subject was measured, the complete recording system was checked by sending a $50-\mu V$, 10-Hz signal from the electrode

3.24-3.25

3.55 and 4.14

figure continued

(Figure 7 continued)

Individual Differences

7

leads through the outputs of the computer's A to D converter. A
specially written Fourier analysis program, independently tested
by others (e.g., G. S. Wolverton, personal communication, February
1981), was used to transform the EEG data into conventional
frequency bandwidths. The EEG recordings were made from two
parietal-temporal sites over Wernicke's area on the left hemisphere
and at the homologous site on the right hemisphere. I chose
Wernicke's area because it appears to be highly important for
semantic processing (Geschwind, 1972).

During the first session, only baseline EEG activity was
recorded. During the second session, baseline activity was recorded,
and then, after the participants had rested for 5 min, EEG activity
was recorded while the participants read and recalled the two
passages. Passages were counterbalanced across subjects, and each
passage appeared, a paragraph at a time, on the computer's
cathode-ray tube terminal, which was placed at eye level 1 m in
front of the subject. Subjects initiated the reading/recall sequence
for each passage by pressing the space bar on the terminal to
present each paragraph. Subjects were instructed to read at their
normal rates. After the subjects finished reading, they were asked
to write down as much of the passage as they could remember, taking
as much time as necessary. They were also instructed to press the

3.93

3.02

4.14

3.24 (one)

3.39

Individual Differences

8

recorded the time interval between bar presses for both
~~read~~ing and recall tasks. Subjects had a rest period of 3 min
~~between~~ the two reading/recall sequences. At the end of the session,
~~the natu~~re of the study was explained to each subject.

~~Sco~~ring

~~Rec~~all data. Because the high-imagery poetry was nonanalytical
~~and se~~quential, none of the existing prose analysis procedures
~~(e.g., Ki~~ntsch, 1974; Meyer, 1975) could easily be used to determine
~~the seman~~tic content of the poem. Instead, three graduate students
~~majoring~~ in English independently ranked sentences in the passage
~~from most~~ important to least important. Other researchers (e.g.,
~~Johnson, M~~cConkie, 1973) successfully used this method to determine
~~the conte~~nt of narrative and expository text. I developed a semantic
~~hierarchy~~ based only on the sentences on which all three graduate
~~students~~ had agreed. The expository "Chemical Pesticides" passage
~~was analy~~zed in an identical manner—even though established
~~prose~~ analysis procedures like Meyer's (1975) could have been
~~used—in~~ order to make the resultant semantic hierarchies as equal
~~as possib~~le. Two independent raters judged subjects' recall protocols
~~and deter~~mined which recalled sentences were contained in the
~~previousl~~y described semantic hierarchies. The scoring method was
~~lenient,~~ and paraphrased versions of the sentences were scored as
~~correct.~~ The reliability of the ratings was acceptable (92.6%),
~~given the~~ scoring procedure. Because the resultant

3.05 and 4.11

3.39

3.55

Individual Differences

9

hierarchies had unequal levels of subordination, the first 10
sentences of each hierarchy were scored as superordinate information,
and the last 15 sentences were scored as subordinate information.
As a result, proportional recall scores were used.

EEG data. Each second of EEG data was checked for muscle artifacts.
If any artifact occurred, that second of a given subject's EEG data
was deleted. Fourier transforms were used to convert the remaining
EEG data into conventional frequency bandwidths within the range
of 1 to 51 Hz.

Results

A Pearson product-moment correlation revealed a substantial relation
between each participant's two alpha power scores, which were taken
a week apart, $\underline{r}(59) = .87$, $\underline{p} < .01$. Therefore, the alpha power scores
were averaged for each subject and served as the basis for
dichotomizing subjects into analytic and holistic groups. Those
subjects whose scores were below the median were classified as
analytic; those whose scores were above the median were classified
as holistic. This procedure has been used to classify analytics
and holistics in past research (e.g., Hymes et al., 1977), which
has demonstrated that alpha power scores are highly reliable.

Recall Data

The proportional recall data were analyzed with a 2 x 2 x 2 (Type
of Processor x Passage x Level of Subordination) mixed analysis of
covariance, with average reading time serving as the covariate

3.54

4.14 (mult)

3.17

Individual Differences

10

and with passage and level serving as repeated measures. Although
several main effects and two-way interactions reached statistical
significance, they were of little interest because a significant
three-way (Type of Processor x Passage x Level of Subordination)
interaction was obtained, $F(1, 58) = 29.93$, $p < .0001$. For ease of
interpretation, Figure 1 shows this interaction as 2 two-way (Passage
x Level of Subordination) interactions, one for each processing
style. The three-way interaction indicates that analytics recalled

———————————

Insert Figure 1 about here

———————————

proportionally more superordinate information from the logically
structured expository text than from the high-imagery poetry. In
contrast, the holistics recalled more of the important information
from the poem than from the expository passage. Simple-effects
tests of the interaction at the .05 level of significance (Kirk,
1968) showed that the analytics' mean recall of important information
from the expository text (.70) was greater than the holistics' mean
recall (.52). Furthermore, the holistics recalled more important
information from the poem than the analytics did (.72 vs. .55).

EEG Data

    Reading data. The bilateral alpha power scores recorded during
reading for each subject were averaged and subjected to a 2 x 2
(Type of Processor x Passage) mixed analysis of variance with

Annotations (pointing to text above): 3.54 and 4.14 · 3.79 · 3.41 · 4.22 · 3.43

Margin note: **Author: Descriptive statistics appear in the figure (see section 3.54).**

Individual Differences

11

repeated measures on passage.[2] The main effect of type of processor
was significant: The holistics' mean alpha score (3.35) was greater
than that of the analytics (1.35), $F(1, 28) = 14.89$, $p < .005$. More
important, the two-way (Type of Processor x Passage) interaction
also yielded significance, $F(1, 168) = 9.49$, $p < .005$. The data in
the top half of Table 1 show that the analytics produced less alpha
activity when they read the expository text than when they read the

———————————

Insert Table 1 about here

———————————

high-imagery poem; the opposite pattern occurred for the
holistics. In addition, the holistics generally appeared to produce
more alpha activity than did the analytics, regardless of the type
of passage. This finding was confirmed with Scheffé's post hoc
tests ($p < .05$).

    Recall data. The recall alpha data were analyzed in the same
way the reading alpha data were analyzed. Type of processor was
again found to be significant, $F(1, 28) = 5.70$, $p < .25$, with the
holistics' mean alpha score (2.30) being greater than the analytics'
(1.12). The two-way interaction was also significant,
$F(1, 168) = 6.23$, $p < .025$, and followed a pattern similar to that
found with the reading alpha data (see the bottom half of Table 1).

Discussion

    The present data are congruent with the bimodal theory of
processing (Deikman, 1971; Dunn, in press; Ornstein, 1977; Paivio,

Annotations: 3.04 and 4.11 · 3.60 · 4.21 · 3.54

Margin note: **Author: Descriptive statistics appear in the table (see section 3.54).**

Individual Differences

12

[5] from which the analytic/holistic dimension was derived.
[...]esized, the analytics recalled more of the important
[...]on from logically structured text (cause followed by
[...]than the holistics did. However, holistics recalled more
[...]mportant information from the less structured and more
[...] text (poetry) than analytics did. This finding is
[...]rly indicated by the relatively poor superordinate recall
[...]oetry passage by high analytics. These recall results cannot
[...]ted for by either reading time (reading time was treated
[...]ariate) or total proportional recall differences. The mean
[...]oportional recall, for example, was approximately the same
[...]analytic and the holistic groups (expository passage: .66
[...]respectively; poetry passage: .59 vs. .60, respectively).
[...]ause both groups recalled more superordinate information
[...]rdinate information, the results seem to demonstrate a
[...]ive rather than a qualitative difference in analytical
[...]g. However, the differential recall of superordinate
[...]on from the expository text and from the poem by the two
[...]rgues against a solely quantitative explanation. As had
[...]nstrated in past research (Dunn et al., 1981), holistics
[...]more alpha activity than did analytics during the reading
[...]l tasks. Furthermore, holistics produced more alpha activity
[...]ding and recalling the expository text than while reading
[...]Because the analytics' alpha activity showed the opposite
[...]I believe that two qualitatively distinct styles were
[...]d.

figure continued

(Figure 7 continued)

Individual Differences

13

Admittedly, the experimental variation of logical structure across the passages in the present experiment was naive. Future research should test the boundary conditions of the analytic/holistic cognitive style continuum by systematically varying both semantic and structural text variables and by varying visuospatial tasks in order to determine their effects on the recall and perceptual performance of analytics and holistics. Also, other promising individual difference constructs, such as extraversion (H. J. Eysenck, 1967; M. W. Eysenck, 1976, 1977) and field dependency (Witkin, Dyk, Faterson, Goodenough, & Karp, 1962), should be compared with the analytic/holistic dimension in terms of success in predicting differential recall.

The present results have a more indirect implication, which is reflected in the following statement by M. W. Eysenck (1976):

In spite of the obvious importance of individual differences in human learning and memory, relatively few investigators incorporate any measures of intelligence, personality, or motivation into their studies. Instead, they prefer to relegate individual differences to the error term in their analyses of variance. (p. 75)

Given the robustness of the present results and the results of others (for reviews see M. W. Eysenck, 1977, and Goodenough, 1976),

3.90

3.34 and 4.13

Typist: Indent block quotations five spaces.

3.95

3.97–3.101 and Table 17

Individual Differences

14

References

4.18

American Psychological Association. (1981). Ethical principles of psychologists (revised). *American Psychologist*, 36, 633–638.

Brown, H., & Milstead, J. (1968). *Patterns in poetry: An introductory anthology*. Glenview, IL: Scott, Foresman.

Cohen, G. (1975). Hemisphere differences in the effects of cuing in visual recognition tasks. *Journal of Experimental Psychology: Human Perception and Performance*, 1, 366–373.

Davidson, R. J., & Schwartz, G. E. (1977). The influence of musical training on patterns of EEG asymmetry during musical and non-musical self-generation tasks. *Psychophysiology*, 14, 58–63.

Deikman, A. J. (1971). Bimodal consciousness. *Archives of General Psychiatry*, 25, 481–489.

Deikman, A. J. (1976). Bimodal consciousness and the mystic experience. In P. R. Lee, R. E. Ornstein, D. Galin, A. J. Deikman, & C. T. Tart (Eds.), *Symposium on consciousness* (pp. 67–88). New York: Viking Press.

Doktor, R., & Bloom, D. M. (1977). Selective lateralization of cognitive style related to occupation as determined by EEG alpha asymmetry. *Psychophysiology*, 14, 385–387.

Dunn, B. R. (in press). Bimodal processing and memory from text. In V. M. Rentel, S. Corson, & B. R. Dunn (Eds.), *Psychophysiological aspects of reading*. Oxford, England: Pergamon Press.

Individual Differences

15

R., Gould, J. E., & Singer, M. (1981). *Cognitive style* rences in expository prose recall (Tech. Rep. 210). n–Champaign: University of Illinois, Center for the Study of g. (ERIC Document Reproduction Service No. ED 205 922)

H. J. (1967). *The biological basis of personality*. field, IL: Charles C. Thomas.

M. W. (1976). Extraversion, verbal learning, and memory. ological Bulletin, 83, 75–90.

M. W. (1977). *Human memory: Theory, research, and* dual differences Oxford, England: Pergamon Press.

(1974). Implications for psychiatry of left and right al specialization. *Archives of General Psychiatry*, 31, 572–583.

N. (1972). Language and the brain. *Scientific American*, , 76–83.

h, D. R. (1976). The role of individual differences in dependence as a factor in learning and memory. *Psychological* in, 83, 675–694.

L. (1980). Expository prose recall by young, hospitalized phrenics (Doctoral dissertation, Florida State University, *Dissertation Abstracts International*, 41, 1011B.

, Dunn, B. R., Gould, J. E., & Harris, W. (1977). s of mode of conscious processing on recall and clustering. presented at the meeting of the Southeastern Psychological ation, Hollywood, FL.

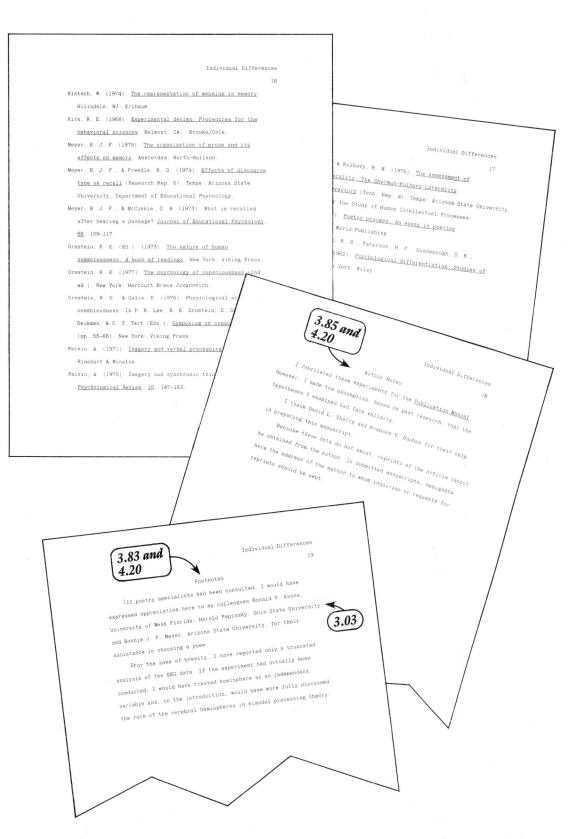

Individual Differences

16

Kintsch, W. (1974). <u>The representation of meaning in memory</u>.
Hillsdale, NJ: Erlbaum.

Kirk, R. E. (1968). <u>Experimental design: Procedures for the</u>
<u>behavioral sciences</u>. Belmont, CA: Brooks/Cole.

Meyer, B. J. F. (1975). <u>The organization of prose and its</u>
<u>effects on memory</u>. Amsterdam: North-Holland.

Meyer, B. J. F., & Freedle, R. O. (1979). <u>Effects of discourse</u>
<u>type on recall</u> (Research Rep. 6). Tempe: Arizona State
University, Department of Educational Psychology.

Meyer, B. J. F., & McConkie, G. W. (1973). What is recalled
after hearing a passage? <u>Journal of Educational Psychology</u>,
<u>65</u>, 109–117.

Ornstein, R. E. (Ed.). (1973). <u>The nature of human</u>
<u>consciousness: A book of readings</u>. New York: Viking Press.

Ornstein, R. E. (1977). <u>The psychology of consciousness</u> (2nd
ed.). New York: Harcourt Brace Jovanovich.

Ornstein, R. E., & Galin, D. (1976). Physiological st
consciousness. In P. R. Lee, R. E. Ornstein, D. G
Deikman, & C. T. Tart (Eds.), <u>Symposium on consc</u>
(pp. 53–66). New York: Viking Press.

Paivio, A. (1971). <u>Imagery and verbal processing</u>
Rinehart & Winston.

Paivio, A. (1975). Imagery and synchronic thin
<u>Psychological Review</u>, <u>16</u>, 147–163.

Individual Differences

17

& Kulhavy, R. W. (1976). <u>The assessment of</u>
erality: The Sherman-Kulhavy Laterality
ventory (Tech. Rep. 4). Tempe: Arizona State University,
r the Study of Human Intellectual Processes.
). <u>Poetic process: An essay in poetics</u>
World Publishing
, R. B., Faterson, H. F., Goodenough, D. R.,
1962). <u>Psychological differentiation: Studies of</u>
York: Wiley

3.85 and 4.20 →

Author Notes   Individual Differences

18

I fabricated these experiments for the <u>Publication Manual</u>.
However, I made the assumption, based on past research, that the
hypotheses I examined had face validity.

I thank David L. Sherry and Frances Y. Dunham for their help
in preparing this manuscript.

Because these data do not exist, reprints of the article cannot
be obtained from the author. In submitted manuscripts, designate
here the address of the author to whom inquiries or requests for
reprints should be sent.

3.83 and 4.20 →

Individual Differences

19

Footnotes

1If poetry specialists had been consulted, I would have
expressed appreciation here to my colleagues Ronald V. Evans,
University of West Florida; Harold Pepinsky, Ohio State University; **3.03**
and Bonnie J. F. Meyer, Arizona State University, for their
assistance in choosing a poem.

2For the sake of brevity, I have reported only a truncated
analysis of the EEG data. If the experiment had actually been
conducted, I would have treated hemisphere as an independent
variable and, in the introduction, would have more fully discussed
the role of the cerebral hemispheres in bimodal processing theory.

figure continued

(Figure 7 continued)

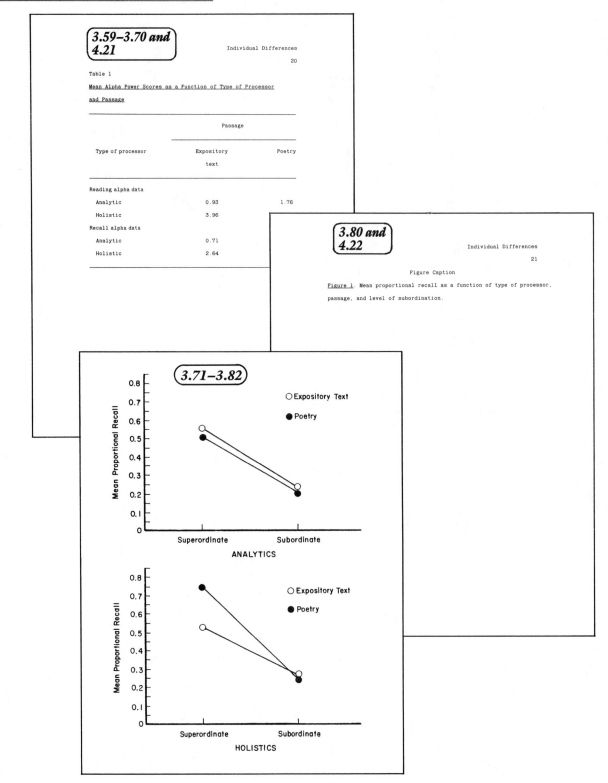

3.59–3.70 and 4.21

Individual Differences

20

Table 1

Mean Alpha Power Scores as a Function of Type of Processor

and Passage

	Passage	
Type of processor	Expository text	Poetry
Reading alpha data		
Analytic	0.93	1.76
Holistic	3.96	
Recall alpha data		
Analytic	0.71	
Holistic	2.64	

3.80 and 4.22

Individual Differences

21

Figure Caption

Figure 1. Mean proportional recall as a function of type of processor,

passage, and level of subordination.

3.71–3.82

FIGURE 8

Outline of the Text of a Sample Two-Experiment Paper

This abridged manuscript illustrates the organizational structure characteristic of multiple-experiment papers. Of course, a complete multiple-experiment paper would include a title page, an abstract page, and so on.

Effect on Prose Recall

3

1.04

Effect on Prose Recall of

Individual Differences in Cognitive Style

Recently researchers have shown increased interest in the

relation between cognitive style differences and comprehension of

text. Several researchers in this area have attempted to show the

relation of locus of control (Wolk & DuCette, 1974) and field

dependency (Annis, 1979; Spiro & Tirre, 1980) to prose encoding or

recall. Taken together, these constructs appear to overlap, in

part, with the cognitive-style dimension termed analytical processing

by Dunn (in press). . . . [section continues].

1.12

Experiment 1

3.30 and 4.10

Method

Subjects. Sixty upper division university students served as

voluntary participants. . . . [section continues].

Materials. Four expository prose passages were used.

[section continues].

Personality/cognitive measurements. A brief descript

three individual-difference constructs measured for each

is given in the following section. . . . [section continues]

Design and procedure. Testing was conducted in two s

In the first session, individual pencil-and-paper persona

inventories were administered and eyes-open electroenceph

(EEG) baseline recordings were made. . . . [section continue

Effect on Prose Recall

4

Results

All data were converted to z scores and, with Pearson product-moment

correlations, a correlation matix was generated (see Table 1).

Because the multiple independent and dependent variables were

---

Insert Table 1 about here

---

related, I analyzed the data using the Statistical Analysis System

canonical correlation routine (Barr, Goodnight, Sall, & Helwig, 1976).

. . . [section continues].

Discussion

The results of Experiment 1 indicate that although locus of

control and field dependency correlated with the set of dependent

variables, they did so only through their correlation with the

alpha activity index of analytical processing.

Because only highly logical verbal materials were used in

Experiment 1, it could be argued that this study measured only

quantitative differences in analytical processing. Experiment 2

was designed to identify qualitative differences between

styles. . . . [section continues].

Experiment 2

1.12

Method

Subjects. Forty upper division, right-handed college students

served as voluntary participants. . . . [section continues].

Effect on Prose Recall

5

Materials. A 205-word poem by Fyodor Sologue (cited in Markov

& Sparks, 1966) entitled "The Devil's Swing" was selected because

three poetry specialists who were consulted agreed that the poem

was full of imagery and nonanalytical content. . . . [section continues].

Design and procedure. The design and procedure were identical

to those of Experiment 1, except that only one passage was given

to the subjects. . . . [section continues].

Data scoring. Two independent raters judged subjects' recall

protocols and determined which recalled sentences were contained in

the previously described semantic hierarchy. . . . [section continues].

Results

4.11

A correlation matrix on the z-transformed data again showed

that the predictor variables—analytical processing, locus of

control, and field dependency—were significantly intercorrelated

($ps < .005$). . . . [section continues].

General Discussion

The results of both experiments strongly suggest that the

analytical processing dimension is a better predictor of individual

differences in the recall of higher order information from text

than are the personality constructs of locus of control and field

dependency. . . . [section continues].

[Follow the form of the one-experiment sample paper to type references, author
notes, footnotes, tables, and figure captions.]

FIGURE 9

Outline of the Text of a Sample Review Paper

This abridged manuscript illustrates the organizational structure characteristic of review or theoretical papers. Of course, a complete review or theoretical paper would include a title page, an abstract page, and so on.

Analytical Cognitive Style

3

1.04

Analytical Cognitive Style as a Factor

in Memory for Text

Cognitive or personality style differences have traditionally been ignored in the field of human learning and memory (Eysenck, 1977). This situation is surprising given the growing body of literature showing that individuals differ in how they encode and retrieve simple and complex verbal information (for summaries see Eysenck, 1977, and Goodenough, 1976). The present review has two purposes: (a) to demonstrate that when the popular personality and cognitive constructs—locus of control (Rotter, 1966) and field dependency (Witkin, Dyk, Faterson, Goodenough, & Karp, 1962)—are used as factors in semantic recall studies, similar results are obtained; and (b) to suggest that this similarity occurs because both constructs overlap with the analytic/holistic cognitive-style dimension.

3.31 and 4.12

3.30 and 4.10

Locus of Control

Rotter (1966) suggested that people with an internal, as opposed to external, locus of control believe that events are contingent on their own actions and abilities rather than chance, or other people. . . . [section continues].

Research on Learning Word Lists

A widely held belief in verbal learning is that subjects use cognitive categories while learning lists of words and that they use those categories as the basis for retrieval (Bousfield,

Analytical Cognitive Style

4

Tulving, 1966). The results of Bartel, DuCette, and Wolk (1972) indicate that only internals use this strategy. . . . [section continues].

Research on Text Recall

The argument that externals and internals use different strategies to encode and retrieve simple word lists can be made when complex material serves as the stimulus material. . . . [section continues].

Field Dependency

A field-independent person, in contrast to a field-dependent person, can overcome an embedding context and can deal with a perceptual field analytically. . . . [section continues].

Research on Learning Word Lists

Researchers obtain results similar to those found in the locus of control literature when they use field dependency as the individual-difference construct in studies employing simple verbal materials. . . . [section continues].

Research on Text Recall

Annis (1979) has found individual differences in field dependency and text recall that parallel those found in a study of locus of control by Wolk and DuCette (1974). . . . [section continues].

Relationship of Locus of Control and Field

Dependency With Analytic Processing

The constructs of locus of control, field dependency, and analytic processing style are related to a certain extent because

Analytical Cogni

the definitions of the constructs overlap. However, the overlap in the constructs occurs because of shared behav referents. . . . [section continues].

Conclusions

Although the constructs of locus of control and fie dependency generally measure different aspects of perso cognitive functioning, they appear to measure the same text encoding. That factor appears to be individual dif analytic and holistic processing. . . . [section continues].

[Follow the form of the one-experiment sample paper to type references, author notes, footnotes, tables, and figure captions.]

5 Submitting the Manuscript and Proofreading

The efficient handling of a manuscript is a responsibility that the author, editor, printer, and publisher share. This chapter describes procedures for submitting the manuscript and, if the manuscript is accepted, for handling the edited manuscript and typeset article. You, the author, can contribute to the efficient processing and publication of articles by following the guidelines provided in this chapter.

The specific requirements for submitting a manuscript may differ between journals. Therefore, before submitting a manuscript, refer to the most recent issue of the appropriate journal. The journal's inside front cover and Instructions to Authors will tell you (a) the journal's area of coverage, that is, what kinds of manuscripts are appropriate for that journal; (b) the current editor's name and address; and (c) instructions for manuscript preparation and submission specific to that journal, including the number of copies you need to submit and whether the journal uses blind review (see section 6.12).

Submitting the Manuscript

5.01 Number of Copies

Each journal editor requires a specific number of copies (usually three or four) of a submitted manuscript. One manuscript must be the original and must include the glossy prints of any figures. The additional copies should be clear photocopies (including a full set of photocopied tables and figures) on paper of good quality. Carbon copies are unacceptable.

The original manuscript is marked by the APA copy editor and used by the typesetter (hereinafter called *printer*); it therefore must withstand repeated handling. The additional copies are for editorial review and for the editor's central file.

5.02 Cover Letter

Enclose a short letter when submitting a manuscript to a journal editor. Give the editor general information about the manuscript: for example, whether it has been presented at a scientific meeting. Inform the editor of the existence of any closely related manuscripts that have already been published or that have been submitted for simultaneous consideration to the same or to another journal. Also, give specific details about the manuscript you are submitting, such as the title, the length, and the number of tables and figures. If the journal offers blind review, say whether you are requesting blind review of the manuscript. Verify that the treatment of participants (human or animal) was in accordance with the ethical standards of the APA (see Principle 9, Research With Human Participants, and Principle 10, Care and Use of Animals, in the "Ethical Principles of Psychologists," APA, 1981). If you are reproducing any copyrighted material, enclose a copy of the permission letter. Include your telephone number and address for future correspondence.

5.03 Contents of Package

After you have proofread the typed manuscript (and have had any necessary corrections retyped) and written the cover letter, the manuscript is ready for mailing. The package should contain
- your cover letter, including a telephone number and address for future correspondence;
- the original manuscript, including all tables and the glossy prints of all figures;
- the number of additional photocopies of the manuscript required by the journal to which the manuscript is being submitted; and
- letters of permission to reproduce any copyrighted material (text, figures, or tables) that appears in the manuscript (see sections 6.06 and 6.07).

Be sure to keep a copy of the entire manuscript, including figures and tables, to guard against loss in the mail.

Do not bind or staple the manuscript pages. Editors and printers prefer to work with loose sheets held together by a paper clip. To protect the manuscript from rough handling in the mail, use a strong envelope stiffened with cardboard or corrugated filler.

Send the manuscript by first-class mail to the journal editor, not to the APA journal office. Because editors and their addresses change, always check the most recent issue of the journal to ascertain the current editor's name and address.

5.04 Editor Acknowledgment of Manuscript Submission

When a manuscript is received in the editor's office, the editor assigns the manuscript a number and, usually within 48 hours, sends an acknowledgment of receipt to the author. (See chapter 6 for the APA publication process.)

5.05 Interim Correspondence

While a manuscript is under consideration, you should inform the editor of any substantive corrections needed, any change of address, and so forth. In all correspondence, include the complete manuscript title, the authors' names, and the manuscript number.

5.06 Copyright Transfer

When a manuscript is accepted for publication (see chapter 6 on APA's publication policies and process), the journal editor sends to the author a copyright transfer form, by which an author transfers the copyright on the published article to APA or specifies that the work was done under United States government contract and is therefore in the public domain. An article will not be published until the editor receives the signed copyright transfer form. APA owns the copyright for 28 years on pre-1978 APA journal articles and for 75 years on subsequent articles. After these time periods, the articles are placed in the public domain.

5.07 Future Correspondence

The journal editor sends manuscripts accepted for publication to the APA journal office for copy editing and production. Correspondence about copy editing of the manuscript, proofs, and other production matters should be sent to the Production Editor, in care of the particular journal, American Psychological Association, 1400 North Uhle Street, Arlington, Virginia 22201. Send correspondence concerning necessary substantive changes to the journal editor. Send address changes to both the journal editor and the APA journal office. In all correspondence, include the complete article title, authors' names, journal name, and manuscript number.

Reviewing the Copy-Edited Manuscript

Both journal editors and copy editors introduce changes in manuscripts to correct errors of form, to achieve consistency with APA style, or to clarify expression. After copy editing, APA usually sends the manuscript back to you, the author, for a review of the editing. You should answer the copy editor's queries or indicate changes to the manuscript neatly in the margins of the manuscript or on the tags attached to the manuscript, using **black pencil only**; detail long responses or changes in a cover letter. Substantive changes must be approved by the journal editor. Do not mark the manuscript

FIGURE 10

Proofreader's Marks

Authors, editors, and printers use proofreader's marks to indicate changes on print-ed proofs. These standard marks are used in pairs, one in the text where the change is to be made and one in the margin closest to the change.

Mark in the margin	Mark in typeset text
ℐ	delete; take it out
◡	close up; print as one word
ℐ	delete and close up
a word	caret; insert here
#	insert a space
eq.#	space evenly where indicated
stet	let marked text stand as set
tr	transpose; change order the
/	used to separate two or more marginal marks and often as a concluding stroke after the final of several marginal marks
⊏	set farther to the left
⊐	set farther to the right
‖	align on margin
⊗	imperfect or broken character
□	indent
¶	begin a new paragraph
sp	spell out (set 2 as two)
ok/?	the printer will underline or circle a typeset word (or words) to alert the author that the copy may be incorrect but has been set as typed on the manuscript
cap	set in capitals (CAPITALS)
lc	set in Lowercase (lowercase)
ital	set in italic (*italic*)
rom	set in *roman* (roman)
bf	set in boldface (**boldface**)
/=/	insert hyphen (self imposed)
∨	superscript (2 as in χ^2)
∧	subscript (2 as in H_2O)
◇	centered (for a centered dot in $p \cdot q$)
∧	insert comma (yes whereas)
∨	insert apostrophe (editors)
⊙	insert period (end Then)
;	insert semicolon (this in)
:	insert colon (Tests Part 1)
⌣/⌣	insert quotation marks (less than comparative)
(/)	insert parentheses only two
[/]	insert brackets (these 12 subjects)

From *Webster's New Collegiate Dictionary*, 1981, Springfield, MA: Merriam-Webster Inc. Copyright 1981 by Merriam-Webster Inc., publisher of the Merriam-Webster® dictionaries. Adapted by permission.

text in response to a query and do not erase the copy editor's marks because such changes often result in typesetting errors. Instead, the copy editor will transfer your changes from the margins, tags, or cover letter to the manuscript.

Take the time to review the edited manuscript carefully. The printer will typeset the manuscript as edited. All changes made later to the typeset proof for a reason other than making the proof agree with the edited manuscript are charged to you as author's alterations (see section 5.09).

It is important to return the copy-edited manuscript to the APA journal office within 48 hours so that the manuscript can be sent to the printer on schedule. Delays in returning the manuscript can result in delayed publication.

Proofreading

5.08 Reading Proofs

After a manuscript is set in type, the printer sends you the manuscript and two sets of typeset proofs (an original proof to read, correct, and return to APA and a duplicate for your files).

First, familiarize yourself with the proofreader's marks in Figure 10 and use them when marking corrections on the page proofs of your article (see Figure 11).

Second, give the printed proofs a literal reading to catch typographical errors. Another person (a copyholder) should read the manuscript aloud slowly while you read the proof. The copyholder should spell out complicated terms letter by letter and call out punctuation to catch all deviations from the manuscript. If there is no copyholder, proofread by reading word for word from the manuscript to the proof.

Limit changes on these printed proofs to corrections of printer's errors and to updates of reference citations or addresses. This is not the time to rewrite the text. Changes that reflect preferences in wording should have been made at the time the edited manuscript was reviewed.

Third, check specific points:
* Are all copy editor's and printer's queries fully answered?
* Are all numbers in text, tables, and mathematical and statistical copy correct?
* Are tables and figures correct? Do they carry correct captions and numbers?

5.09 Author's Alterations

The purpose of proofreading is to make the printed page similar to the edited manuscript. A change made on the proof for a reason other than achieving agreement with the manuscript is an author's alteration. All changes at the proof stage that result from your own error, omission, or failure to review the edited manuscript are charged to you as author's alterations; such charges include changing the edited version at the proofreading stage to reinstate the wording before editing.

The cost of author's alterations is computed according to the number of printed lines and pages affected by a change, and such

FIGURE 11

Marking Proofs

Sample of a Proof Marked for Correction

Make all marks in black pencil only (never in ink or colored pencil). Mark all corrections on the proofs; never alter the manuscript when correcting proofs. Because the original proofs are used by the Printer, mark neatly, using conventional proofreader's marks (see Figure 10. When you find an error, make two marks, one in the text in the exact plce where the correction is to be made and one in the margin next to the line in which the error occurs. Together the marks show exactly what is to be done. In the margin, circle words or abbreviations that are instructions. Do not circle words that new copy and do not circle symbols. For more than one correction in a single line, markthe corrections from left to right in the nearest margin and separate them by a slanted line (/) for clarity. do not try to squeeze corrections between the printed lines. Include any special instructions or questions in accompanying letter; do Not write them on the proofs.

Sample of a Corrected Proof

Make all marks in **black pencil only** (never in ink or in colored pencil). Mark all corrections on the proofs; never alter the manuscript when correcting proofs. Because the original proofs are used by the printer, mark them neatly, using conventional proofreader's marks (see Figure 10). When you find an error, make two marks, one in the text in the exact place where the correction is to be made and one in the margin next to the line in which the error occurs. Together the marks show exactly what is to be done. In the margin, circle words or abbreviations that are instructions. Do not circle words that are new copy and do not circle symbols. For more than one correction in a single line, mark the corrections from left to right in the nearest margin and separate them by a slanted line (/) for clarity. Do not try to squeeze corrections between the printed lines. Include any special instructions or questions in an accompanying letter; do *not* write them on the proofs.

alterations are costly. For example, the insertion or deletion of a single word may involve resetting several lines and remaking several pages. When a change on the proofs is essential, you should plan the alteration to minimize cost and confusion. For example, count the number of characters and spaces to be removed and make an insertion that will use as nearly as possible the same number of characters and spaces. Type or print all changes clearly in the margin of the proof or, if the changes are long, on a separate sheet attached to the proof. Indicate clearly on the proof where the correction is to be inserted. Any change in a figure means that you need to arrange to have the figure redrawn and to submit a new glossy print of the figure. Because the printer must remake the negative of the figure, corrections to figures are especially costly. If you make extensive additions or deletions on the proof, the journal editor must approve the changes. Numerous author's alterations not only are costly but also can cause delays in publication and often lead to new errors. You can easily avoid alteration charges if you carefully review the edited manuscript before it is typeset.

5.10 Returning Proofs and Manuscript

Copy all corrections on the original proofs onto your duplicate proofs (or make a photocopy of the corrected proofs) and retain the duplicate proofs for reference. Mail the original proofs *and the manuscript* within 48 hours to the Production Editor, in care of the particular journal, American Psychological Association, 1400 North Uhle Street, Arlington, Virginia 22201. If you do not return proofs promptly, publication may be delayed.

5.11 Reprints

You may order reprints of your article from the printer. A reprint order form is sent when your proofs are mailed to you. To obtain any reprints, you must return the completed form *to the printer* when you return the proofs and the original manuscript *to APA*. Reprint rates vary according to the length of the article and the number of copies ordered. Reprints are usually delivered 6–8 weeks after publication of the article. Problems with reprint orders should be referred to the Managing Editor of APA's journal office.

Authors who publish articles in APA journals are permitted to reproduce their own articles for personal use without obtaining permission from APA as long as the material incorporates the copyright notice that appears on the original publication. Reproduction of your own articles for other than personal use requires written permission from APA. (See section 6.06 for more information on permission to reproduce APA-copyrighted material.)

After the Article Is Published

5.12 Retaining Raw Data

It is traditional in scientific publication to retain data, instructions, details of procedure, and analyses so that copies may be made available in response to inquiries from interested readers. Therefore, you are encouraged to retain these materials for a minimum of 5 years after your article has been published.

5.13 Correction Notices

From time to time, errors occur in published journal articles. The APA is not obligated to publish corrections for minor errors, but it will publish a correction promptly when an important piece of information in a journal article is incorrect, misleading, incomprehensible, or omitted. The decision to publish a correction rests with the journal editor unless the error is typographical, in which case the APA journal office and the journal editor determine whether a published correction is warranted.

If you detect an error in your published article and think that a correction notice is required, submit a proposed correction notice to the journal editor. The notice should contain the following elements: (a) full journal title and year, volume number, issue number, and inclusive page numbers of the article being corrected; (b) complete article title and names of all authors, exactly as they appear in the published article; (c) precise location of the error (e.g., page, column, line); (d) exact quotation of the error or, in the case of lengthy errors or an error in a table or figure, an accurate paraphrasing of the error; and (e) concise, unambiguous wording of the correction. Because it is not the purpose of corrections to place blame for mistakes, correction notices do not identify the source of the error.

The cost of typesetting a notice to correct your own error is charged to you as an author's alteration. Such a notice can be expensive, particularly if the correction requires the resetting of tables or the reshooting of figures. You are more likely to avoid the kinds of errors requiring a correction notice if you carefully prepare the manuscript, carefully review the copy-edited manuscript, and carefully review the article proofs.

6 Journal Program of the American Psychological Association

The American Psychological Association, founded in 1892 and incorporated in 1925, is the major organization of psychologists in the United States. More than 54,000 psychologists are members. The purpose of the APA is to advance psychology as a science, as a profession, and as a means of promoting human welfare. One way the APA accomplishes this purpose is by disseminating psychological information through its publication program, of which scholarly journals are a major component.

Policies Governing the Journals

The policies and practices of the APA journals are based on formal actions of APA's governing bodies and on informal consensus and tradition. The Association's Bylaws and Rules of Council state general journal policies enacted by APA's Council of Representatives. The Publications and Communications Board is one of several boards reporting to the APA Board of Directors, which in turn reports to the Council of Representatives. The Publications and Communications Board regularly assesses trends in the major areas of psychology and in specific journals and recommends the establishment, modification, or discontinuation of journals. The Council of Editors, a permanent committee established under the Publications and Communications Board, includes the editors of all journals published by the Association. It meets to discuss commonly shared editorial problems and to make recommendations about specific journal policies and practices.

Thus, the Publications and Communications Board and the Council of Editors together establish specific policies for the journals. Journal editors and APA staff concerned with the publication of the journals implement the policies. Editors, operating within the framework of the general policies described in this chapter, select the manuscripts to be published in the journals. The APA staff produces the journals. Authors should review the policies described here for general orientation and also should note specific instructions published in every journal and policies of style and manuscript preparation described in the preceding chapters of the *Manual*.

6.01 Selection of Editors

The Publications and Communications Board appoints the editors of journals on the recommendation of search committees that actively seek nominations of persons who have attained recognition in a journal's special area and are members of APA. Editors normally serve terms of 6 years. The editor appoints the number of associate editors authorized for the journal and selects as many consulting or advisory reviewers and ad hoc reviewers as are needed for the effective functioning of the journal. As many as 3,000 persons may participate each year as editors, associate editors, consulting or advisory reviewers, and ad hoc reviewers.

6.02 Page Allocations

Each year the Publications and Communications Board provides an allotment of printed pages for each of the journals. In making such allocations, the Board considers the number of manuscripts submitted to a journal, the journal's acceptance rate and publication lag, the availability of other publication outlets, and the potential loss to psychology from delays in publication or from rejection of manuscripts caused by restrictions on the journal's page allocation. The Board requires each editor to adhere to the journal's page allocation and to keep publication lag from being unduly long.

6.03 Publication Lag

The interval between the date an acceptable manuscript is received in an editor's office and the date the manuscript is published is the publication lag. The publication lag varies from journal to journal but normally does not exceed 12 months. The publication lag of each of the journals is given in the Summary Report of Journal Operations, which appears each year in the June issue of the *American Psychologist*.

6.04 Primary Publication

Members of the scientific community generally agree that the characteristics of primary, or original, publication are (a) that articles represent research not previously published (i.e., first disclosure); (b) that articles are reviewed by peers before being accepted or rejected by a journal; and (c) that articles are archival (i.e., retrievable for future reference). (Also see Day, 1980, "Keeping Primary Publication Primary.")

Like a wall that is built one brick at a time, the peer-reviewed literature in a field is built by single contributions that together represent the accumulated knowledge of a field. Each contribution must fill a place that before was empty, and each contribution must be sturdy enough to bear the weight of contributions to come. To ensure the quality of each contribution—that the work is original, valid, and significant—authorities in the subspecialities of a field carefully review submitted manuscripts. The peer-reviewed journals in which the literature is preserved thus serve as "journals of record, that is, authoritative sources of information in their field" (Orne, 1981, p. 3). In the APA primary journals, the standard of primary publication is supported by the peer-review system and protected by policies that prohibit multiple submission and duplicate publication.

Multiple submission. An author must not submit the same manuscript for concurrent consideration by two or more journals. If a manuscript is rejected by one journal, an author may then submit it to another. Before resubmitting a rejected manuscript, however, an author is expected to revise it according to the editor's suggestions.

Duplicate publication. An author must not submit to an APA primary journal a manuscript that has been published in whole or in substantial part in another journal or in any readily available work, in English or in another language. This policy does not necessarily exclude articles previously published in summarized or abstracted form (e.g., in the proceedings of an annual meeting) or in a periodical with limited circulation or availability (e.g., in a report by a university department or by a government agency). The policy does exclude articles that have appeared in a publication that has been offered for public sale; such a publication does not meet the criterion of "limited circulation." Therefore, the author must inform an editor of the existence of any similar manuscripts that have already been published or that may be submitted for concurrent consideration to the same journal or to another journal.

Whether the publication of two or more reports based on the same or on closely related research constitutes duplicate publication is a matter of editorial judgment. Substantial overlap in material submitted to the same or to different journals may render a manuscript unacceptable. Problems of duplicate publication may arise when material is published simultaneously in a popular journal or magazine and in a scientific journal or when publication in a popular form precedes publication in a journal. These circumstances, or other ambiguous cases, such as the same or overlapping material published in book chapters, brief reports, and other outlets, should be reported to the editor of the journal to which the material is to be submitted. If, during the review or production process, a manuscript is discovered to be in violation of duplicate publication policies and the author has failed to inform the editor of the possible violation, then the manuscript is rejected without further consideration. (Publication of a brief report in an APA journal is with the understanding that a more extended report will not be published.)

Piecemeal publication of several reports of the results from a single data base is undesirable and may be judged as duplicate publication. APA editors encourage the submission of articles that integrate several research studies and that consider broad implications of results, although many journal editors also accept reports of single studies. An author who wishes to divide the report of a study into more than one article should inform the editor before preparing the articles or, if the articles are already prepared, submit all the articles at the same time to the editor. Repeated publication from a longitudinal study may be justified if the data from different times justify further publication, but descriptions of the nature of the study and its design and methods should not be repeated.

6.05 Author's Copyright on an Unpublished Manuscript

Authors are protected by federal statute against unauthorized use of their unpublished manuscripts. Under the Copyright Act of 1976 (title 17 of the United States Code), an unpublished work is copyrighted from the moment it is fixed in tangible form, for example, typed on a page. Copyright protection is "an incident of the process of authorship" (U.S. Copyright Office, 1981, p. 3). Until the author formally transfers copyright (see section 5.06), the author owns the copyright on an unpublished manuscript, and all exclusive rights due the owner of the copyright of a published work are also due the author of an unpublished work.

An author need not register the copyright to secure copyright protection. However, registration is usually a prerequisite for any legal action and does provide a public record of the copyright. Nor need an author affix the notice of copyright to unpublished works, although the notice must appear on published works.

Editorial review of a manuscript requires that the editors and reviewers circulate and discuss the manuscript. When submitting a manuscript to an APA journal, an author implicitly consents to the handling necessary for review of the manuscript. However, editors and reviewers may not, without the author's explicit permission, quote from a manuscript or circulate copies for any purpose other than that of editorial review. In addition, editors and reviewers may not use the material from an unpublished manuscript to advance their own or others' work without the author's consent. Suspected infringements of the author's copyright on a manuscript submitted to an APA journal should be referred to the Chair of the APA Publications and Communications Board.

6.06   Copyright and Permission to Reproduce APA Material

APA owns the copyright on material published in its journals (see section 5.06 on the author's transfer of copyright to APA). Therefore, authors who wish to reproduce an APA article in full, to quote text of more than 500 words, or to copy two or more tables or figures must secure written permission from APA and from the author of the reproduced material. APA normally grants permission contingent upon permission by the author, inclusion of the APA copyright notice on the first page of reproduced material, and payment of a per-page fee. Requests for permission to reproduce material should be directed to APA's Permissions Office.

APA requires no written permission or fees when
- authors reproduce a *single* table or figure from an article, provided that the author's permission is obtained and that full credit is given to the author and to APA as copyright holder through a complete and accurate citation;
- authors reproduce their own material for personal use (e.g., to prepare reprints); however, if they use their own material commercially, authors must secure prior written permission from APA;
- instructors and educational institutions photocopy isolated articles for nonprofit classroom or library reserve use; and
- abstracting and information services use abstracts.

Libraries are permitted to photocopy beyond the limits of U.S. copyright law provided that the per-copy fee is paid through the Copyright Clearance Center, 21 Congress Street, Salem, Massachusetts 01970.

6.07   Other Copyrighted Material

Material copyrighted by sources other than APA. Copyright policies vary among publishers. Authors submitting manuscripts to APA who wish to reproduce material from non-APA-copyrighted sources must contact the copyright holders (usually the publishers) to determine their requirements.

Permission. It is the author's responsibility (a) to obtain letters of permission from copyright holders to reproduce copyrighted material and (b) to enclose copies of these letters with the submitted manuscript. The author must acknowledge the copyright holder in a note that accompanies the reproduced material (see section 3.69 for format).

Editorial Management of Manuscripts

6.08   Editorial Responsibilities

The *editor* of each journal is responsible for the quality and content of the journal within the framework of the policies and rules of procedure established for the journals by the APA. An *associate editor* of a journal assists the editor in the editorial management of the journal and usually has responsibility for a specific content area of the journal or for a portion of the manuscripts submitted to the journal. An associate editor may act as editor in all stages of the consideration of a manuscript, including communication with an author regarding acceptance, rejection, or required revision of a manuscript. *Consulting* and *advisory reviewers* and *ad hoc reviewers* review manuscripts and make recommendations to editors or to associate editors concerning the disposition of manuscripts.

The *managing editor, production supervisors,* and *production editors* (also called *copy editors*) are on the staff of the APA Central Office. They copy edit, proofread, and manage the production of APA journals.

6.09 Date of Receipt of Manuscripts

When a manuscript is received in an editor's office, its date of receipt is noted, and, usually within 48 hours, the editor sends an acknowledgment of its receipt to the author. The date that an accepted manuscript is originally received in the editor's office appears with the printed article. Most articles now carry a second date (i.e., the "revision received" date), the date on which an acceptable revision of the manuscript is received. When an article carries two receipt dates (i.e., receipt of the original manuscript and receipt of the acceptable revision), publication lag is calculated from the date of the receipt of the revision. The *American Psychologist* and *Contemporary Psychology* do not publish receipt dates.

6.10 Order of Publication of Articles

Most APA editors publish articles in the order of their receipt. However, editors may (a) advance or delay publication of an article for the purpose of assembling issues on related topics or (b) advance publication of an article for reasons such as timeliness (e.g., brief articles of comment and rejoinder) or importance of material. The APA staff may, with the editor's knowledge, advance or delay publication of an article in the interest of making up an issue with the most economical number of pages determined by printing requirements.

The order of publication of articles in the *American Psychologist* is determined by the requirements of official APA documents and by the necessity for timely publication of certain reports and articles.

6.11 Procedures in Editorial Review

After the editor has acknowledged the receipt of a manuscript, the manuscript is reviewed (see Figure 12 on the APA publication process). By submitting a manuscript to an APA journal, an author implicitly consents to the circulation of copies and to the discussion of the manuscript that are necessary for editorial review. The editor may accept or reject a manuscript outright, that is, before its review by an associate editor or by reviewers. Most of the time, however, the editor sends the manuscript to an associate editor or to reviewers. Editors and associate editors usually send manuscripts to two reviewers, sometimes to more than two. Some editors routinely use a

FIGURE 12

The APA Publication Process

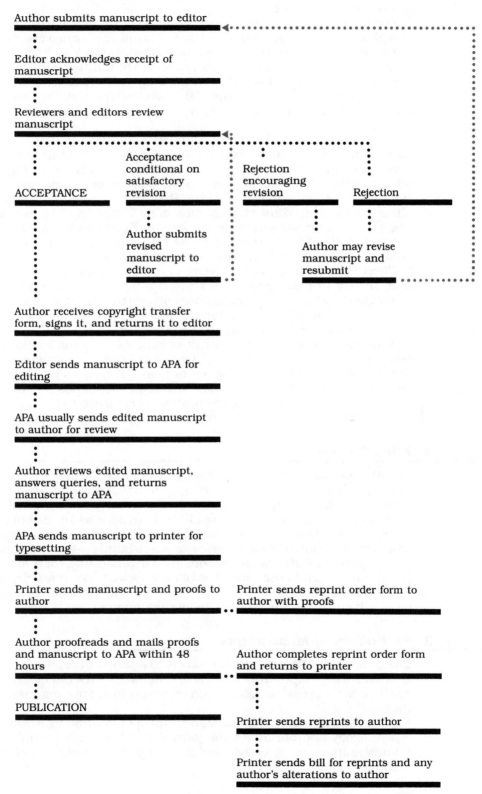

system of blind review; others use blind review at the author's request (see section 6.12).

The period of review can vary, depending both on the length and complexity of the manuscript and on the number of reviewers asked to evaluate it; but the review process typically takes 2 to 3 months. After 2 or 3 months, the author can expect to be notified either of the action taken on the manuscript or, if a delay occurs before or during the review process, of the status of the manuscript. If not notified in 3 months, the author may appropriately contact the editor for information.

Reviewers provide the editor with an evaluation of the manuscript's quality and appropriateness for the journal. The decision to accept a manuscript, to reject it, or to ask for revision is the responsibility of the editor (or, in some cases, of an associate editor); and the editor's decision may differ from the recommendation of any or all reviewers. The editor may accept a manuscript on the condition that the author make satisfactory revisions. Such conditional acceptances may involve, for example, reanalysis, reinterpretation, or correction of flaws in presentation and organization.

When necessary revisions involve correcting basic flaws in content, the editor may reject the manuscript but invite resubmission of a revised manuscript. If the author chooses to submit a revision of a previously rejected manuscript, the revised manuscript is treated as a new manuscript and requires new review.

If the editor rejects a manuscript or returns it to the author for revision, the editor explains why the manuscript is rejected or why the revisions are required. The editor does not have to provide the reviewer's comments to the author but frequently chooses to do so.

If a manuscript is rejected, the original is returned to the author, the journal editor retains one copy, and other copies are destroyed.

6.12 Blind Review

The APA journal editors, either routinely or at the author's request, may use blind review. Blind review requires that the identity of the author of a manuscript be concealed from reviewers during the review process. Authors should read the Instructions to Authors, a statement published in every issue of every journal, to determine whether a journal uses blind review or offers blind review to authors who request it. Authors are responsible for concealing their identities in manuscripts that are to be blind reviewed: For example, author identification notes must be typed on the manuscript's title page, which the editor removes before the manuscript is reviewed.

6.13 Evaluation of Manuscripts

The goal of the APA primary journals is to publish information that is "*new, true, important,* and *comprehensible*" (DeBakey, 1976, p. 30). For this reason, editors and reviewers look for a manuscript that

- makes an original, valid, and significant contribution to an area of psychology appropriate to the journal to which it is submitted;
- conveys its message clearly and as briefly as its content permits; and

- is in a form that maintains the integrity of the style described in the *Publication Manual*.

A manuscript that does not meet the first criterion is rejected. A manuscript that does not fully meet the second criterion but is otherwise acceptable is returned to the author for revision prior to further editorial consideration. A manuscript that does not meet the third criterion may be returned for revision prior to any editorial consideration. Some specific questions that may help the author assess the quality of a manuscript against these general criteria are given in the sections on quality of content and quality of presentation in chapter 1.

Most manuscripts need to be revised, and some manuscripts need to be revised more than once. Initial revisions of a manuscript may reveal to the author or to the editor and reviewers deficiencies that were not apparent in the original manuscript, and the editor may request further revision to correct these deficiencies. During the review process, an editor may ask an author to supply material that supplements the manuscript (e.g., complex statistical tables, instructions to subjects).

Editors do not undertake the major editorial revision of manuscripts. Authors are expected to follow editors' detailed recommendations for revision, condensation, or correction and retyping in order to conform with the style specified by the *Manual*. Should editors wish to undertake major changes themselves, they will consult the author.

The APA Journals

Since 1925 APA has published scientific journals, acquiring some (by gift, purchase, or merger) and creating others. As the list of journals has grown, the Association has adapted its journal coverage policies to fit the needs occasioned by the growth of psychology as a science and a profession.

The areas of psychology that the journals presently cover are described in the following editorial statements. Familiarity with these statements, as well as with the journals, should help prospective authors choose the appropriate journal for their manuscripts. Because journal policies may change after the publication of the *Manual*, authors should always examine the editorial policy statements and Instructions to Authors in current issues of the journals to become familiar with each journal's specific content and any special instructions. These policy statements and Instructions to Authors refer readers to recently published editorials in which editors may expand or introduce policies.

6.14 Policy Statements on Journal Coverage

The ***American Psychologist*** is the official journal of the American Psychological Association and, as such, contains the Association's archival documents. It also contains articles that (a) inform psychologists and the public about psychology's impact and potential regarding issues and problems facing psychology; (b) identify and discuss trends, issues, and policies that affect the Association; (c) examine the relation between psychology and society; and (d) present the status of substantive areas of psychological knowledge and of diverse applications of psychological knowledge in a form appropriate to the general membership.

Behavioral Neuroscience (formerly contained within the *Journal of Comparative and Physiological Psychology*) contains original research papers in the broad field of the biological bases of behavior. Occasional review articles and theoretical papers are also acceptable for publication if they are judged to make original and important conceptual contributions to the field. Studies covering the entire range of relevant biological and neural sciences, for example, anatomy, chemistry, physiology, endocrinology, and pharmacology, are considered if behavioral variables are measured or manipulated or if the work has relevance to behavior. Studies on the genetic, evolutionary, and developmental aspects of behavior are also appropriate, as are behavioral studies, if they have clear implications for biological processes or mechanisms.

Single-experiment papers are just as acceptable as multiple-experiment papers. Good experimental design, proper controls and procedures, importance or significance, and careful scholarship are the major criteria for acceptance. The journal also contains a "Brief Communications" section of shorter articles.

Contemporary Psychology contains critical reviews of books, films, tapes, and other media relevant to psychology. Material reviewed is intended to present a cross section of psychological literature suitable for a broad readership. *All reviews are written by invitation.* Readers are welcome to submit brief letters commenting on the substance of reviews or on the policies of the journal.

The ***Journal of Abnormal Psychology*** contains articles of research and theory on abnormal behavior, its determinants, and its correlates. The following general topics fall within its area of major focus: (a) psychopathology, (b) normal processes in abnormal individuals, (c) pathological or atypical behavior in normal persons, (d) experimental studies on disordered emotional behavior or pathology, (e) social or group effects on pathological processes, and (f) tests of hypotheses from psychological theories that relate to abnormal behavior. Each article should increase understanding of abnormal behavior in its etiology, description, or change. The journal also contains a "Short Reports" section of shorter articles. The editor of the *Journal of Abnormal Psychology* considers manuscripts dealing with the etiology or descriptive pathology of abnormal behavior but not articles dealing with diagnosis or treatment of abnormal behavior, which are more appropriate to the *Journal of Consulting and Clinical Psychology*. Articles that appear to have a significant contribution to both of these broad areas may be sent to the editor of either journal for an editorial decision.

The ***Journal of Applied Psychology*** is devoted primarily to original investigations that contribute new knowledge and understanding to any field of applied psychology except clinical psychology. The journal contains quantitative investigations of interest to psychologists doing research or working in such areas as universities, industry, government, urban affairs, police and correctional systems, health and educational institutions, transportation and defense systems, and consumer affairs. A theoretical or review article may be accepted if it represents a special contribution to an applied field. The journal also contains a "Short Notes" section of shorter articles.

The *Journal of Comparative Psychology* (formerly contained within the *Journal of Comparative and Physiological Psychology*) contains laboratory and field studies of the behavioral patterns of various species as they relate to evolution, development, ecology, control, and functional significance. Comparison of the behavioral patterns of different species is appropriate and desirable, but not requisite, for publication. Observations of animals freely behaving in the field and in controlled laboratory studies are given equal status. Applications of behavioral principles are as acceptable as tests of theory. Explanations in terms of adaptation, evolution, ontogenesis, and learning are equally acceptable, as is any method that yields valid empirical information.

The *Journal of Consulting and Clinical Psychology* contains original contributions on the following topics: (a) studies of the development, validity, and use of techniques of diagnosis and treatment in disordered behavior; (b) studies of populations of clinical interest, such as hospital, prison, rehabilitation, geriatric, and similar samples; (c) cross-cultural and demographic studies of interest for the behavioral disorders; (d) studies of personality and of its assessment and development where these have a clear bearing on problems of consulting and clinical psychology; or (e) case studies pertinent to the preceding topics. The journal also contains a "Brief Reports" section of shorter articles. The editor of the *Journal of Consulting and Clinical Psychology* considers articles dealing with the diagnosis or treatment of abnormal behavior but not manuscripts dealing with the etiology or descriptive pathology of abnormal behavior, which are more appropriate to the *Journal of Abnormal Psychology*. Articles that appear to have a significant contribution to both of these broad areas may be sent to the editor of either journal for an editorial decision. Papers of a theoretical nature occasionally will be considered within the space limitations of the journal.

The *Journal of Counseling Psychology* contains articles on counseling of interest to psychologists and counselors in schools, colleges, universities, private and public counseling agencies, and commercial, industrial, religious, and military settings. Particular attention is given to articles reporting the results of empirical studies about counseling processes and interventions, theoretical articles about counseling, and studies dealing with the evaluation of applications of counseling and counseling programs. Also considered are studies on the selection and training of counselors, the development of counseling materials and methods, and applications of counseling to special populations and problem areas. Also published occasionally are topical reviews of research and other systematic surveys, as well as research methodology studies directly related to counseling. The journal also contains a "Brief Reports" section of shorter articles.

Developmental Psychology contains articles that advance knowledge and theory about human development across the life span. Although most papers address directly the issues of human development, studies on other species are appropriate if they have important implications for human development. The journal includes significant empirical contributions to the study of growth and development and, occasionally, scholarly reviews, theoretical articles, and social policy papers. Studies of any variables that affect human psychological development—whether proximal or distal causes or whether efficient, final, or formal causes—are considered. In the case of laboratory experimental studies, preference is given to reports of series of studies, and the external validity of such studies is a major consideration. Field research, cross-cultural studies, and research on socially important topics are especially welcome.

The *Journal of Educational Psychology* contains original investigations and theoretical papers dealing with learning and cognition, especially as they relate to problems of instruction, and with the psychological development, relationships, and adjustment of the individual. Journal articles pertain to all levels of education and to all age groups.

The *Journal of Experimental Psychology: General* contains articles in any area of experimental psychology when the articles involve a longer, more integrative report than the usual journal article, leading to an advance in knowledge that is judged to be of interest to the entire community of experimental psychologists. The journal includes articles such as those that have appeared as *Journal of Experimental Psychology* monographs and as chapters in contemporary books of "advances." Republishing a limited number of data may be permitted if the data are necessary to make the article complete and definitive.

The *Journal of Experimental Psychology: Learning, Memory, and Cognition* contains articles discussing original experimental studies and extensive theory development on fundamental encoding, transfer, memory, and cognitive processes in human behavior. Articles include quantitative models where appropriate. The journal also contains brief articles.

The *Journal of Experimental Psychology: Human Perception and Performance* contains studies of perception, verbal or motor performance, and related cognitive processes. The journal also contains brief articles of commentary and criticism.

The *Journal of Experimental Psychology: Animal Behavior Processes* contains experimental studies that contribute significantly to the understanding of learning, memory, perception, motivation, and performance, especially as revealed in the behavior of nonhuman animals.

The *Journal of Personality and Social Psychology* contains original papers in all areas of personality and social psychology. Although empirical reports are emphasized, specialized theoretical, methodological, and review papers may be included. The journal is divided into three independently edited sections:

Attitudes and Social Cognition includes papers on attitudes dealing with such topics as the formation or change of beliefs and attitudes, measurement of attitudes, and the relation between attitudes and behavior. Papers on social cognition deal with the formation and utilization of knowledge about the social world and embrace such topics as social and person perception, attributional processes, and information processing.

Interpersonal Relations and Group Processes contains articles that focus on the interaction between two or more people. Included in this section are papers on group structure, helping and aggression, group decision making and task performance, leadership, cooperation and competition, in-group/out-group relations, and the like.

Personality Processes and Individual Differences contains papers on all aspects of personality psychology as traditionally defined. These aspects include personality assessment, measurement, structure, and dynamics. The editor considers all methodological approaches.

Professional Psychology: Research and Practice (formerly titled *Professional Psychology*) contains articles on the application of psychology, including the scientific underpinnings of the profession. Both data-based and theoretical articles on techniques and practices used in the application of psychology are included. Appropriate topics include research and theory on public policy as it affects the practice of psychology; current advances in applications from such fields as health psychology, community psychology, clinical neuropsychology, family psychology, and forensic psychology; standards of professional practice and delivery of services in a variety of contexts; education and training of professional psychologists; and research and theory as they concern the interests of those in the practice of psychology.

Psychological Bulletin contains evaluative and integrative reviews and interpretations of substantive and methodological issues in scientific psychology. Original research is reported only for illustrative purposes. *Substantive Contributions*: Integrative reviews that summarize a body of literature may set forth major developments within a particular research area or provide a bridge between related specialized fields within psychology or between psychology and related fields. In all cases, reviews that develop connections between areas of research are particularly valuable. Expository articles may be published if they are deemed accurate, broad, clear, and pertinent. Articles should aim at a broad range of psychologists. *Methodological Contributions*: Descriptions of quantitative methods and research designs, whether expository or critical, should be clear and understandable to a wide range of research psychologists for whom they are pertinent. Articles on broadly applicable methods are encouraged, but the range of application and any limitations should be carefully spelled out.

Original theoretical articles should be submitted to the editor of the *Psychological Review*, even when they include reviews of research literature. Literature reviews should be submitted to the editor of the *Bulletin*, however, even when they develop an integrated theoretical statement.

Psychological Review contains articles that make theoretical contributions to any area of scientific psychology. Preference is given to papers that advance theory rather than review it and to statements that are specifically theoretical rather than programmatic. Papers that point up critical flaws in existing theory or demonstrate the superiority of one theory over another are also considered. Papers devoted primarily to surveys of the literature, problems of method and design, or reports of empirical findings ordinarily are not appropriate. However, discussions of previously published articles are considered for publication as Theoretical Notes on the basis of the scientific contribution represented.

Journal-Related Periodicals

APA publishes periodicals in addition to its journals. These journal-related periodicals are briefly described here.

Psychological Abstracts Information Services (PsycINFO) publishes periodicals and other specialized products, maintains the PsycINFO Database of abstracts, and provides searches of its database. The PsycINFO products and services are briefly described here.

Psychological Abstracts is a periodical of nonevaluative abstracts of the world's literature in psychology and related disciplines. In addition to the monthly publication of abstracts, PsycINFO publishes semiannual volume indexes and 3-year cumulative indexes of *Psychological Abstracts*. Since 1967, the abstracts published in *Psychological Abstracts*, as well as some material that does not appear in *Psychological Abstracts*, have been entered in the PsycINFO Database and have been made available on machine-readable tapes. PsycINFO provides customized computerized literature searches of the PsycINFO Database, a service called PASAR (PsycINFO Assisted Search and Retrieval). Vendors who obtain PsycINFO's tapes through a lease or license also offer automated search and retrieval services.

The *PsycSCAN* series comprises quarterly publications of abstracts in a specific area: In 1982, four PsycSCANs were published, one each in the areas of applied, clinical, and developmental psychology and one in the area of learning and communication disorders/mental retardation. All items printed in the PsycSCAN publications have appeared previously in *Psychological Abstracts*, and therefore they also appear in the PsycINFO Database. Future PsycSCANs are anticipated in other areas of psychology. (For further information, contact APA's PsycINFO Division.)

Other PsycINFO specialized printed products include the *Thesaurus of Psychological Index Terms* and the *PsycINFO Psychological Abstracts Information Services Users Reference Manual*.

Psychological Documents (formerly titled the Journal Supplement Abstract Service [JSAS] and the JSAS *Catalog of Selected Documents in Psychology*) combines characteristics of informal communication networks and conventional journals. It is a catalog of synopses of manuscripts that have been reviewed and accepted in the customary way and an on-demand publication service, by which readers can order full-text copies of accepted documents in microfiche or hard copy.

Original, previously unpublished materials of all types, formats, lengths, and psychological content are appropriate for submission, for example, educational materials, massive data collections, methodological techniques and procedures, major projects in progress, descriptions of effective techniques or programs, technical reports, fresh looks at controversial issues, invited lectures, demands on psychology, management of psychological resources, APA task force reports, bibliographies, information on psychology and public policy, literature review, well-designed studies that are "near replications," and well-designed studies with negative results.

Printed with each synopsis in the catalog is a notation of document length, price per copy, and receipt date. See a recent issue of the *Psychological Documents* catalog for manuscript submission requirements.

The **APA Monitor** is the monthly newspaper of the Association. It contains nonarchival news stories about psychology and current APA activities. It also contains news about government and legislative activities relating to psychological issues as well as current listings of employment opportunities and professional meetings.

7 Bibliography

The bibliography is in three sections: The first section, which gives the historical background of the APA Publication Manual, *lists the predecessors of this edition in chronological order. The second section is an alphabetical listing of all references cited in the* Manual. *The third section, which is subdivided and annotated, suggests further reading.*

7.01 History of the *Publication Manual*

Instructions in regard to preparation of manuscript. (1929). *Psychological Bulletin, 26*, 57–63.

Anderson, J. E., & Valentine, W. L. (1944). The preparation of articles for publication in the journals of the American Psychological Association. *Psychological Bulletin, 41*, 345–376.

American Psychological Association, Council of Editors. (1952). Publication manual of the American Psychological Association [Supplement]. *Psychological Bulletin, 49*, 389–449.

American Psychological Association, Council of Editors. (1957). *Publication manual of the American Psychological Association* (rev. ed.). Washington, DC: Author.

American Psychological Association. (1967). *Publication manual of the American Psychological Association* (rev. ed.). Washington, DC: Author.

American Psychological Association. (1974). *Publication manual of the American Psychological Association* (2nd ed.). Washington, DC: Author.

7.02 References Cited in This Edition

American Psychological Association. (1981). Ethical principles of psychologists (revised). *American Psychologist, 36*, 633–638. (This is a 1981 revision of the *Ethical Standards of Psychologists*, and reprints can be ordered from APA's Order Department.)

Bartol, K. M. (1981, August). *Survey results from editorial board members: Lethal and nonlethal errors.* Paper presented at the meeting of the American Psychological Association, Los Angeles, CA.

Bass, B. M. (1979). Confessions of a former male chauvinist. *American Psychologist, 34*, 194–195.

Bruner, K. F. (1942). Of psychological writing: Being some vale-dictory remarks on style. *Journal of Abnormal and Social Psychology, 37*, 52–70.

Day, R. A. (1980). Keeping primary publication primary. *CBE Views, 3*, 4–8.

DeBakey, L. (1976). *The scientific journal: Editorial policies and practices.* St. Louis, MO: Mosby.

Ehrenberg, A. S. C. (1977). Rudiments of numeracy. *Journal of the Royal Statistical Society A, 140*(Part 3), 277–297.

Holt, R. R. (1959). Researchmanship or how to write a dissertation in clinical psychology without really trying. *American Psychologist, 14*, 151.

Instructions in regard to preparation of manuscript. (1929). *Psychological Bulletin, 26*, 57–63.

Lasiter, P. S., & Glanzman, D. L. (1982). Cortical substrates of taste aversion learning: Dorsal prepiriform (insular) lesions disrupt taste aversion learning. *Journal of Comparative and Physiological Psychology, 96*, 376–392.

Maher, B. A. (1974). Editorial. *Journal of Consulting and Clinical Psychology, 42*, 1–3.

McCall, R. B. (1981, September). *Writing strategy and style.* Unpublished manuscript.

Mendelson, M. J., Haith, M. M., & Goldman-Rakic, P. S. (1982). Face scanning and responsiveness to social cues in infant rhesus monkeys. *Developmental Psychology, 18*, 222–228.

Mullins, C. J. (1977). *A guide to writing and publishing in the social and behavorial sciences.* New York: Wiley.

National Bureau of Standards. (1979, December). Guidelines for use of the modernized metric system. *Dimensions/NBS*, pp. 13–19.

Orne, M. T. (1981). The why and how of a contribution to the literature: A brief communication. *International Journal of Clinical and Experimental Hypnosis, 29*, 1–4.

Poizner, H., Bellugi, U., & Tweney, R. D. (1981). Processing of formational, semantic, and iconic information in American Sign Language. *Journal of Experimental Psychology: Human Perception and Performance, 7*, 1146–1159.

Polyson, J., Levinson, M., & Miller, H. (1982). Writing styles: A survey of psychology journal editors. *American Psychologist, 37*, 335–338.

PsycINFO Psychological Abstracts Information Services Users Reference Manual. (1981). Washington, DC: American Psychological Association.

Reisman, S. J. (Ed.). (1962). *A style manual for technical writers and editors.* New York: Macmillan.

Salthouse, T. A., Ellis, C. L., Diener, D. C., & Somberg, B. L. (1981). Stimulus processing during eye fixations. *Journal of Experimental Psychology: Human Perception and Performance, 7*, 611–623.

Schlosberg, H. (1965). Hints on presenting a paper at an APA convention. *American Psychologist, 20,* 606–607.

Skillin, M. E., & Gay, R. M. (1974). *Words into type* (3rd ed.). Englewood Cliffs, NJ: Prentice-Hall.

A uniform system of citation (13th ed.). (1981). Cambridge, MA: Harvard Law Review Association.

University of Chicago Press. (1982). *The Chicago manual of style* (13th ed., rev.). Chicago: Author.

U.S. Copyright Office. (1981). *Circular R1: Copyright basics* (Publication No. 341–279/106). Washington, DC: U.S. Government Printing Office.

Webster's new collegiate dictionary (8th ed.). (1981). Springfield, MA: Merriam-Webster.

Webster's third new international dictionary, unabridged: The great library of the English language. (1976). Springfield, MA: Merriam-Webster.

Woodside, B., Leon, M., Attard, M., Feder, H. H., Siegel, H. I., & Fischette, C. (1981). Prolactin-steroid influences on the thermal basis for mother–young contact in Norway rats. *Journal of Comparative and Physiological Psychology, 95,* 771–780.

7.03   Suggested Reading

General

American National Standard for the preparation of scientific papers for written or oral presentation (ANSI Z39.16-1979). (1979). New York: American National Standards Institute. (Available from American National Standards Institute, Inc., 1430 Broadway, New York, NY 10018)

Official standard of the American National Standards Institute; outlines specific guidelines for the preparation of scientific articles for publication.

Day, R. A. (1979). *How to write and publish a scientific paper.* Philadelphia, PA: ISI Press.

Provides complete instructions for the writing, preparation, and submission of manuscripts for publication.

Skillin, M. E., & Gay, R. M. (1974). *Words into type* (3rd ed.). Englewood Cliffs, NJ: Prentice-Hall.

Detailed guide to the preparation of manuscripts, the handling of copy and proofs, copy-editing style, typographical style, grammar and word usage, and typography and illustration.

University of Chicago Press. (1982). *The Chicago manual of style* (13th ed., rev.). Chicago: Author.

A standard reference for authors, editors, printers, and proofreaders that provides clear and simple guidelines for preparing and editing copy. Discusses the technicalities of preparing copy, such as mathematical material, for scientific publication.

..

Parts of a Manuscript

Cremmins, E. T. (1982). *The art of abstracting.* Philadelphia, PA: ISI Press.
Describes in detail how to create an abstract; focuses on the cognitive skills used, that is, reading, thinking, writing, and editing.

Writing Style

Bates, J. D. (1980). *Writing with precision: How to write so that you cannot possibly be misunderstood* (3rd ed.). Washington, DC: Acropolis Books.
Discusses the principles of clear, effective writing; offers help on preparing and writing specific kinds of material, such as letters, memoranda, and reports.

Bernstein, T. M. (1971). *Miss Thistlebottom's hobgoblins.* New York: Farrar, Strauss & Giroux.
Subtitled as "the careful writer's guide to the taboos, bugbears, and outmoded rules of English usage."

Boring, E. G. (1957). CP speaks . . . . *Contemporary Psychology, 2,* 279.
An editorial on psychologists and good writing by the first editor of *Contemporary Psychology.*

Copperud, R. H. (1980). *American usage and style: The consensus.* New York: Van Nostrand Reinhold.
Compares the judgments of leading authorities and sources on points of usage and style.

Fowler, H. W. (1965). *A dictionary of modern English usage* (2nd ed.). New York: Oxford University Press.
A classic dictionary of usage; offers detailed information on grammar and style, on spelling and pronunciation, and on punctuation.

Harlow, H. F. (1962). Fundamental principles for preparing psychology journal articles. *Journal of Comparative and Physiological Psychology, 55,* 893–896.
An editor's humorous remarks on the content and style of scientific reporting.

Ross-Larson, B. (1982). *Edit yourself.* New York: Norton.
Shows how to recognize and correct the common problems in writing; describes techniques editors use to make writing clear and clean.

Strunk, W., Jr., & White, E. B. (1979). *The elements of style* (3rd ed.). New York: Macmillan.
A classic that offers concise, clear advice on writing well.

Trimble, J. R. (1975). *Writing with style: Conversations on the art of writing.* Englewood Cliffs, NJ: Prentice-Hall.
Offers informal advice on the fundamentals of writing, on how to begin and how to proceed, and on the importance of clear thinking to clear writing; also offers specific advice on punctuation, quotations, and general usage.

Woodford, F. P. (1967). Sounder thinking through clearer writing. *Science, 156,* 743–745.
Suggests that a graduate course on scientific writing can strengthen and clarify scientific thinking.

Zinsser, W. (1980). *On writing well: An informal guide to writing nonfiction* (2nd ed.). New York: Harper & Row.
Informal discussion of principles that are basic to strong, uncluttered writing.

Nondiscriminatory Language

Bass, B. M. (1979). Confessions of a former male chauvinist. *American Psychologist, 34,* 194–195.
Personal account of the author's experience of applying guidelines for nonsexist language, with suggestions for their implementation.

International Association of Business Communicators. (1982). *Without bias: A guidebook for nondiscriminatory communication* (2nd ed.). New York: Wiley.
Provides guidelines for language that is free of bias of ethnicity, sex, age, and disability.

Moore, R. B. (1976). *Racism in the English language.* New York: Council on Interracial Books for Children/Racism and Sexism Resource Center for Educators.
Includes an essay on embedded as well as obvious racism in the English language and a lesson plan designed to help students and teachers recognize and eliminate racism in language.

Moulton, J., Robinson, G. M., & Elias, C. (1978). Sex bias in language use: "Neutral" pronouns that aren't. *American Psychologist, 33,* 1032–1036.
Reports data demonstrating that even when used in a supposedly neutral context, "generic" male terms induce people to think of males.

National Committee on Women in Public Administration of the American Society for Public Administration. (1979). *The right word: Guidelines for avoiding a sex-biased language.* Washington, DC: American Society for Public Administration.
Guidelines for the use of nonsexist language in administrative and legislative contexts.

Metrication

Goldman, D. T. (1981). SI: Prognosis for the future. *Journal of College Science Teaching, 10,* 222–225.
Outlines history of the adoption of the International System of Units (SI) and discusses potential modifications of the SI.

National Bureau of Standards. (1979, December). Guidelines for use of the modernized metric system. *Dimensions/NBS,* pp. 13–19.
Briefly describes the history of the International System of Units (SI) and provides tables of SI units and equivalencies as well as guidelines on metric writing style.

Page, C. H., & Vigoureux, P. (Eds.). (1972). *The International System of Units (SI)* (National Bureau of Standards Special Publication 330). Washington, DC: U.S. Government Printing Office.
The approved translation of the French *Le Système International d'Unités*. Contains the resolutions and recommendations of the General Conference on Weights and Measures on the SI, as well as recommendations for the practical use of the SI.

Standard for metric practice (ASTM E-380-79). (1979). Philadelphia, PA: American Society for Testing and Materials.
Includes sections on SI units and symbols, rules for SI style and usage, rules for conversion and rounding, as well as an appendix of conversion factors.

Mathematics

American Institute of Physics. (1978). *Style manual* (3rd ed., rev.). New York: Author.
Includes detailed instructions for the presentation of mathematical expressions, as well as an appendix of special characters and signs available for typesetting.

Swanson, E. (1979). *Mathematics into type* (rev. ed.). Providence, RI: American Mathematical Society.
Offers detailed, practical instructions on preparing mathematical copy.

University of Chicago Press. (1982). Mathematics in type. In *The Chicago manual of style* (13th ed., rev.) (pp. 351–373). Chicago: Author.
Discusses how to prepare mathematical copy.

Figures

Hill, M., & Cochran, W. (1977). *Into print: A practical guide to writing, illustrating, and publishing*. Los Altos, CA: William Kaufman.
Includes general and technical information on the preparation of photographs, drawings, graphs, and charts.

Houp, K. W., & Pearsall, T. E. (1980). *Reporting technical information* (4th ed.). New York: Macmillan.
Discusses kinds of illustrations (tables as well as figures) and the importance of selecting the appropriate type of illustration; provides guidelines for ensuring that the graphical presentation is simple and clear.

Illustrations for publication and projections (ASA Y15.1-1959). (1959). New York: American National Standards Institute. (Available from American National Standards Institute, Inc., 1430 Broadway, New York, NY 10018)
Explains and illustrates the preparation of legible and effective diagrams and graphs for technical publications or with oral presentations.

Strong, C. W., & Eidson, D. (1971). *A technical writer's handbook.* New York: Holt, Rinehart & Winston.
Offers detailed information on types of graphic aids; describes the drawing materials needed and provides step-by-step instructions for the preparation of drawings.

Typing

Dunford, N. J. (1964). *A handbook for technical typists.* New York: Gordon & Breach.
Contains helpful instructions on typing mathematical and other technical material.

Editorial Policies

DeBakey, L. (1976). *The scientific journal: Editorial policies and practices.* St. Louis, MO: Mosby.
Offers guidelines for editors, reviewers, and authors in such areas as review of manuscripts, duplicate publication, and style and format.

Maher, B. A. (1978). A reader's, writer's, and reviewer's guide to assessing research reports in clinical psychology. *Journal of Consulting and Clinical Psychology, 46,* 835–838.
Outlines specific criteria for the evaluation of the content and presentation of research reports in clinical psychology.

Student Papers

Baker, S. (1981). *The practical stylist* (5th ed.). New York: Harper & Row.
Explains in clear and direct language how to write an expository piece, from picking a thesis and constructing the argument to putting the ideas on paper, from researching methodically to writing well and with style.

Barrass, R. (1978). *Scientists must write.* New York: Wiley.
Advises students and their professors on the writing of scientific papers; describes the parts of a research report, provides guidelines on writing and on the use of illustrations, and includes a manuscript preparation checklist.

Maimon, P., Belcher, G. L., Hearn, G. W., Nodine, B. F., & O'Connor, F. W. (1981). *Writing in the arts and sciences.* Boston: Little, Brown.
Introduces students to the processes of library and laboratory research in the sciences; provides step-by-step instructions on preparing the research paper, from draft through final stages.

Turabian, K. L. (1973). *A manual for writers of term papers, theses, and dissertations* (4th ed.). Chicago: University of Chicago Press.
Based on the University of Chicago Press *Chicago Manual of Style*, provides style guidelines for the typewritten presentation of formal papers.

Woodford, F. P. (1967). Sounder thinking through clearer writing. *Science, 156,* 743–745.
Argues that good scientific writing both reflects clear thinking and avoids condescension and pretentiousness.

Yates, B. T. (1982). *Doing the dissertation: The nuts and bolts of psychological research.* Springfield, IL: Charles C. Thomas.
Describes the dissertation process; provides practical, step-by-step instructions for the preparation and presentation of the dissertation.

APA Publications

For free information on ordering APA publications and on information services, write the APA Order Department, 1400 North Uhle Street, Arlington, Virginia 22201.

Appendix:
Material Other Than
Journal Articles

The APA Publication Manual *is intended primarily as a guide to preparing manuscripts for journal publication. However, authors also use the* Manual *to prepare theses, dissertations, and student papers; papers for oral presentation; and papers published in abbreviated form. This appendix therefore briefly explains some of the differences between these materials and journal articles.*

Theses, Dissertations, and Student Papers

A.01 Final Manuscript

The author of a thesis, dissertation, or student paper produces a "final" manuscript; the author of a journal article produces a "copy" manuscript (which will become a typeset article). The differences between these two kinds of manuscripts help explain why the requirements for theses, dissertations, and student papers are not necessarily identical to the requirements for manuscripts submitted for publication in a journal.

Copy manuscripts have been described throughout the *Manual*. Their life span is short; they are normally read by editors, reviewers, and compositors only and are no longer usable after they have been typeset. Copy manuscripts must conform to the format and other policies of the journal to which they are submitted.

Final manuscripts, however, reach their audiences in the exact form in which they are prepared. Final manuscripts have a long life span; they may be read by many people over a long time. The difference between how copy manuscripts and final manuscripts are used is one reason for the differences between the preparation of journal articles and the preparation of theses, dissertations, and student papers. A number of variations from the requirements described in the *Manual* are not only permissible but also desirable in the preparation of final manuscripts.

Many psychology departments require that theses and dissertations be prepared according to the *Publication Manual*. Use of the *Manual* in the production of these papers is excellent preparation for a research-productive career. However, theses and dissertations are submitted to the student's graduate school, not to a journal. Therefore, they must satisfy the graduate school's specific requirements, even if these requirements depart from the style outlined in the *Manual*. Graduate schools should provide students (and typists) with written guidelines that explain all modifications to APA style. (*Note:* A thesis or dissertation in its original form is not acceptable to APA journals.)

Many departments have also adopted the *Manual* for undergraduate senior theses, term papers, laboratory reports, and the like. The *Publication Manual* is not intended to cover scientific writing at an undergraduate level because preferences for style at that level are diverse. Instructions to students to "use the *Publication Manual*" should be accompanied by specific guidelines for its use.

A.02 Content Requirements

The purpose of theses, dissertations, and student papers and the nature of the reading audience (professor or committee members) may dictate variations from the requirements for manuscripts submitted for publication. The following discussion describes the sections of a typical thesis, dissertation, or student paper and touches on some of the common variations among psychology departments. Psychology departments should inform students of any special requirements.

Preliminary pages. Introductory material for a thesis or dissertation usually includes a title page, an approval page, an acknowledgment page, a table of contents, a list of tables and figures, and an abstract. Requirements for these items vary between institutions. Because requirements for the length of abstracts often vary the most, some common guidelines on length are given here.

Many institutions require that abstracts be prepared according to the requirements of *Dissertation Abstracts International*. The maximum length for a dissertation abstract submitted to *Dissertation Abstracts International* is 350 words, far longer than the maximum of 100–150 words for most abstracts in APA journals.

In psychology dissertations, the abstract is now often substituted for the summary, but the author and the dissertation committee usually make the choice. In general, standards for theses and dissertations are similar. Abstracts for student laboratory reports are more often expected to follow APA limits on length.

Introduction. The introduction in a thesis or dissertation is similar to that in a journal article (see section 1.08), except that the author of a thesis or dissertation may be expected to demonstrate familiarity with the literature by developing the background more comprehensively. The decision about length is usually delegated to the chair of the department or dissertation committee; thus, requirements vary widely.

Students writing laboratory reports are often permitted to cite material from secondary sources with appropriate referencing. This practice is not encouraged in journal articles, theses, or dissertations.

Method, results, and discussion. The content of these sections in undergraduate and graduate papers is similar to that in journal articles (see sections 1.09, 1.10, and 1.11).

Summary. As noted, the trend is to substitute the abstract for the summary.

References. Generally, only references cited in the text are included in the reference list; however, an occasional exception can be found to this rule. For example, committees or departments may require evidence that students are familiar with a broader spectrum of literature than that immediately relevant to their research. In such instances, the reference list may be called a bibliography.

Appendixes. Although space and content requirements usually limit the use of appendixes in journal articles, the need for complete documentation often dictates their inclusion in undergraduate and graduate papers. The following materials are appropriate for an appendix: verbatim instructions to subjects, original scales or questionnaires, and raw data. In addition, psychology departments may require subject sign-up sheets or informed consent forms and statistical calculations in appendixes to laboratory reports.

A.03 Typing Requirements

Each university has requirements for the format of theses, dissertations, and student papers, which may or may not differ from those in the *Manual*. The purpose of these requirements is to impose uniformity in manuscripts by individuals from a variety of disciplines.

The following are guidelines for typing a typical undergraduate or graduate paper. These guidelines may not be applicable to laboratory reports because in laboratory courses students are often expected to prepare reports in the style required for actual submission to an appropriate journal. *The student should find out whether (or in what respects) the university's or department's requirements for theses, dissertations, and student papers take precedence over those of the* Manual.

As writers apply these guidelines to typing, they should be aware that the typewritten copy is the *final* copy. Because the manuscript will not be set in type, the typewritten copy must be as readable as possible.

Paper, corrections, copies, and margins. Most requirements for rag content and weight of paper are established to provide durable copies of theses and dissertations for the library. Only corrections that do not mar the appearance or lessen the durability of the manuscript are permitted. Some universities still require carbon copies, but most universities now permit photocopies. The left-hand margin must be wide enough for binding, usually $1\frac{1}{2}$ in. (4 cm). The top margin on the first page of a new chapter (section) may be wider than other margins. Typists should observe requirements carefully because some of each margin is trimmed in the binding process.

Chapters. The sections of a research report (Introduction, Method, Results, and Discussion) are frequently regarded as chapters; each begins on a new page. They may or may not include a chapter number.

In APA style, the introduction is not labeled. However, the arrangement of pages or sections in most theses and dissertations may require that the introduction be labeled because no other heading appears on that page.

Figures, tables, and footnotes. In a manuscript submitted for publication, figures, tables, and footnotes are placed at the end of the manuscript; in theses and dissertations, such material is frequently incorporated at the appropriate point in text. This placement is a convenience to readers, particularly when they are reading the manuscript in microform. Short tables may appear on a page with some text. Each long table and each figure is placed on a separate page immediately after the page on which the table or figure is first mentioned. Figure captions are typed below the figure or, in some cases, on the preceding or facing page. Footnotes to the text are typed at the bottom of the page on which they are referenced.

Pagination. Preliminary pages usually carry lowercase roman numerals. Throughout the manuscript, certain pages may be counted in the numbering sequence without actually carrying a number. The position of numbers on the first pages of chapters or on full-page tables and figures may differ from the position of numbers on other pages. Page numbers continue throughout the appendix.

Spacing. Double-spacing is required throughout most of the manuscript. When single-spacing would improve readability, however, it is usually encouraged. Single-spacing can be used for table titles and headings, figure captions, references (but double-spacing is required *between* references), footnotes, and long quotations. Long quotations may also be indented five spaces.

Judicious triple- or quadruple-spacing can improve appearance and readability. Such spacing is appropriate after chapter titles, before major subheadings, before footnotes, and before and after tables in the text.

Material for Oral Presentation

If you are active in research, you will probably have occasion to present a paper at a convention, symposium, workshop, seminar, or other gathering of professionals. The following hints for preparing a paper for oral presentation are taken from an unpublished manuscript on writing strategy and style by Robert McCall (1981) and from an article by Harold Schlosberg in the July 1965 *American Psychologist* (pp. 606–607).

Material delivered verbally should differ from written material in its level of detail, organization, and presentation. Therefore, prepare an oral presentation differently than you would prepare a manuscript. Concentrate on only one or two main points and keep reminding the audience what the central theme is by relating each major section of the presentation to the theme. The speaker's traditional strategy is still valid: Tell the audience what you are going to say, say it, and then tell them what you have said.

Omit most of the details of scientific procedures because a listener cannot follow the same level of detail as a reader can. The audience wants to know (a) what you studied and why, (b) how you went about the research (give a general orientation), (c) what you discovered, and (d) the implications of your results. A verbal presentation should create awareness about a topic and stimulate interest in it;

colleagues can retrieve the details from a written paper, copies of which you may want to have available.

Do not read your presentation. Reading a paper usually induces boredom and can make even the best research sound second-rate. Instead, tell your audience what you have to say, just as you would in conversation. Having written notes in front of you while speaking will help you keep your focus, but use an outline of topic sentences rather than a complete manuscript so that you are not tempted to begin reading the paper.

Finally, rehearse your presentation until you can speak comfortably and look at your notes only occasionally. If your presentation includes slides, posters, or other visuals, be sure that they are readable and comprehensible from a distance and that their timing is appropriate. The best rehearsal is under conditions similar to the actual presentation. You are prepared for the oral presentation when you can succinctly tell your audience, eye-to-eye, what you want them to know.

Material Published in Abbreviated Form

In addition to publishing research in its entirety as journal articles, authors may make their research available through these means:
• APA's *Psychological Documents*
• brief reports in APA journals
• National Auxiliary Publications Service (NAPS)

A.04 *Psychological Documents*

Psychological Documents (formerly the Journal Supplement Abstract Service [JSAS] and the JSAS *Catalog of Selected Documents in Psychology*) is an on-demand publication service from which readers can order documents in microfiche or hard copy. Materials available from *Psychological Documents* are announced in a catalog of synopses of accepted manuscripts. Original, previously unpublished material of all types, formats, lengths, and psychological content are appropriate for submission (see a recent issue of the catalog, *Psychological Documents*, for manuscript submission requirements).

Psychological Documents combines characteristics of communication networks and conventional journals. It is a publication service developed to
• provide ready access to diverse materials unavailable through journals;
• make available items of value to a small, specialized audience;
• encourage submission of materials not normally considered because they are too bulky for standard publication and uneconomical for large distribution.

A.05 Brief Reports

Studies of specialized interest or limited importance are published as brief reports in some of the APA journals. A brief report, usually one to three typeset journal pages, summarizes the procedure and results of a study. Refer to the appropriate journals for details on preparing brief reports.

A.06 NAPS

The National Auxiliary Publications Service is operated as a service of the American Society for Information Science. Authors may deposit with NAPS any supplementary materials, such as original observations, extensive calculations, or detailed drawings, that cannot be included economically in a printed article or that may be of interest to only a few readers. So that readers may order copies, the author includes with the printed article a footnote indicating that materials are available from NAPS. The author is responsible for depositing the materials with NAPS, at his or her own expense. Authors should direct all inquiries to ASIS/NAPS, c/o Microfiche Publications, P.O. Box 3513, Grand Central Station, New York, New York 10163.

Index

Abbreviations, 63–65
  in abstract, 23
  acronyms, 23, 63
  of corporate author's name,
    109–110
  in figures and tables, 64, 86–87
  hyphenation with, 59
  International System of Units,
    75
  introduction of, 54, 63
  Latin, 64
  of metric units, 64, 75
  of nonmetric units, 64
  periods with, 65
  plurals of, 65
  in references and citations,
    110, 112
  of states' names, 112, 113
  statistical, 62, 81–82
  style changes from 1974 *Manual*,
    13
  of technical terms, 63
  in article and table titles, 23, 87
Abstracts, 23–24, 178
  abbreviations in, 23
  length of, 24, 190
  reference citations for, 122, 123
  of thesis or dissertation, 190
  typing, 144
Abstracting and information
    services, 22, 23, 178, 193, 194
Acknowledgments, 20, 106–107,
    145, 190
Acronyms, 23, 63 (*see also*
    Abbreviations)
Adjectives, 39–40, 49
  compound, 57
  phrases used as, 56
  proper, 59, 73
Adverbs, 39–40
  hyphenation of, 56
  as introductory or transition
    words, 40
Affiliation, author's, 23, 106
  typing, 143–144
Agreement
  of noun and pronoun, 38
  of subject and verb, 37–38
Algebraic variables, italics for, 61,
    81–82
Alphabetizing
  authors' names, 107–110
  foreign names, 115
  reference list, 115–116

Alterations, author's, 161–164
Although vs. *while*, 40–41
American Psychological
    Association, 9–10 (*see also*
    Journal program, APA)
  address of, 159, 163
  copyright policies of, 71, 93, 169
  editorial style, defined, 12–14,
    51
  governance structure of, 166
  journal policy of, 166, 173–179
  journal program of, 12, 165–179
  Monitor, 179
  Publication Manual, history of,
    9–10, 181
  publication process, 171
American Psychologist, 173–174
  order of articles in, 170
  publication of future style
    changes in, 13
  receipt dates in, 170
American Society for Information
    Science (ASIS), 194
  NAPS, 83, 105, 193–194
Ampersand (&) in citations and
    references, 108, 119
Analysis
  chi-square, 13, 81
  factor, capitalization in, 60–61
Animals
  as research subjects, 26, 158
  relative pronouns to refer to, 38
Anonymous
  as author, 109, 116
  review (*see* Blind review)
Antecedents (*see* Referents)
Anthropomorphism, 35
APA (*see* American Psychological
    Association)
Apparatus, description of, 25, 26,
    33, 59
Appendixes, 26, 28–29, 105, 138,
    191
  citing in text, 106
  tables in, 86
  for theses and dissertations, 191
  typing, 145
Arabic vs. roman numerals, 74,
    112
Art (*see* Figures)
Articles (*a, an, the,* etc.)
  capitalization of, in titles, 58
  surnames with, alphabetizing
    references, 115

Articles, journal (*see also*
Manuscript; Papers;
References)
empirical studies, 20–21, 24
length of, 22
multiexperiment, 28
reproduction of, 163
review of, 21, 24, 33, 156
sections of, 22–29
theoretical, 21, 24
types of, 21–22
Artist, guidelines for, 95, 100
As well as with *both*, 42
ASIS (American Society for
Information Science), 194
Asterisk, to indicate probability
levels, 91
Author (*see also* Authorship;
By-lines)
address of, 23, 106, 158
affiliation of, 23, 106, 143–144
anonymous, 109, 116
author identification notes,
106–107, 145
copyright of, on unpublished
manuscript, 168–169
corporate, 108–109
correspondence with editor,
157–159
degrees and titles of, 23
of a direct quote, 69–70
instructions to, 157, 172
multiple, citation of, 107–109,
115–116
names, form of, 23
names, order of, 20, 107–110,
115–116
in reference list, examples of,
119
references without, 109
reprinting own material, 163,
169
responsibilities of, 20, 80, 112,
136, 157–159
single, 107, 115
title page, 23, 143
Author–date method of citation,
107
Author identification notes,
106–107, 145
Author's alterations, 161–164
Authorship, 11, 18, 20–21, 23
(*see also* Author; By-lines)
guidelines on determining, 20
joint, 20

Because, 32
with *reason*, 34

Because *(continued)*
vs. *since*, 41
Behavioral Neuroscience, 174
Between and *and*, 41–42
Bias, sexual or ethnic, avoidance
of, 43–49
Bibliography (*see also* References)
differences from reference list,
111
of the *Manual*, 181–188
for student papers, 191
Blind review, 136, 145, 157, 158,
172
Block quotations, 68–70, 152
Board of Directors, APA, 166
Boldface type, 81, 101
Book reviews (*see* References)
Books (*see* References)
Both and *and*, 41–42
with *as well as*, 42
Brackets, 55, 141
in equations, 55, 82–83
with parentheses, 55, 82–83
in quotations, 69, 70
Brand names, capitalization of, 59
Breaks, end-of-line, 137, 148
Brief reports, 21, 135, 193
By-lines, 20, 23 (*see also* Author;
Authorship)
order of names in, 20

Capitalization, 57–61, 139
of academic courses and
departments, 59
after colon, 53, 58
beginning a sentence, 57
of brand names, 59
of factors, variables, and effects,
60–61
in figures, 58, 101, 147
of group names, 60
in headings, 58
of hyphenated words, 58, 59
of laws, theories, or hypotheses,
59
of major words, 58
of metric units, 75
of nouns followed by numerals
or letters, 60
of proper nouns and adjectives,
58–60, 72, 73
in quotations, 70
in references, 120, 124
in tables, 58, 90, 146
of tests, 60
of titles, 58
Captions, figure, 93, 103–104
capitalization in, 58

Captions *(continued)*
  typing, 146–147
Case histories, 21
Cassettes *(see* References)
Cells, in tables, 89, 90
Chapters
  abbreviation for, 110, 112
  numbers, 72–73
  in student papers, 191–192
  titles of, cited in text, 53
Characters
  number of in running head, 23, 136
  per typed line, 137
Charges to authors *(see* Author's alterations)
Charts, 98 *(see also* Figures)
Checklist for manuscripts, inside front and back covers of the *Manual*
Chemical terms
  not italicized, 62
  spelling of, 56
Chicago Manual of Style, 51, 183
Chi-square statistics *(see* Statistical copy)
Circulation, works of limited, 106 *(see also* References)
Citations in text *(see* Reference citations in text)
Clauses
  final, 53
  independent, 52
  nonrestrictive, 41, 52
  restrictive, 40, 52
Clichés, 43, 44
Collective nouns, 37
Colloquialisms, 34–35, 53
Colon, 53
  capitalization after, 53, 58
  in reference list, 53, 124
  spacing after, 140
Comma, 52
  in numbers, 52, 74–75
  with quotation marks, 70
  in reference citations, 55, 107, 109–110, 111
  in reference list, 119–120, 126
  in series, 52, 68
  spacing after, 140
Comments and replies, 21
Communications, personal, citation of, 110, 112
Comparatives, no hyphens with, 56
Compound terms, hyphenation of, 55–57
Computer-generated figures, 100
Computer programs *(see* References)

Conclusions
  in abstract, 24
  in Discussion section, 27–28
  verb tense for, 33
Conjunctions
  coordinating, 41–43
  subordinate, 40–41
  in titles, 58
Contemporary Psychology, 174
  abstracts in, 23
  receipt dates in, 170
Content
  evaluating, 19
  of manuscript, 17–20
  of student papers, 190–191
Conventions, 192–193 *(see also* References)
Conversations *(see* Personal communications)
Copies of manuscripts, 158
Copy editing, 159, 161, 170
Copy editor, 137, 159–161, 170
Copyright, 71, 93, 103, 158, 163
  of APA-copyrighted material, 71, 93, 169
  permission footnotes, 71, 93–94, 106, 145–146
  transfer form, 159, 168
Copyright Act of 1976, 168
Corporate author, 108–109 *(see also* References)
Corrections
  to edited manuscript, 159, 161
  to typed manuscript, 136, 138, 191
  to proofs, 161–163
  to published journal article, 163–164
Correlation matrixes, 90
Correspondence
  between author and journal editor, 157–159
  personal communications, citation of, 110, 112
Cost charged to authors *(see* Author's alterations)
Council of Editors, APA, 9, 10, 166
Council of Representatives, APA, 166
Court cases
  cited in text, 110–111
  in reference list, 113–114
Cover letters for manuscripts, 158
Credit
  authorship, 11, 18, 20–21, 23
  copyright permission footnotes, 71, 93–94, 106
  for quotations, 69–71, 106
  for reprinted figures, 93, 103–104, 145

Credit *(continued)*
  for reprinted tables, 93–94
Cropping figures, 102–103 (*see also* Figures)

Dash, 53
  capitalization after, 58
  in table, 90
  typing, 140, 145
Data, verb agreement with, 37
Data (*see also* References)
  in figures, 27
  in Results section, 27
  retaining after publication, 80, 163
  in tables, 27
Dates
  numerals for, 72, 75
  of receipt of manuscript, 159, 170
  in text citations, 69, 70, 107
  in reference list, 120
Decimal fractions, 74
  precision of measurement in, 74, 90
  in tables, 90
  use of zero before decimal point in, 74, 80
Degrees, author's, 23
Degrees of freedom (*see* Statistical copy)
Demographic characteristics of subjects, reporting, 26
Departments, university
  in by-line, 23
  capitalization of, 59
Dependent variables, in figures, 95, 102 (*see also* Variables)
Descriptive statistics (*see* Statistical copy)
Design
  experimental, 19–20, 24
  of tables, 84, 93
Developmental Psychology, 175–176
Dictionary used by APA, 55
Discussion, 27–29
  verb tense for, 33
Displayed equations, 55, 82, 83, 142–143
Dissertation Abstracts International, 130, 190
Dissertations
  abstract of, 190
  preparation of, 189–192
  reference for, 118, 130
  typing, 191–192
Double-spacing, 137

Drawings, 98 (*see also* Figures)
Drugs
  capitalization of, 59
  dosage of, 24
  generic names for, 23
Duplicate publication, 19, 167–168

Editing, copy, 159, 161, 170
Editor
  address of, 158–159
  associate, 166, 169–170, 172
  copy, 137, 159–161, 170
  journal, 158–159, 166, 169–173
  publication credit for, 20
Editorial policies of APA journal program, 166–173
Editorial style, defined, 12–14, 51
Educational Resources Information Center (ERIC) report (*see* References)
Either and *or,* 41–42
Ellipses, 70, 141
Empirical articles, 20–21, 24
Enumeration (*see* Numbering; Series)
Equations (*see also* Mathematical copy; Statistical copy)
  displayed, 55, 82, 83, 142–143
  in the line of text, 82–83
  punctuation of, 82
  statistical symbols in, 81–82
Equipment used in experiment, 25, 26, 59
ERIC report (*see* References)
Et al., 64, 107–108
"Ethical Principles of Psychologists"
  Principle 7f: 20
  Principle 9: 26, 158
  Principle 10: 26, 158
Ethics
  of authorship, 20–21
  in treatment of subjects, 20, 26, 158
Ethnic bias, avoidance of, 43, 44–45
Experimental groups
  abbreviating, 63
  not capitalized, 60
Experiments
  design of, 19–20, 24
  multiple, 28, 65, 155
  single vs. multiple, 168

Factor, 60–61
Figures, 94–105

Figures *(continued)*
 abbreviations in, 63–64
 axes in, 102
 camera-ready, 100
 captions for, 93, 103–104,
  146–147
 charts, 98
 checklist for, 105
 citing in text, 103, 146–147
 color vs. black-and-white prints,
  102
 computer-generated, 100
 cost of correcting proof, 162
 cropping, 102–103
 drawings, 98
 glossy print, 102, 104
 graphs, 95–97, 100–102
 halftones, 98
 identifying, 103, 147
 legends for, 58, 100, 103–104
 lettering, 100–101
 maps, 98
 numbering, 103, 146–147
 paper size, 104
 pen-and-ink, 100
 photographs, 98, 102–103
 photomicrographs, 103
 preparation of, 95, 100–102
 reduction and enlargement of,
  98, 100–101
 reprinted, permission for, 93–
  94, 104, 145
 scaling, 102
 shading, 101
 size of, 98, 100
 in student papers, 192
 vs. tables, 27
 vs. text, 80
 typing, 146–147
 use of, 27
Films *(see* References)
First person vs. third, 35
Footnotes, 105–107 *(see also*
  Notes)
 content, 105–106
 copyright permission, 71, 93–
  94, 106
 NAPS deposit, 194
 numbering, 106, 145
 in student papers, 192
 in text, 105–106
 typing, 145–146
 unnumbered notes *(see* Notes)
Foreign words
 abbreviations of, 64
 not hyphenated, 56
 not italicized, 62
 names, alphabetizing in
  reference list, 115

Foreign words *(continued)*
 plurals of, 37
Formulas
 displayed equations, 82–83,
  142–143
 statistical, 80
Fractions
 decimal, 72, 74, 90
 figures to express, 72
 in line of text, 82–83
 words to express, 73
F ratios *(see* Statistical copy)

Gender of pronoun, 38
Genera, italics for, 61
Government reports *(see*
  References)
Grammar, 36–43
Grants, acknowledgment of, 106–
  107
Graphs *(see* Figures)
Greek letters, 62, 81–82, 142
Guidelines for Nonsexist
  Language in APA Journals,
  43–44, 45–49

Halftones, 98
Headings, in articles, 65–67
 capitalization of, 58
 levels of, 66–67
 selection of, 22, 26, 51
 typing, 139–140
Headings, in tables, 87–90
 column heads, 87–90
 decked heads, 88
 spanners, 87–88
 stubheads, 87
 typing, 146
Hopefully, 40
Humans
 as experimental subjects, 26
 relative pronouns for, 38
Hyphen, typing, 140
Hyphenation of compound terms,
  55–57, 58, 59
 with abbreviations, 59
 and capitalization, 58, 59
 chemical terms, 56
 with comparatives, 56
 foreign phrases, 56
 with *-ly* endings, 56
 with numbers, 56, 59
 with participles, 56
 with prefixes, 58, 59
 with *self-,* 59
Hypotheses, not capitalized, 59
  (see also Research, scientific)

I, use in scientific writing, 35
Illustrations (*see* Figures; Tables)
Indentation, 138
  of abstracts, 138, 144
  of figure captions, 138, 147
  of footnotes, 138, 145–146
  of headings, 66–67, 138, 139
  of paragraphs, 138
  of quotations, 68–69, 138, 141
  in reference list, 138, 145
  in tables, 85, 138, 146
Independent variables, 87, 95, 102
  (*see also* Variables)
Index to table of reference
  examples, 118–119
Inferential statistics (*see* Statistical
  copy)
Information and abstracting
  services, 22, 23, 178, 193, 194
Initials, author's, 23, 109, 119, 125
  periods with, 65
  typing, 140
In-press references, 109, 120 (*see
  also* References)
Institutional affiliations (*see*
  Author)
Instructions to Authors, 157, 172
International System of Units (SI),
  75–79
Interviews (*see* References)
Introduction, 21, 24–25
  without heading, 66
  in student papers, 190
Italics, 54, 61–62
  for algebraic variables, 61, 81–
    82
  for anchors of a scale, 54
  for genera, 61
  to introduce key term, 54
  for linguistic examples, 54
  to prevent misreading, 53
  in quotations, adding emphasis,
    70
  in reference list, 120, 124, 126,
    127
  in statistics and equations, 81–
    82
  of titles of publications, 61
  underlining words, 61
Items in a series, 42, 67–68

Journal articles (*see also*
  References)
  titles of, in reference list, 120
  titles of, in text, 58
  types of, 21–22
Journals, APA, coverage of
  American Psychologist, 173–174

Journals (*continued*)
  Behavioral Neuroscience, 174
  Contemporary Psychology, 174
  Developmental Psychology,
    175–176
  *Journal of Abnormal
    Psychology*, 174
  Journal of Applied Psychology,
    174–175
  *Journal of Comparative
    Psychology*, 175
  *Journal of Consulting and
    Clinical Psychology*, 175
  *Journal of Counseling
    Psychology*, 175
  *Journal of Educational
    Psychology*, 176
  *Journal of Experimental
    Psychology: Animal Behavior
    Processes*, 176
  *Journal of Experimental
    Psychology: General*, 176
  *Journal of Experimental
    Psychology: Human
    Perception and
    Performance*, 176
  *Journal of Experimental
    Psychology: Learning,
    Memory, and Cognition*, 176
  *Journal of Personality and
    Social Psychology*, 176–177
  *Professional Psychology:
    Research and Practice*, 177
  Psychological Bulletin, 177
  Psychological Review, 177
  Journal Supplement Abstract
    Service (JSAS) (*see
    Psychological Documents*)
Journal program, APA
  blind review, 172
  copyright policy of, 169
  duplicate publication, 167–168
  editorial management in, 169–
    170
  editors, 158–159, 166, 169–
    170, 172
  Instructions to Authors, 157,
    172
  multiple submission, 167
  order of publication of articles,
    170
  page allocations, 166
  piecemeal publication, 19, 168
  policies governing, 166–169
  primary publication, 167–168
  publication lag, 167
  publication process, 171
  requirements for submission of
    work, 157

Journal program, APA
    (continued)
    review process, 170, 172
    types of articles for, 21–22
Journal-related periodicals,
    APA, 178–179
JSAS *(see Psychological
    Documents)*

Key words
    in abstract, 24
    introduction of, 54, 61

Language, sexist, 43–49
Latin terms
    abbreviations of, 62, 64, 65
    plurals of, 37
Laws and theories, not capitalized,
    59
Legal references
    in reference list, 113–115
    in text, 110–111
Legends, figure, 58, 100, 103–104
Length *(see also* Size)
    of abstracts, 24, 190
    of line of type, 137
    lines per manuscript page, 137
    of manuscripts, 22, 33–34
    of paragraphs, 34
    of printed pages, 22
    of quotations, 68–69, 71, 141
    of sentences, 34
    of tables, 83, 93
    of titles, 23, 58
    of typewritten pages, 137
Letter
    as linguistic example, 54, 61
    Greek, 62, 81–82, 142
    group or condition, designation
        of, 60
    in mathematical copy, 81–83,
        142
    subscript, 62
    superscript, 91
    as symbol or variable, 62
Lettering for figures, 101
Letters
    to journal editor, 157–159
    permission, 71, 93, 103, 158
    personal, citation in text, 110,
        112
Line art, 98 *(see also* Figures)
Literature, review of, 21, 24, 33

Magazine articles *(see* References)
Mailing
    manuscripts, 157–159

Mailing *(continued)*
    proofs, 163
Man (see Guidelines for Nonsexist
    Language in APA Journals)
Manuscript
    abstract in, 23–24, 137, 144
    appendix to, 26, 28–29, 138,
        145, 191
    author's copyright on, 168–169
    checklist for *(see* inside front
        and back covers of the
        Manual)
    date of receipt of, 159, 170
    Discussion section in, 27–28
    editing of, 159, 161, 170
    editorial review of, 170, 172–173
    evaluation of, 15, 19, 29, 172–
        173
    final, 189–191
    length of, 22, 33–34
    Method section in, 21, 25–26
    organization of, 17–29, 65–67
    parts of, 21, 22–29, 143–147
    receipt of by editor, 159, 170
    Reference section in, 28, 111–
        113, 118–119, 145, 191
    rejection of, 19, 171, 172
    Results section in, 21, 27, 28
    revision of, 172–173
    sample, 135, 147–156
    submission of, 157–159
    title page in, 22–23, 143–144
    typing, 135–156
    unpublished *(see* References)
Maps, 98 *(see also* Figures)
Margins in manuscript, 137, 191
Mathematical copy, 61, 72, 80–83,
        142–143 *(see also* Fractions;
        Numbers; Statistical copy)
    equations, 55, 61, 82–83, 142–
        143
    italics in, 61, 81–82
    parentheses in, 55, 82
    subscripts, 62, 82, 142
    superscripts, 82, 142
    typing, 141–143
Matrixes, correlation, 85, 87, 90
Means *(see* Statistical copy)
Measurement
    abbreviations, 64–65
    metric, 75–79
    nonmetric, 75, 79
    precision of, 74, 90
Media, nonprint *(see* References)
Meetings, papers presented at,
        192–193 *(see also* References)
Memos *(see* Personal
        communications)
Method, experimental, 25–26

Method *(continued)*
  mentioned in abstract, 24
  verb tense for, 33
Metrication, 75–79
  abbreviations, 64–65
  tables, 76–79
Microfilm publications *(see* References)
Minus sign, typing, 140
Modifiers
  adjectives, 39–40, 56, 57, 59
  adverbs, 39–40, 56
  compound, 55–57
  dangling, 39–40
  with numbers, 56–57, 59–60, 74
  misplaced, 39
Money, expressing sums of, 72
Monitor, APA, 179
Monograph, 21, 22, 67 *(see also* References)
Multiexperiment papers, 28, 67, 155
Multiple submission, 167

Names
  alphabetizing, 110, 115–116
  authors' *(see* Author; Authorship; By-lines)
  trade or brand, 59
NAPS *(see* National Auxiliary Publications Service)
National Auxiliary Publications Service (NAPS), 83, 105, 193–194
  address, 194
National Technical Information Service (NTIS) report *(see* References)
Negative results, 28
Neither and *nor*, 38, 41–42
None, verb agreement with, 37–38
Nonsexist language, guidelines for, 43–44, 45–49
Nor, verb agreement with, 38
Not only and *but also*, 41–42
Notes, 105–107 *(see also* Footnotes)
  to acknowledge contributions, 20, 106–107, 190
  author identification, 20, 106–107
  copyright permission, 93–94, 106
  to tables, 91–92, 93–94, 106
  typing, 145–146

Nouns
  agreement with pronoun, 38
  collective, 37
  foreign, plurals of, 37
  proper, 59
  verb agreement with, 37–38
NTIS (National Technical Information Service) report *(see* References)
Number
  agreement of subject and verb, 37–38
  agreement of noun and pronoun, 38
Numbering
  equations, 83
  figures, 103, 146–147
  footnotes, 93, 106, 145
  manuscript pages, 137–138, 192
  a series, 67–68, 72–73
  tables, 86, 146
Numbers, 71–75 *(see also* Mathematical copy; Statistical copy)
  chapter, 72–73
  commas in, 74–75
  expressed in numerals, 71–73
  in hyphenated words, 57, 59
  numbered series, 67–68
  ordinal, 74
  page, 138
  plurals of, 75
  in reference list, 112
  spelled out, 73–74
Numerals
  arabic vs. roman, 74, 112
  as numerals, 72

Omission
  of verbs, 35, 38
  of material in a quotation, 70
One, spelled out, 73
Only, placement of, 39
Or, verb agreement with, 38
Oral presentations, 192–193 *(see also* References)
Order
  of articles, 170
  of citations in text, 107–110
  of manuscript pages, 137–138
  of names in by-line, 20
  of reference-list entries, 115–116
Ordinal numbers, 74
Organization of manuscript, 17–29, 65–67
Original publication *(see* Primary publication)
Outline of paper, 35, 65–66

Outline of paper *(continued)*
use in oral presentations, 193

Page numbers of manuscript,
137–138, 192
Page numbers of sources
for quotations, 69, 70–71
in reference list, 120, 126
in text citations, 110
Papers *(see also* Manuscript)
oral presentation of, 192–193
student, 189–192
unpublished *(see* References)
Paragraphs
indentation of, 138
length of, 34
series of, 68, 140
Parallelism, 41–43
Parentheses, 54–55
abbreviations in, 63, 64
vs. brackets, in quotations, 70,
141
in equations, 82–83
with other punctuation, 140
in text citations, 107, 111
Participants *(see* Subjects)
Participle, present, 39
Peer review, 167
Percent, symbol for, 81
Percentage, 81
Periods, 52
in abbreviations, 65
in ellipses, 70, 141
with parentheses, 140
with quotation marks, 70,
141
Periodicals *(see* References)
Permission to reproduce
APA-copyrighted material, 71,
93, 169
figures, 93, 104
footnote for, 71, 93–94, 106,
145–146
letter of, 71, 93, 158
photograph of person, 103
quotation, 71, 106
tables, 93–94
Person, first vs. third, 35
Personal communications, citation
of, 110, 112
Phenomena, verb agreement with,
37
Photocopies of manuscripts, 158,
191
Photographs, 98, 102–103 *(see
also* Figures)
cropping, 102–103
Photomicrographs, 103

Phrases, compound, hyphenation
of, 56
Plurals
of abbreviations, 65, 76
of metric units, 76
of nouns of foreign origin, 37
of numbers, 75
of verbs, 37
Policies, APA journal program *(see*
Journal program, APA)
Population vs. sample statistics
(see Statistical copy)
Prefixes
hyphenation with, 57, 58, 59
metric (SI), 77
Prepositions
capitalization of, in titles, 58
in foreign names, alphabetizing,
115
Present participle, 39
Previous publication, 167–168
Primary publication, 167–168
Prime, in mathematical copy, 82
Principles, ethical *(see* "Ethical
Principles of Psychologists")
Printed pages, calculating number
of, 22
Printer
errors, 161, 163
ordering reprints from, 163
Prints *(see also* Figures)
color vs. black and white, 102
cropping, 102–103
glossy, 102, 104
Probability levels *(see also*
Statistical copy)
in abstract, 24
in results, 27
in tables, 91–92
in text, 80–81
Procedure *(see* Method,
experimental)
Proceedings, of meetings and
symposia *(see* References)
*Professional Psychology: Research
and Practice,* 177
Pronouns, 38–39
agreement with noun in number
and gender, 38
none, 37–38
referents, 35, 38
relative, 38, 40–41
Proofreader's marks, 160, 161, 162
Proofreading, 160–163
Proofs, 161, 163
Proportions
colon in, 53
in figure reduction and
enlargement, 98, 100, 101

Psychological Abstracts, 178
Psychological Abstracts
    Information Services
    (PsycINFO), 178
Psychological Bulletin, 177
Psychological Documents, 178–
    179, 193
Psychological Review, 177–178
Psychology, departments of, in
    by-line, 23
PsycINFO (Psychological Abstracts
    Information Services), 178
PsycINFO Assisted Search and
    Retrieval (PASAR), 178
*PsycINFO Users Reference
    Manual,* 178
PsycSCAN, 178
Publication, credit for, 20 (*see
    also* Journal program, APA)
Publication lag, 166–167, 170
Publication Manual
    bibliography of, 181–188
    history of, 9–10, 181
    how to use, 14–15
    students' needs, 9–11, 189–192
    style changes in third edition,
        12–14
Publications of limited circulation
    (*see* References)
Publications and Communications
    Board, APA, 9, 10, 166, 169
Publisher name in a book
    reference, 124 (*see also*
    References)
Punctuation, 52–55 (*see also*
    under individual marks)
    brackets, 55
    colon, 53
    comma, 52
    dash, 53
    with footnote superscripts, 145
    hyphens, 55–57
    in mathematical and statistical
        copy, 82–83, 141–142
    with other punctuation, 70–71,
        140, 141
    parentheses, 54–55
    period, 52
    quotation marks, 53–54, 70
    semicolon, 52
    in titles, 53
    typing, 140–142, 145

Queries, copy editor's, 159–161
Quotation marks, 53–54
    double, 53–54, 70
    with other punctuation, 70, 141
    in quotations, 70, 141

Quotation marks (*continued*)
    single, 70
Quotations, 68–71
    adding emphasis in, 70
    brackets in, 69, 70
    capitalization of first word in, 70
    changes from original, 70
    citation of sources for, 70–71
    display or block, 68–69, 70, 141
    ellipsis points in, 70, 141
    length of, 68–69, 71, 141
    insertions in, 70, 141
    omissions in, 70, 141
    page numbers for, 70–71
    permission for, 71, 106
    punctuation in, 69–71, 141
    quoted material in, 70
    typing, 141

Ratios, 72
    colon in, 53
    spacing in, 140
Reason with *because,* 34
Receipt date, 170
Reduction of figures, 98–100, 101
    (*see also* Figures)
Redundancy, 23, 33–34
Refereeing of manuscripts (*see*
    Review)
Reference citations in text, 107–
    111 (*see also* References)
    in abstract, 23–24
    agreement with reference list,
        111
    ampersand (&) vs. *and* in, 108
    author–date method, 107
    corporate author, 108–109
    in footnotes, 108
    initials in, 109
    et al. in, 107–108
    in press, 109
    legal, 110–111
    multiple authors of one work,
        107–108
    multiple works, 109–110
    no author, 109
    order of, 109–110
    page numbers in, 55, 69–71
    in parentheses, 54–55, 111
    of personal communications,
        110, 112
    of quotations, 55, 68–71
    of specific part of a source, 110
References, in reference list, 28,
    111–133 (for Index to specific
    reference examples, *see* 118–
    119) (*see also* Reference
    citations in text)

References *(continued)*
abbreviations in, 112
alphabetizing, 115–116
ampersand (&) vs. *and* in, 119,
126
arabic vs. roman numerals in,
112
authors in, 119, 123
capitalization in, 120, 124
date of publication in, 120
discontinuous pages in, 121
editors in, 123, 125–126
examples of, specific, 118–133
initials of authors, 119, 125
italics in, 120, 124
legal, 113–115
location of publisher in, 124,
128
no author, 119
order of, 115–116
page numbers in, 120, 126
publisher in, 124, 128
punctuation in, 119–120, 123–
124, 126, 127–128
reference notes, 13
for student papers, 191
style for, APA, 112
titles in, 120, 124, 127
typing, 145
volume numbers in, 120, 124
Referents, 32, 35
for pronouns, 32, 35, 38
Rejection of manuscripts, 170–172
Reports *(see References)*
Reprinting material *(see
Copyright; Permission to
reproduce)*
Reprints
of article, ordering, 163
requests, address for, 106–107
Research, scientific
design and reporting of, 19,
21–22, 43
hypothesis, 19, 24–25, 27, 29
Research reports *(see References)*
Responsibilities
author's, 136, 157–164
editorial, 169–170
typist's, 136
Results of a study, 27
combined with Discussion, 27,
28
negative, 28
verb tense for, 33
Review
blind, 136, 145, 158, 172
of copy editing by author, 159–
161
editorial, 168–169, 170–172

Review *(continued)*
peer, 167
Review articles, 21, 24
Reviewers, ad hoc and advisory,
166, 170
Revision of manuscripts, 170–172
Roman vs. arabic numerals, 74,
112
Roman typeface, 81, 101
Ruling of tables, 93, 146
Running heads, 23, 136, 144

Sample paper and outlines, 147–
156
Sample vs. population statistics
(see Statistical copy)
Sample sizes *(see* Statistical copy)
Scales
capitalization of, 60
italics for, 62
with numbers, 72
Secondary sources *(see* References)
Self- compounds, 59
Semicolon, 52
with a series, 52, 68
in text citation, 110
Seminars, oral presentation to,
192 *(see also* References)
Sentences
length of, 34
used as linguistic examples, 54,
61
punctuation with, 52–53
Series, 67–68
punctuation of items in, 52, 54,
68
typing, 140
Sexist language, avoiding use of,
43–44, 45–49
Short article title vs. running
head, 23, 138
Short reports, 21, 135, 193
SI (International System of Units),
75–79
Sic, 69
Significance levels *(see* Probability
levels; Statistical copy)
Signs *(see* Symbols)
Since, 32
vs. *because,* 41
and *while,* 40–41
Size *(see also* Length)
of figures, 98, 100, 104
of statistical samples, 72, 81
of tables, 93
of typewriting paper, 136
Slang, quotation marks to
indicate, 53

Source (*see* Permission to reproduce)
Spacing
  of manuscripts, 137
  of mathematical copy, 82–83
  of metric units, 76
  after punctuation, 140
  in reference lists, 112, 145
  for student papers, 192
  in tables, 84, 93
Speaking, at professional gathering, 192–193
Species, 26
  italics for, 61
Spelling, 55–57
  standard reference for, 55
Standard deviations (*see* Statistical copy)
Standards, ethical (*see* "Ethical Principles of Psychologists")
States, abbreviations for, 112, 113
Statistical copy (*see also* Data; Mathematical copy)
  changes in style, 13
  chi-square statistics, 27, 81
  commas in, 74–75
  degrees of freedom, 27, 74–75, 80–81
  descriptive statistics, 27, 80, 151
  equations, 82–83
  formulas, 80
  F ratios, 80–81
  Greek letters, 62, 81–82
  inferential statistics, 27, 80
  italics in, 61–62, 81–82
  means, 27, 80–81
  multiple-range test, 92
  references for, 80
  in Results section, 27
  sample sizes, 81
  sample vs. population statistics, 81
  significance levels, 24, 27, 80–81, 91–92
  spacing of, 82
  standard deviations, 27, 80
  symbols, 62, 65, 81–82, 86
  typing, 141–143
  zero before decimal in, 74, 80
Statutes
  cited in text, 111
  in reference list, 114–115
Stencil, 101
Student papers, 189–192
Studies, empirical, 20–21, 24
Style
  changes from 1974 *Manual*, 12–14

Style (*continued*)
  consistency of, 11
  editorial, defined, 51
  for typing manuscript, 135–156
  writing, 22, 31–36
Subheadings, 25–26 (*see also* Headings, in articles; Headings, in tables)
Subjects
  agreement with verbs, 37–38
  pronouns as, 38–39
Subjects, research, 25–26
  in abstract, 24
  animal, 26
  describing, 25–26, 43–45, 64
  ethical treatment of, 20, 26
  human, 26
  other terms for, 64
  sample size, 81
Subjunctive, 36–37
Submission of manuscript, 157–159
Subscripts, 62, 82, 142
Subsections of Method section, 25–26
Subtitle, capitalization of, 120
Suffix letters in references, 110, 116
Summaries (*see* Abstracts)
Superlatives in compound adjectives, 56
Superscripts
  in footnotes, 71, 93, 145
  in mathematical and statistical copy, 82, 142
  in tables, 91
Supplemental material, 173
Symbols (*see also* Variables)
  Greek letters, 62, 81–82
  identifying, for editor and printer, 82, 142
  italics for, 61–62, 81–82
  metric, 76–78
  percent, 81
  statistical, 81–82
  typing, 141–143
Symposia, oral presentations to, 192–193 (*see also* References)
Synonyms, 33

Tables, 83–94
  abbreviations in, 64, 87
  in appendix, 86
  body of, 90–91
  capitalization in, 58, 90
  checklist for, 94
  citing in text, 84–86
  combining, 86
  correlation matrixes, 85, 87, 90

Tables *(continued)*
    data in, 27, 90–91
    decimals in, 90
    vs. figures, 27
    headings in, 87–90, 146
    metric, 76–79
    notes to, 91–92, 93–94, 146
    numbering, 86, 146
    organization of, 84
    permission to reproduce, 93–94
    probability levels, notes for, 91–92
    in Results section, 27
    rules in, 93, 146
    samples of, 84, 85, 89
    size of, 93
    for student papers, 192
    vs. text, 80, 83–84
    titles of, 58, 86–87
    typing, 85, 93, 146
    word tables, 90–91
Technical reports *(see* References)
Tense, verb *(see* Verbs)
Tests
    in abstract, 24
    scores on, 72
    titles of, 23, 60
Tests, statistical *(see* Statistical copy)
Text citation *(see also* Reference citations in text)
    of figures, 103, 146–147
    of tables, 85–86, 146
That vs. *which,* 40–41
Theoretical articles, 21, 24
Theories, not capitalized, 59
Theses, 189–192 *(see also* References)
Third person vs. first, 35
Time, units of, 64, 72
Titles
    abbreviations in, 23, 87
    figure, 93, 103–104, 146–147
    manuscript, 22–23
    method or *results,* not used in, 23
    short, 22, 23, 138
    table, 58, 86–87
    title page, 22–23, 143–144
    typing, 143
Titles *(see also* References)
    authors' degrees, 23
    capitalization of, 58
    italics for, 61
    punctuation of, 53
Trade names, capitalization of, 59
Transfer of copyright, 159, 168
Transition words, 32–33, 40
Translations *(see* References)

Typeface *(see also* Italics)
    boldface, 81, 101
    for figures, 101
    italic, 81–82
    for mathematical and statistical copy, 81–82
    roman, 81, 101
    for typing manuscript, 136–137
Typing the manuscript, 135–156
    abstract, 144
    appendix, 145
    for blind review, 136, 143
    brackets, 141
    by-line, 143–144
    capital letters, 139, 140
    copyright permission footnotes, 145
    corrections, 138, 191
    displayed expressions, 142–143
    double-spacing, 137
    ellipsis points, 141
    figure captions, 147
    figures, 146–147
    footnotes, 145–146
    headings, 139–140
    indentation, 138
    margins and spacing, 137
    of mathematics, 141–143
    order of pages, 137–138
    page numbers, 138
    paper size and quality, 136, 191
    punctuation, 140, 141
    quotations, 141
    reference list, 145
    running head, 144
    sample papers, 147–156
    seriation, 140
    spacing, 137, 140
    statistical copy, 141–143
    student papers, 191–192
    tables, 85, 93, 146
    text, 144
    title page, 143–144
Typist's responsibilities, 136

Underlining *(see* Italics)
A Uniform System of Citation, 110, 113
Universities
    in by-line, 23
    capitalization of, 59
    student paper requirements, 189–191
University Microfilms *(see* References)
Unpublished manuscript, author's copyright on, 168 *(see also* References)

Variables (*see also* Symbols)
capitalization of, 60–61
identifying, for editor and
printer, 82, 142
italics for, 61–62, 81–82
research, 24, 25, 26
in tables and figures, 87, 95,
102
typing, 141–143
Varieties, italics for, 61
Vectors, 82
Verbs, 36–39
agreement with subjects, 37–38
compound predicate, 52
mood, 36–37
omission of, 35, 38
subjunctive, 36–37
tense, 24, 32–33, 36–37
voice, 24, 36, 39–40
Volume numbers
arabic numerals for, 112, 124
italics for, 62, 120

We, use in scientific writing, 35
*Webster's New Collegiate
Dictionary*, 55, 64
Which vs. *that*, 40–41
While
vs. *although*, 41
and *since*, 40, 41
Who vs. *whom*, 38–39, 40
Word breaks, 137
Word tables, 90–91
Words as words, italics for, 54, 61
Words into Type, 51, 183
Workshops, oral presentations at,
192–193
Would, 37
Writing style, 31–36

Year of publication, 69–70, 107,
120

Zero, spelled out, 73
Zero, use before decimal point, 74